TEACHING
TECH-SAVVY
KIDS

JESSICA K. PARKER

FOREWORD BY GLYNDA HULL

TEACHING TECH-SAVVY KIDS

Bringing Digital Media Into the Classroom, Grades 5–12

CORWIN
A SAGE Company

For information:

Corwin
A SAGE Company
2455 Teller Road
Thousand Oaks, California 91320
(800) 233-9936
Fax: (800) 417-2466
www.corwin.com

SAGE Ltd.
1 Oliver's Yard
55 City Road
London EC1Y 1SP
United Kingdom

SAGE India Pvt. Ltd.
B 1/I 1 Mohan Cooperative
   Industrial Area
Mathura Road, New Delhi 110 044
India

SAGE Asia-Pacific Pte. Ltd.
33 Pekin Street #02-01
Far East Square
Singapore 048763

Printed in the United States of America

Library of Congress Cataloging-in-Publication Data

Parker, Jessica K.
Teaching tech-savvy kids: bringing digital media into the classroom, grades 5–12/
Jessica K. Parker; foreword by Glynda Hull.
     p. cm.
Includes bibliographical references and index.
ISBN 978-1-4129-7150-8 (pbk.)

   1. Educational technology—Study and teaching (Elementary)—United States.
2. Educational technology—Study and teaching (Secondary)—United States. 3. Digital media.
4. Internet in education. I. Title.

LB1027.P27 2010
371.33′4464—dc22   2010003019

This book is printed on acid-free paper.

10   11   12   13   14   10   9   8   7   6   5   4   3   2   1

Acquisitions Editor:	Debra Stollenwerk
Associate Editor:	Desirée Bartlett
Editorial Assistant:	Kimberly Greenberg
Production Editor:	Amy Schroller
Copy Editor:	Tomara Kafka
Typesetter:	C&M Digitals (P) Ltd.
Proofreader:	Eleni Georgiou
Indexer:	Sylvia Coates
Cover Designer:	Scott Van Atta

Contents

Foreword   vii
  Glynda Hull

Preface   xi

Acknowledgments   xv

About the Author   xvii

About the Contributors   xix

1. **Understanding Youth and Digital Media**   1
   Jessica K. Parker

2. **Hanging Out With Friends: MySpace, Facebook, and
   Other Networked Publics**   15
   danah boyd and Jessica K. Parker

3. **YouTube: Creating, Connecting, and Learning
   Through Video**   37
   Patricia G. Lange and Jessica K. Parker

4. **Wikipedia: The Online Encyclopedia Based on
   Collaborative Knowledge**   65
   Jessica K. Parker

5. **Role-Playing: Writing and Performing Beyond
   the Classroom**   83
   Becky Herr-Stephenson and Jessica K. Parker

6. **Virtual Worlds: Designing, Playing, and Learning**   113
   Jessica K. Parker and Maryanne Berry

7. **Remix Culture: Digital Music and Video Remix, Opportunities for Creative Production**   **143**
    Erin B. Reilly

8. **Conclusion**   **167**
    Jessica K. Parker

Glossary   **175**
Index   **181**

Foreword

History reminds us of the uneasy, ambivalent, and yes, sometimes decidedly negative relationship that has existed between educational technologies and technology-centric practices for education, on the one hand, and teachers and their visions for their classrooms and students on the other. Presented with the latest claims of how a new technology turned to an educational purpose can, indeed must, transform teaching and learning—be it radio, filmstrips, an overhead projector, computers, or now Web 2.0 technologies—teachers sometimes feel relegated to the sidelines, where they must stand, metaphorical arms akimbo, critically evaluating what seems close to hyperbole and resisting pressures to just get on board. There have indeed been some ill-conceived attempts over the years to remove human agency from the educational equation, including what appeared as the replacement of teachers with individualized computer-based instruction, or "teaching machines" as they were once called, or the reduction of teachers to monitoring the real providers of instruction, modules delivered online. Paulo Freire (Donegan, R., Shilton-Martin, A., and Martin, D., 1978) decried such attempts 30 years ago in a now vintage film entitled *Starting with Nina: The Politics of Learning* (Toronto: Education Development Center). And now as our 21st century school systems are beset with pressures to improve test scores by any means available, questionable efforts in this tradition continue, however well-intentioned. The introduction of technologies into classrooms, both historically and currently, let us admit, has too often been wrongheaded, and accompanied by unmet expectations, increased and intensified demands, insufficient support preservice and inservice, and retrograde theories of knowledge and pedagogy.

Now enter youth media. Now peruse Jessica Parker's *Teaching Tech-Savvy Kids: Bringing Digital Media Into the Classroom, Grades 5–12*. Now ponder the research sponsored by the McArthur Foundation on which the book is based. Now locate the respectful and sensible representation of teachers and teaching in relation to new media in Parker's work. And then join me in contemplating a cautious but hopeful sea of change concerning, if not the automatically transformative impact of digital tools, then their helpful, pivotal use when paired with informed educational practices that are themselves inspired by youth's use of new media in their everyday worlds. I should be clear that we don't have in this book a panacea for longstanding intractable educational ills, nor is one promised. The institution of schooling in the United States and elsewhere is too complicated and entrenched, too much a piece of a larger social and political fabric of finances, cultures, ideologies, and traditions, to be easily or quickly shifted, no matter the individual vision or tool. However, what is possible, in the microcosm of a classroom and more rarely a school or even a school system, is the sustenance of venues in which creating, communicating, and learning can indeed flourish—in part, and in large part, via the employ of, knowledge of, the most powerful semiotic tools at hand in a given historical moment. An important available resource for re-understanding and re-imagining, among other things, language use, participant structures, identity formation, and social relationships, as Parker and colleagues vibrantly describe in this book, is youth's digital practices out-of-school.

A hallmark, then, of the digital practices described for us in *Teaching Tech-Savvy Kids* is that they originated in domains of play, work, and social activity outside of school. Learning what it means to come of age in a digital world—by documenting the social, literate, and creative activities of young people as these are mediated by the Internet, cell phones, social networks, multiple digital modalities, and a range of related tools and practices—is a super starting point, perhaps the most important one, for rethinking how to engage young people in traditional school settings and the knowledge of texts and disciplines to be acquired therein, and also in gaining insights into how such settings could themselves do with alteration and transformation. This was the late Professor Peter Lyman's brilliant conceptualization of the "Digital Kids" project, which resulted in the research on which this book is based. We come to know through Parker's book some of the young people that the researchers came to know through their long-term participation in a variety of communities, with a variety of youth: multimodal and inventive composers; incessant communicators, communally inclined; creators and purveyors of popular culture; media-driven multitaskers; inveterate symbolizers; valuers par excellence of friends, social connections, and collaboration. These hopeful, talented, and challenging adolescents are also of necessity engaged in imagining social futures in a changing and uncertain world. The focus of this text is research on youth in the United States, but for me the shadows of youth from all over the world loom large in its background, a reminder that they too are, or desire to be, producers and recipients of and participants in a digitally oriented global youth culture, and that increasingly they will become the digitally mediated interlocutors of American youth.

Parker's important contribution in this volume is to represent to educators, clearly, accessibly, humanely, and respectfully, the digitally mediated literate and creative practices of youth. Her approach is to throw bright light on productive pathways and directions, but not to prescribe specific steps or dictate a precise destination. What underpins this book, and what is by contrast absent in much of the literature that offers guidance for teachers who didn't come of age in a digital world, is a clear-eyed sense of the big questions, of what is at stake in taking into account in our classrooms and in our own lives the new media practices that so engage young people. The questions that she invites us to consider are no less than what is literacy, what is learning, and what is knowledge? She addresses these questions, however, not through abstractions, but by research-based portraits of digitally driven youthful practices and relationships, and through examples provided by teachers who've successfully and joyfully incorporated the communicative and creative practices of youth in their classrooms.

Perhaps best of all, Parker's approach in *Teaching Tech-Savvy Kids* invites educators to themselves contribute to the new worlds of digital media. There is much to be done and even more to be imagined, prompted and inspired by the research and the pedagogical portraits in Parker's volume. If social networking sites are used by and large to extend existing friendship networks, what instructional scaffolds might increase their reach and function, and to what pedagogical, epistemological, and ethical ends? If youthful communication across modes and platforms tends to brevity and the phatic, in what contexts and for what purposes and in what modes might young people's discourse become more sustained and multiply purposed? Since many youth spend enormous amounts of time on creative arts-based, digitally enabled projects, how might we incorporate within our own classrooms understandings of literacy that foreground an appreciation of the aesthetic? What youthful practices should remain youthful practices, allowed to flourish in out-of-school contexts untouched by school-based purposes, and where might sturdy bridging be built? At what point do the changes in communication and knowledge creation in a digital and global world, reflected in youth's new media practices, make current conceptualizations of schooling's architectures, subject matters, and disciplinary routines outmoded? If that moment is now, as I believe it is, then how do we best proceed, especially given the resistance to change that characterizes institutions and bureaucracies along with strong current pressures to test the measurable and to certify knowledge and achievement accordingly? Works like Parker's *Teaching*

Tech-Savvy Kids cover considerable persuasive distance—by illustrating the changes in communication and knowledge construction that now illumine our global world, and by introducing us to the inventive practices of youth that likewise signal important changes in how we might learn, relate, and create together.

—*Glynda Hull*

New York University

REFERENCE

Donegan, R., Shilton-Martin, A., & Martin, D. (Producers & Directors). (1978). *Starting with Nina: The politics of learning* [Motion picture]. Toronto: Education Development Center.

Preface

*T*eaching Tech-Savvy Kids: Bringing Digital Media Into the Classroom, Grades 5–12 focuses on the intricate and maturing relationship between youth and their digital media practices. Given that this phenomenon has primarily developed outside of school walls, educators can utilize characteristics of digital media such as collaboration, creativity and peer sharing and feedback, in an effort to offer more engaged, student-centered learning opportunities within our schools. Surprisingly, it is through an understanding of how young people learn and participate in our shifting media landscape that philosophical questions regarding learning and literacy in the 21st century can be addressed and new ideas regarding pedagogy and curriculum development can emerge.

Drawing on studies of youth and their experiences outside of school, I initially asked myself, "What are students doing with new media?" The answer, I realized, was centered on engaging and complex literacy and learning opportunities in which students were avid writers and readers outside of school and also producers of many different kinds of media texts such as original stories, Wikipedia entries and documentary videos. I was amazed and impressed by the sheer amount of time and devotion students put into their collaborative, detailed and intense non-school projects. I then asked myself, "What can classroom teachers in Grades 5–12 learn, both personally and professionally, from the study of new media environments?"

This book is an attempt at answering the former question, and has resulted in a compilation of resources and insights based on current research from a number of sources including projects funded by the MacArthur Foundation and leaders in the fields of new media and education. As such, each chapter includes vignettes and quotes from personal interviews and written materials from various sources. Additionally, educators such as classroom teachers, counselors and technology specialists helped to connect current academic research to the realities of today's schools with their own stories and reflections, as they highlighted what they saw as a rich and rewarding relationship between their students and digital media. I hope this will be the start of a long and prosperous discussion concerning new media in our society and its impact on learning and adolescence. I view this as a conversation among learners, rather than a book that grants correct answers or cut-n-paste activities.

GOALS FOR THE BOOK

This book is designed for teachers who are interested in understanding the ins and outs of digital media, such as Wikipedia, YouTube and MySpace, and are also curious as to how their students are using these social media in their daily lives. This is not your typical teacher's guide with an expert detailing unit and lesson plans on one particular subject. I understand most teachers' guides are grade and content specific, but I have designed this book as a practice-based guide not a content-based guide. There are activities for teachers to try in order to navigate their way through the abundance of new media in their students' lives and contribute to an online community of teachers. As such, the book's focus is to encourage teachers to explore new media in their personal lives and in their classrooms, and to help them rethink their practices and relations not their content: from teacher-centered to student-centered activities, from individualistic pursuits to collaborative efforts, and from teacher-as-the-audience to teachers and peers-as-audience members armed with feedback and critique.

One of the goals for this book is to inspire fifth through twelfth grade teachers to understand both the relationship between their students and digital media and how to make use of this relationship when designing learning opportunities for their students. By focusing on literacy and learning through a different lens, as described by the numerous out-of-school media practices of youth captured throughout these chapters, teachers can work to offer educational environments in which a 21st century student is entitled. This book does not advocate "replacing" face-to-face learning or teachers themselves with new educational platforms or online environments. On the contrary, the goal is to learn about the culture of new media as it pertains to specific friendship- and interest-based practices, and through awareness and dialogue educators can apply characteristics of new media in their classroom. The classroom activities put forth in this book are not "the answers" nor are they meant to be a laundry list of activities for teachers to implement the following school day. This book is about understanding how the study of new media environments can help to broaden our understanding of literacy, promote a much-needed dialogue concerning new media technologies, and high-light the changing nature of learning.

AUDIENCE OF THIS BOOK

This book speaks to teachers of fifth through twelfth graders, regardless of one's technological competence or interest. Novices will find these chapters offer explanations of specific sites such as Facebook and Wikipedia, definitions of key terms and even activities to try out personally and in the classroom. Tech-savvy teachers will have access to the latest research and current on- and offline resources to further their knowledge of the field. Beginning teachers can take away implications for their pedagogical practice and mull over a changing communicative landscape. And veteran teachers can broaden their understanding of interesting phenomena such as virtual worlds and remix culture. Additionally, teachers and educators will have access to our online community forum!

ORGANIZATION OF THE BOOK

Teaching Tech-Savvy Kids: Bringing Digital Media Into the Classroom, Grades 5–12 is organized thematically and encompasses popular youth activities found online and/or with other computer applications. Focusing on key characteristics of new media environments such as a community of learners, creative production, peer sharing and feedback, themes of this book include:

- Social network sites: MySpace and Facebook (Chapter 2) and YouTube (Chapter 3)

These sites are ***networked publics*** (***bolded italicized*** words are defined in the glossary) which offer young people active participation—whether friendship driven or interest driven—to produce, share and publish media and youth culture. These two chapters offer educators a chance to learn about prized aspects of youth culture while also pondering how characteristics such as peer sharing and feedback can enhance student learning.

- Communities in cyberspace: Wikipedia (Chapter 4) and online role-playing (Chapter 5)

Collaborative wikis and online role playing are sites that cater to particular interests such as adding or editing entries in Wikipedia or exploring informal story telling through online role playing games. These two chapters provide insight into user-generated content and offer teachers a glimpse into online participation and membership.

- Creative media productions: Virtual worlds (Chapter 6) and remix culture (Chapter 7)

Remix culture and virtual worlds, such as *Second Life*, *Final Fantasy XI*, and *Quest Atlantis*, allow students to become active producers rather than passive recipients of media. These two chapters offer examples of ***participatory culture*** and outlines how educators can capitalize on specific characteristics of this culture.

Chapter Sections include

- An *Introduction* that provides key terms and a description of how a medium is used or phenomenon is appealing.
- *Myth and Reality Sidebar* that outlines common misconceptions surrounding youth and digital media and shares a more sophisticated understanding of these experiences.
- A *Story From the Field* that details current research of youth experiences with new media.
- *Pedagogical Implications* that highlight classroom practices such as activities and creative ideas for teachers to test, reflect, and share.
- *References and Helpful Resources* that contain key readings, Web sites and other resources for teachers.

Special Features of the book include

- *Bits and Bytes of Research.* These are short vignettes based on current research and address potential implications for teachers. Topics include safe spaces to connect for gay, lesbian, bisexual, transgendered, and queer (GLBTQ) youth; class issues regarding the purchase of a family computer; and familial interactions with media in the home.
- *Online Community Forum.* Why not use technology to further our professional development and create an online community of educators? My hope is that from this online community comes a rich and diverse space in which to upload, download and discuss content-based activities, best practices and struggles with digital media. I invite educators to continue this journey online at www.teachingtechsavvykids.com.
- *Glossary.* Located in the back of the book, this glossary is based on the ***bolded italicized*** words and phrases seen throughout these pages.

Acknowledgments

This publication would not have been possible without the generosity of a number of scholars from the University of California, Berkeley, and the University of Southern California. First, I would like to thank Mimi Ito, Michael Carter, and Barrie Thorne for their trust and guidance throughout the writing of this book. To Peter Lyman who had the passion and foresight to put this idea into motion, I am thankful for his unwavering commitment to classroom teachers. I am also indebted to the researchers listed below who sat down with me on numerous occasions to update me on their research. This included sharing their ethnographic investigations and the concepts and phenomena concerning kids and their new media use. Not only did these researchers trust me to convey their research but they also devoted their personal excerpts to the book without hesitation. These scholars are truly pioneers in the study of youth and new media, and I look forward to following their future discoveries:

danah boyd	C. J. Pascoe
Megan Finn	Dan Perkel
Becky Herr-Stephenson	Rachel Cody Pfister
Heather A. Horst	Laura Robinson
Patricia G. Lange	Christo Sims

Erin Reilly, Amira Fouad, Maryanne Berry, and Sasha Barab were also supportive of my efforts to write this book. I would also like to personally acknowledge the love and support of Stephanie Fox, Amanda Godley, Nora Kenney, Glynda Hull, and my parents, Jackie Nystrom Parker and Thomas and René Parker.

Publisher's Acknowledgments

Corwin acknowledges and thanks the following reviewers:

Beverly Adams
Science Teacher
Payson Unified School
    Districts
Payson, AZ

David Brock
High School Science Teacher
Roland Park Country School
Baltimore, MD

Jason Cushner
Math and Science Teacher
Presidential Awardee in Math
    and Science Education
Vermont Commons School
Burlington, VT

Jolene Dockstader
Grade 7 Language Arts
    Teacher
Jerome Middle School
Jerome, ID

Sheila Gragg
Educational Technology
    Integration Coach
Ashbury College
Ottawa, Ontario

Jamie Jahnig
English Teacher
Cheyenne Central High School
Cheyenne, WY

Cheryl Oakes
Collaborative Content Coach
    for Technology
Wells Ogunquit Community
    School District
Wells, ME

Rebecca Rupert
English Teacher
Monroe County Community
    School Corporation
Bloomington, IN

About the Author

 **Jessica K. Parker** is currently an assistant professor at Sonoma State University, and she studies how high schools integrate multimedia literacy into academic literacy learning. She has taught middle school, high school, and college students for over a decade and has also created and taught professional development courses for teachers. She has published teacher-researcher articles in *English Journal* and has presented at national conventions such as AERA, National Media Education Conference, NCTE Assembly for Research, and many others. Jessica completed her undergraduate and graduate work at U. C. Berkeley; she has a BA in media studies and an MA and a PhD in education.

Contributors

Corwin and the author would like to thank the following individuals for their contributions to the book:

Diana J. Arya is currently a doctoral candidate at the University of California, Berkeley, where she lives with her husband and their puppy. She teaches reading and science methods classes for a graduate teaching program at U.C. Berkeley.

Phoebe Ayers is a reference librarian at U.C., Davis, where she specializes in science and engineering resources. She is a longtime contributor to Wikipedia, an organizer of the site's annual international conferences, and co-author of *How Wikipedia Works: And How You Can Be a Part of It*, published by No Starch Press in 2008. To learn more about her, visit http://phoebeayers.info. To learn more about her book, visit http://howwikipediaworks.com.

Rick Ayers received his master's in education at Mills College in 1997 and taught at Berkeley High School from 1995 to 2006, where he founded the Communication Arts and Sciences small school. He is co-author (with Amy Crawford) of *Great Books for High School Kids: A Teacher's Guide to Books That Can Change Teens' Lives* (2004), author of *Studs Terkel's Working: A Teaching Guide* (2000) and co-creator (with students) of the *Berkeley High Slang Dictionary* (2003). He is involved with teacher education at U.C. Berkeley and the University of San Francisco and can be reached at rayers@berkeley.edu.

Sasha Barab is a professor in learning sciences, instructional systems technology and cognitive science at Indiana University. He also holds the Barbara Jacobs Chair of Education and Technology, and is the director of the Center for Research on Learning and Technology. His current work involves the research and development of rich learning environments, frequently with the aid of technology, that are designed to assist children in developing their sense of purpose as individuals, as members of their communities, and as knowledgeable citizens of the world.

Maryanne Berry enjoys a high school teaching career that has spanned a quarter of a century. The longer she teaches, the more fascinated she becomes with the ways young people learn. She is currently a doctoral candidate in the Graduate School of Education at U.C. Berkeley.

danah boyd is a researcher at Microsoft Research New England and a fellow at the Harvard University Berkman Center for Internet and Society. She recently completed her PhD in the School of Information at U. C. Berkeley. Dr. boyd's dissertation research focuses on how American youths use networked publics for sociable purposes. She examines the role that social network sites like MySpace and Facebook play in everyday teen interactions and social relations.

David Conlay has been teaching at Estancia High School for nine years. He has taught every level of English except for the freshman and sophomore honors courses, and he currently teaches comparative literature as well as AP English language and composition. He received his BA degree in English language arts with a minor in Spanish from U. C. Irvine.

Amy Crawford has been teaching English since 1994 and at Berkeley High since 1997. She is also a teacher consultant with the Bay Area Writing Project.

Leslie Finamore is a coworker of Roman Gonzalez and her experience and expertise has helped tremendously in his special education classes. She has worked with Roman for two years and has contributed to making the Nintendo Wii a major force for interaction among special and general education students.

Megan Finn is a doctoral candidate at U.C. Berkeley's School of Information. Her current research is about how information influences people's experiences with disasters.

Brett J. Freccia is a graduate of the University of Delaware with a bachelor's degree in history education and a master's degree in educational instruction. In addition to his Web site and teaching duties he has been involved in curricular activities at the state, district, and school level centered around using technology as a way to improve existing teaching strategies. He lives in Delaware with his wife Diana.

Roman Gonzalez has been teaching students with severe disabilities for the past nine years. He currently teaches at Clovis North High School in Clovis, California. Each year he tries new and creative ways to include special education students with the general education population. The Nintendo Wii has been an instrumental part of this effort.

Philip Halpern is the lead teacher of Communication Arts and Sciences, a small school within Berkeley High School, where he teaches a variety of English and communications classes. He graduated from Georgetown University and Teachers College, Columbia University, with a BA in English and a master's degree in the teaching of English. He traces his interest in media education to the weekly television news program he helped produce while in high school back in the earliest days of videotape. He lives in Berkeley, California, with his wife, Mary Patterson, and their three children, Julian, Elias, and Mara.

Becky Herr-Stephenson is a postdoctoral researcher at the Humanities Research Institute at U.C. Irvine. Her research interests include media literacy, teaching and learning with popular culture, and youth media production. She recently completed her PhD in communication at the Annenberg School for Communication at the University of Southern California.

Heather A. Horst is a sociocultural anthropologist at U. C. Irvine. She is coauthor of *Hanging Out, Messing Around and Geeking Out: Living and Learning with New Media* (2010), *The Cell Phone: An Anthropology of Communication* (2006) and *Jamaican-Americans* (2007), a book written for middle school students that chronicles the Jamaican experience in North America.

Patricia G. Lange is an anthropologist conducting research at the Institute for Multimedia Literacy at the University of Southern California. She explores issues of video reciprocity, creative self-expression, online sociality, and technical identity negotiation in video cultures on YouTube and among video bloggers. Having researched online interaction for over 10 years, her work has appeared in numerous journals including, *the Anthropology of Work Review*, and *The Journal of Computer-Mediated Communication*. Her website is www.patriciaglange.org.

Ann Y. Lauriks has been passionately working with adolescents for over 12 years; first as an eighth-grade teacher and then as a middle school counselor. In 2006 she received her master's in counseling from Saint Mary's College where she had previously completed her Single

Subject Teaching Credential as well as her Pupil Personnel Services Credential.

Andy Maul lives with his wife and puppy in Berkeley, California. He is an instructor of statistics at San Jose State University.

Ricardo Navarro went to both private catholic school and public high school in the Bay Area. His life experiences have affected his work in film. He now attends San Francisco State University and is planning to major in cinema.

Rik Panganiban is the assistant director of the Online Leadership Program at Global Kids, a New York City-based nonprofit that helps thousands of underprivileged kids in New York and beyond to learn about global issues and act to make their community a better place. He has helped expand Global Kids' work to the virtual world, launching a range of innovative educational projects from a virtual fossil dig to an online conversation with a Ugandan teen about AIDS in Africa. He is spearheading a new program to help nonprofits explore virtual worlds and think strategically about how they can integrate these cutting-edge social media tools into their missions.

C. J. Pascoe is a sociologist who is interested in sexuality, gender, youth, and new media. Her book on gender in high school, *Dude, You're a Fag: Masculinity and Sexuality in High School*, recently received the 2008 Outstanding Book Award from the American Educational Research Association. She is currently investigating how teenagers navigate digital technology and how new media have become a central part of contemporary teen culture with a particular focus on teens' courtship, romance, and intimacy practices. Along with Dr. Natalie Boero she is writing a book on pro-eating disorder online communities. She is currently an assistant professor of sociology at Colorado College.

Dan Perkel is a doctoral candidate at U.C. Berkeley's School of Information. His research explores how young people use the Web and other technologies as a part of their everyday media production activities. His ongoing dissertation research investigates the mutual shaping of young people's creative practices and the social and technical infrastructure that support them. In 2000 he received his BA in science, technology, and society from Stanford University and his master's in information management and systems from U.C. Berkeley's School of Information in 2005.

Rachel Cody Pfister is a graduate student in the department of communication at U.C., San Diego. Her research includes ethnographic work with online anime fan communities and gaming communities in *Final Fantasy XI* and *World of Warcraft*.

Erin B. Reilly is the research director for Project New Media Literacies first at MIT and now at USC She is a recognized expert in the design and development of thought-provoking and engaging educational content powered by virtual learning and new media applications, known best for her work with women and girls in Zoey's Room. She currently lives in Massachusetts with her husband, Shane, and media-savvy son, Ocean (five years old).

Laura Robinson earned her PhD in sociology from UCLA in 2006. She is assistant professor of sociology at Santa Clara University. Prior to joining the sociology department, she carried out two years of postdoctoral research on digital inequality. Her published work analyzes new media, digital inequality, culture, communication, and cross-national use of new media in the United States, Western Europe, and Latin America. Her work has appeared in a number of peer-reviewed journals including *Qualitative Sociology*, *The Social Science Computer Review*, *New Media and Society*, and *The Journal of Computer-Mediated Communication*. Her Web site is www.laurarobinson.org.

Ronald Nobu Sakamoto is a classically trained pianist, a filmmaker, and a media consultant. He was an instructional media technician and media specialist at Berkeley High School from 2005 to 2008.

Christo Sims is a doctoral candidate at U.C. Berkeley's School of Information. His fieldwork focuses on the ways youth use new media in everyday social practices involving friends, family, and intimates. He received his master's degree from U.C. Berkeley's School of Information in the spring of 2007 and his bachelor's degree from Bowdoin College in the spring of 2000.

Marlo Warburton is a National Board Certified algebra teacher in Berkeley, California.

This book was written because Peter Lyman wanted the
fruits of his labors and that of his team to be available to teachers
as soon as they could, and Blaise Simqu figured out a way to do that.
We owe them both.

Understanding Youth and Digital Media

Jessica K. Parker

Today's student is likely to engage daily in numerous literate practices, from print to film to multimodal forms such as Web sites and video games. She lives in a media saturated world and averages nearly six and a half hours a day with media.[1] She is a media multitasker, watching television as she instant messages and completes her homework. When she plays video games, she usually works as a member of a team and with intense concentration even on these long, time-consuming projects. She searches for information on the Internet, displays herself on myspace.com, and takes pictures on her cell phone, then chooses between a number of media sharing sites in which to upload them. She can simultaneously be an actor, director, editor, and publisher with the movie software that came with her computer. She expects her teachers to guide her through this information era, not dictate "correct" answers to rote questions that Google can provide in seconds through multimodal means, e.g., text, video, and digital images.

For educators, this student is a symbol of ongoing change in which new media technologies offer emergent modes of communication, learning, and play. *Teaching Tech-Savvy Kids: Bringing Digital Media Into the*

---

1. I created this student based on research from A Kaiser Family Foundation Study (2005) titled, *Generation M: Media in the Lives of 8–18 Year-Olds.* Download the study at http://www.kff.org/entmedia/7251.cfm.

Classroom, Grades 5–12 addresses how new media technologies are altering and expanding literate practices among our everyday acts of communication, our informal learning environments and our leisure activities. We are living in both an exciting and nerve-wracking time as notions such as space and time shift, issues such as portability and interconnectedness become widespread and standardized, and long-standing divisions between private and public spheres are blurred (Burbules & Callister, 2000). These issues, as well as the experiences of the student described above, push educators to question how to think about the changes happening beyond school walls and how these changes affect school-based learning. The answers to these questions cannot be to ignore these changes or to be satisfied with superficial solutions such as wired classrooms or additional hardware. When educators discuss and analyze emergent modes of communication, learning, and play, we are forced to rethink long-standing practices and relations within schools.

TOUGH QUESTIONS EDUCATORS MUST ADDRESS

One of our goals as educators in understanding youth and digital media should be to frame our discussion around learning, literacy and knowledge rather than merely concentrating on the integration of and access to technological tools. For this reason I believe educators need to ask themselves and discuss collectively some tough questions:

1. What does learning look like in the 21st century?

2. What does literacy look like in the 21st century?

3. What is knowledge in the 21st century? (Or what does it mean to *know* something in our mediated culture?)

These are three questions we must ponder, rethink, and explore within ourselves, with colleagues and parents, and with students. Pedagogy, curriculum, and assessments are important philosophical issues and determining factors within education, but the most basic issues we as teachers need to address are our core assumptions around learning, literacy, and knowledge and the relationship between the three. The technological changes that are currently taking place—and will continue to do as they have throughout human history—are reshaping everyday practices and relations. As teachers we must try to understand this phenomenon in order to grow professionally, to continue to have influence over our teaching environments, and to support student learning. This book will assist you in understanding these changes, help you adopt some of these new media practices as your own, and present tangible ways for you to incorporate these issues into your teaching. Additionally, the book can help stimulate your thinking around learning, literacy, and knowledge in the 21st century.

Addressing these three questions will test our ability as educators to see past our training, to see past our own experiences with technology and to see past the fear and uncertainty of institutional change in order to create learning environments and interventions based on the most recent and the most informed research on youth. It is pertinent to discuss education and schooling in the 21st century, for our schools are neither situated in a vacuum nor immune to changes and conditions impacting the rest of our lives. Historically the educational system in the United States has not been prone to change, and for administrators and teachers to offer competitive, engaging classrooms, we need to account for the massive technological changes currently taking place. This is not meant to scare but to motivate us. The chapters in this book bring together the latest research on youth and digital media and offer educators opportunities to understand and explore this relationship both personally and professionally. If we are working and teaching in an institution still wedded to a dated vision of schooling, we have the ability to learn from research, ask ourselves tough questions, and strive to create learning environments in which a 21st century student is entitled.

I realize these questions do not have easy *answers* and one of the arguments of this book is to move away from an outdated school-based view that there is "one right answer" or one "right" way to learn. We must shift our understanding of learning and literacy as:

- *Broadly* conceived and not easily defined or standardized
- *Complex* and not based on effortless transmission
- *Socially and ideologically constructed* and not merely neutral entities (Street, 1995)
- *Inclusive* of the intellectual funds students gain at home and from youth culture (Moll, Amanti, Neff, & Gonzalez, 1992)
- *Changing* over time and not limited to static definitions

When we shift our understandings of learning and literacy to encompass these characteristics, educators can come to view new media through a relational lens and avoid discussions in which new media technologies are presented as an either-or proposition.

Unfortunately the current discourse around youth and new media technologies is based on extreme views. One extreme suggests that kids' use of digital media is dumbing down an entire generation, while the other side suggests that school is now irrelevant and should be replaced with kids directing their own learning online. Educators cannot continue to get caught in a polarized debate only to judge if school-based learning is better or worse than informal learning. This dichotomy will not allow us to initiate a dialogue regarding new media; it will only condone or condemn such learning experiences. Starting with three tough questions about the state and nature of learning, literacy, and knowledge in the 21st century can open up new spaces for discussion, queries, insights, and change.

WHAT IS NEW MEDIA?

What is new media or digital media? *New media* is an umbrella term used to describe technologies of the late 20th century and that are *new*. This currently includes but is not limited to the Internet, cellular phones, interactive television, computer games, and virtual worlds. New media is relative though; radio was considered new in the early 1900s, although it was not considered new in the early 2000s. As new technologies are integrated into our daily lives, they become part of our everyday experiences and, as the years go by, are viewed as commonplace and unoriginal—almost invisible as a technology, e.g., writing, pencils, paper, and chalkboards.

Adding the term *digital* to the phrase digital media signals a form of content that is created and distributed electronically based on binary codes. Digital media is currently the predominant form of new media. Due to its digital code, content such as a digital video or e-mail can be edited, shared, and even in some cases—such as in virtual world—interactive. Social networks and Web sites in which people can read and generate content are possible due to digital computers. But I do not want to simply focus on a laundry list of digital media nor do I want to focus on technical definitions. For teachers it is important to concentrate on how new media technologies are being integrated into our daily lives. This includes how our cell phones, our laptops, our iPods, our video game players, and even our digital video cameras get woven into the ways we develop and maintain our relationships, negotiate our social status and our ability to communicate. From this **relational perspective** (Burbules, & Callister, 2000) we can discuss students' participation with digital media including how they produce and distribute media and engage in appropriating, recirculating, archiving, and annotating media content in powerful new ways (Jenkins, 2006). By discussing how new media influences our lives, teachers can come to appreciate how learning, literacy, and knowledge in new media environments differ from traditional school-based experiences.

But the terms *new media* and *digital media* should not imply that all forms of mediation are new. For instance, students seem to be addicted to text messaging with their cell phones, but writing is not a new medium. What's new is the fact that we can write to each other on our cell phones, since the telephone was previously limited to verbal communication. When I was growing up in the 1980s, the phone was something I used while at home. I was delighted when my parents finally bought a cordless phone so I could talk to friends in the comfort of my own room. Yet the cordless phone created tension and often times disagreements between my parents and me: when I was in my room with the door locked, my parents were less likely to monitor my conversations with peers and evaluate my overall time on the phone and ostensibly away from my homework. So new media can affect communicative practices and relations. Currently the age of kids who have their own cell phones keeps getting younger and younger and they often carry them at all times (and seem to be texting all the time) even though they are still using language and words to communicate.

And don't think these text messages are unsophisticated. In fact, they are just the opposite. Christo Sims, a doctoral candidate at University of California, Berkeley's School of Information, studies how kids use technologies such as cell phones and instant messenger as part of their everyday lives and that using lower and upper case letters, misspellings, and the casual appearance of a text message can often be quite purposeful (personal communication, December 12, 2007). From a teacher's perspective, text messages can appear sloppy and rushed. It might seem as if the student may not know how to spell or rarely puts energy into composing a legitimate sentence. Here is our (adult) mistake. We want to judge our students' text messages based upon standards for written English. In fact, we should take the perspective that our students are communicating much more about themselves than just their mastery of English (Baron, 2008).

Christo Sims (personal communication, December 12, 2007) argues that the casual, even sloppy, appearance can be seen as an attempt to explore social connections without exposing, too quickly, the degree to which they are emotionally invested in the outcome. He draws a comparison between such writing practices and that of youth fashion. In both cases the display is highly crafted and yet done in a way that hopes to suggest casualness and ease; as many youth say to suggest "no big deal." For youth it can be scary to put oneself out there when trying to develop friendships and, as such, youth often appear casual as a way to hide the degree to which they are invested in their friendships. Thus they slowly feel out the other person. They get to know each other by writing short messages, ones where what is said can be carefully controlled. Remember when we were teenagers and there were high stakes involved with making new friendships, being accepted by peers, publicly humiliated, or scrutinized? Those days were potentially horrible, and today's youth use text messaging to allow conversations to develop more slowly and allow rejection to be carried out more silently. Essentially sloppy text messages may be a way for youth to protect themselves.

> **MYTH:** Today's high school students should be called the "look at me" generation. They are self-absorbed, superficial, narcissistic teens who are always online for no apparent reason. Their behavior is baffling.
>
> **REALITY:** Our students' forms of expression have changed from when we were kids. Once we come to understand how our students are using digital media, then their behavior becomes incredibly familiar. They may be online and texting all the time, but they are actively working to promote a social identity and, of course, maintain their friendships.
>
> For a video interpretation of this "reality," go to YouTube and watch "Are Kids Different Because of Digital Media?" from the MacArthur Foundation: (http://tiny.cc/teachtech_1_1).

At the most basic level, today's students' ability to communicate and hang out with one another looks different from our educational vantage point and may even appear like a waste of time or unproductive and does not equate with *real* learning. The questions and concerns around their communication practices are understandable. Hopefully after reading this book, today's teenagers will look less like *failures* and more like typical teenagers who are interesting in dating, flirting, having fun, and creating and reinforcing their own creative youth culture. As today's students develop a sense of self and identity, they become heavily invested in establishing and preserving relationships with peers; however, the way they go about maintaining their relationships just looks different from previous generations. Although these communication patterns may feel foreign and off-putting, the main thing to remember is that their forms of communication are often based on how they want to present themselves to other teenagers.

KEY CHARACTERISTICS OF NEW MEDIA

I was fortunate enough to be a collaborator on a research project titled, "Kids' Informal Learning with Digital Media: An Ethnographic Investigation of Innovative Knowledge Cultures." This project was funded by a grant from the John D. and Catherine T. MacArthur Foundation and jointly carried out by researchers from U. C. Berkeley and the University of Southern California. One of the goals of the project was to put current academic research on the learning and new media practices of youth into the hands of classroom teachers and educators. As such, this book draws extensively from the three-year ethnography of the "Kids' Informal Learning with Digital Media" project and represents the most current instantiation of research on youth new media practices. I also drew from other research projects from the MacArthur Foundation and educational leaders in the field of new media and learning. Thus, each chapter includes stories and quotes from interviews and written materials from various sources.

From this broad research corpus, it becomes apparent that new media environments foster and support a *community of learners*, a shared culture of participation in which youth contribute their knowledge of the world and simultaneously demonstrate a keen sense of creativity within these mediated experiences. In these new media environments, youth are usually invested in *friendship-driven* and *interest-driven practices* where peer-based learning is the norm (Ito et al., 2008). According to Ito et al., friendship-driven practices of youth are based on the "day-to-day negotiations with friends and peers" (p. 9). These negotiations take place between age-based friends and peers from school, religious groups, sports, and other local activity groups. Ito et al. argue that these local friendship groups, from which youth navigate affiliations, friendships, and romantic partners, reflect their lives online. So a student's friend and peer group at school (or other local activity groups) is most likely to be the primary source for the student's friends' list on social network sites such as MySpace and Facebook.

Interest-driven practices, according to the authors, place "specialized activities, interests, or niche and marginalized identities first" (Ito et al., 2008, p.10). Hence, *friendship* is not necessarily the driving force behind the formation of these peer networks rather the specific interest is foremost. For instance, digital video (Chapter 3) production and online role playing (Chapter 5) are popular interests in which youth can pursue self-directed learning, develop online friendships and affiliations, and gain recognition. These specialized interests are the impetus for an online social group to come together (Ito et al., 2008).

CHARACTERISTICS OF NEW MEDIA ENVIRONMENTS

A community of learners usually includes:

- Peer-based learning (Ito et al., 2008; Jenkins et al., 2006)
- Collaboration
- Creativity
- Interest-driven practices (Ito et al., 2008)
- Friendship-driven practices (Ito et al., 2008)

Peer-based learning is a common characteristic of new media environments. In these mediated settings, peer feedback and critique are highly prized. Although these environments are usually informal and less structured than school-based settings, a culture of shared participation helps to nurture a sense of membership and identity; thus youth can become heavily invested and committed to sharing their creative efforts and resources and providing feedback and critique to peers. Specifically in interest-driven settings, self-motivated learners can observe and communicate with people engaged in the same interests (Ito et al., 2008). As a result, youth can learn skills, receive recognition for their work, gain status as experts, and promote an ongoing identity based on a shared interest. In friendship-driven settings, youth can learn cultural norms of online interaction and gain valuable and sometimes painful lessons in growing up (Ito et al., 2008).

The characteristics of new media environments are ripe for integrating into the classroom as they foster engaging, student-centered learning experiences. Although I have intentionally separated each chapter into a discussion about a specific medium or media, these characteristics are the threads that weave the chapters of this book together to create a snapshot of youth and their new media practices: In Chapter 2, Christo Sims highlights Lynn—a young girl who is home-schooled—and her friendship-driven practices on a social network site that allow her to stay connected to her current group of friends from church and the local area; in Chapter 3, Patricia G. Lange details the story of Wendy who uses her interest in documentary video to engage in the civic issue of maintaining and enjoying local facilities such as parks; in Chapter 5, C. J. Pascoe chronicles the story of Clarissa, an avid writer and reader who finds an online writing community in which to create fabulous fictional stories and receive insightful feedback from peers. These examples and the other research-based Stories from the Field demonstrate that teenagers, when given the opportunity to pursue their interests in a communal space and receive support and feedback from peers, are hungry for chances to express themselves in creative ways.

Educators have an opportunity to tap into this hunger in the form of a community of learners, peer collaboration and feedback and interest-based subject matter. Our classrooms can be sites in which collaboration is demonstrated through sharing knowledge, creativity is demonstrated through production and publication, and students are asked to respond to peers with authentic feedback and critique. Teachers do not necessarily need to rely on the latest and most expensive technology to incorporate the key characteristics of digital media into their classrooms. It is feasible to foster a classroom environment based on a community of learners, peer collaboration and feedback, and creativity without the help of the latest and most expensive technology. Educators do not have to get weighed down by a need to adopt technology at a record pace. Instead, start with the assumption that youth culture and its new media practices are a point for learning, discovery, and interest-based pursuits in which youth are agents in their own education. From this vantage point, it can become much easier to find a balance between integrating characteristics of new media environments into the curriculum and incorporating technology into classrooms.

WHAT TEACHERS CAN GET OUT OF THIS BOOK

Although Christo Sims's insights into youth and their text messaging exchanges are interesting, how can teachers benefit from this book? What can teachers get out of a book that focuses on digital media practices? There are several answers to these questions. First and unfortunately, there remains a gap between our students' participation with new media in school and outside of school. If many of our students are engaging in new forms of play, new online communities, and new types of communication, these technological distinctions are important for teachers to understand. This book will assist you in adopting and converting these new relationships with new media into your personal and professional lives and help you bridge this gap and discuss with your students the digital era and its impacts on the ways in which we live.

Second, our jobs as teachers are drastically improved if we can come from a perspective that understands the behaviors of our students. If all we see from our students are behaviors that appear foreign or are prohibited by the school, e.g., cell phones and texting, then we are missing out on myriad ways to connect with our students and their youth culture. I am not suggesting that teachers adopt youth culture as their own. Rather, I am suggesting that making a conscious effort to empathize with life for today's teenagers is a prerequisite for good teaching.

Third, we are currently living in a digital age and there is new affiliation for, and new meaning associated with, geek status. It's now extremely cool to be a geek. To "geek out" is to "dive into a topic or talent" as Ito et al. (2008, p. 2) describe it. For youth, to engage interest-driven practices is to throw themselves into open-ended projects that are time consuming and focused on gaining deep knowledge and expertise within a specific area. While providing a social space with access to peer support and feedback, these interest-based practices also promote self-directed learning (Ito et al., 2008). Interest-driven engagements provide educators with examples of how youth geek out, and for educators looking for ways to motivate students, these insights are invaluable.

Fourth, Henry Jenkins (2006), a media educator, suggests that we need adults to help mentor and guide teens with their media-laden experiences. He is not advocating for a surveillance culture. Rather, Jenkins suggests that there are ethical concerns when chatting online or posting a video of one's self and adults, such as teachers, can assist teenagers in this uncharted territory. Additionally, youth can assist adults in their quest to understand new media and participatory culture. Thus, there is a need for cross-generational perspectives when discussing new media environments.

By focusing on new media practices, teachers can harness the communicative practices of youth within the classroom. Read how Maryanne Berry uses *instant messaging*, or *IMing* in her twelfth-grade English class.

A TEACHER'S PERSPECTIVE

Online Conversations Support Student Engagement With Literature

By Maryanne Berry, English Teacher

As educators, we generally assume that the incessant texting, messaging, and e-mailing that students conduct distracts from learning. But what if this fast paced style of communication could be used to foster conversations that supported learning? About five years ago, I decided to experiment by assigning online conversations in response to an independent reading project on contemporary novels. For years I had assigned my Advanced Placement Literature and Composition students reader response journals as a way of following students' progress through their books. While reading their chosen novels, twelfth graders would periodically jot down questions, predictions, observations and insights. They would copy powerful passages from the text and analyze them. Some of the journals had a kind of "canned" quality; the predictions were safe, the interpretations bland. Sometimes I suspected that students used supplementary sources in order to fake their way through the process. Though students exchanged journals in class with peers who had read the same book, the conversations generated by these exchanges lacked the liveliness one experiences when reading a book with someone equally engaged. A student whose journal was weak might learn something by reading stronger writing but when she went back to the book after class would she have been given the support she needed to engage more confidently with the novel? Could the interest of the struggling reader be sustained?

I told the students that they were welcome to form their own groups (of two to four people) but that I wanted all groups to be coed. I'd read a little research about the differences in the way boys and girls interacted in online settings that suggested that all male groups might be less successful than mixed or female groups and I also wanted students to extend a bit beyond their single gender friendships to include students with whom they had not previously worked. Once the groups were formed, each member was responsible for researching book reviews in order to propose a novel to the group. This part of the project, though time consuming, allowed students to discuss the kinds of books they enjoyed and to acquaint them with the process of researching various media in order to discover acclaimed contemporary fiction. Students ultimately selected novels and set reading schedules that would allow them to meet the goal of completing their reading within the time frame of the quarter semester.

After reading a designated number of pages, they chose either to e-mail journal responses to one another or to meet online to discuss their reading using an IM or chat room program. All groups were required to respond to their books a minimum of four times and to submit the transcripts to me. I read the transcripts and asked questions and made comments that I hoped would provoke further thought and analysis. A few class periods were devoted to discussing the critiques I provided and pursuing discussions generated in the online sessions.

Seven of the 10 groups chose instant messaging as their chief mode of response. The dialogue texts that they produced were generally longer than those who contributed e-mailed journal responses. In a few cases, students who instant messaged were able to code their responses by the minute of each exchange and I was surprised to find that several groups would meet as long as an hour at a time. Transcripts of those students who opted to instant message revealed lively exchanges and while there were digressions—mostly about homework—students stayed largely on track.

With those who instant messaged, it was easy to see how one student's ideas influenced another's; the exchanges were lively, sometimes antagonistic or erratic, punctuated with "lol" the term for "laughing out loud." The e-mailed journal (e-journal) responses were more deliberative. Students often responded to each other's points specifically, giving the exchanges a dialogic quality. One drawback, however, was that the first sender's responses seemed to prompt his peers to respond only to the issues he generated. Though the writers of e-journals made reference to specific aspects of the novels they read, the structured nature of the "paragraph response" demanded that students develop a "take" on a character, event, or description, so that the journals did little to reveal questions or misunderstandings. Instant messaged dialogic texts created a different structure, the screen became a space where students could talk/write in a free flowing negotiation their interpretations of text. The e-mailed journal responses resembled short written letters between readers, while the instant messaging resembled spoken conversations.

(Continued)

(Continued)

While e-journal accounts read much like other assignments submitted for a grade, transcripts of the instant messaged dialogue offer greater insight into reading as a social process as it unfolds over time. I noticed a number of interesting features of students' digitally mediated experience. First, it is interesting to note that the students, while not close friends, seemed very natural in their exchange; the transcript suggests that the exchange was lively and convivial. Second, students used the process of creating a dialogue to reveal both their understanding and their questions about the book they read. Finally, they moved from character analysis of the protagonist, a low level of interpretation, through empathetic and personal responses, until they arrived at more abstract and complex understanding of the novel's central questions.

In all online conversations students complemented one another's understanding and took turns leading each other. Together they constructed a process of shared questioning, similar in style to the one we practiced in our English class, a kind of spiraling activity mediated by the novel they read and their written responses to each other's thoughts. Both the affordances and constraints of instant messaging shaped the ways that they responded to each other. The intimacy of the virtual "space" in which instant messaging is conducted created an opportunity for my students to demonstrate aspects of their learning rarely witnessed in classroom settings. The transcripts revealed both students as actively engaged in making meaning of the shared experiences of reading and writing.

Teachers need to investigate the possible uses of online communication rather than dismiss them out of hand. I have facilitated this project over the last five years, sometimes modifying it, in order to discover how it can be most effective with a particular group. The instant message program was not devised with literary analysis in mind. In order to be successful using instant messaging to discuss a text, students need to bend the rules of the program; they need to slow down the rate of exchange and allow each other to complete their thoughts. The results offer us an unusual and telling look at a process of communication that clearly supports learning. We owe it to ourselves and our students to encourage them to think with the tools they love to use.

Issues to Consider:

- Though this project focuses on works of literature, any work of length might be an apt substitute for novels in an online conversation project. Students appreciated the support of the members of their group in meeting reading deadlines. One student told me, "I kept up with the reading because I didn't want to let my group down."
- Students can often suggest methods for convening in an online setting. Both Google (googlegroups.com) and Facebook (facebook.com) offer free tools for forming collaborative groups.
- Teachers can rely on instant messaging to foster both free-form and directed (the teacher offers guiding questions) discussions. In this manner, virtual spaces are created for collaborative learning that can continue outside the classroom.

This book is designed to give teachers access to the latest research about what kids are doing in their everyday lives with digital media, discuss potential implications for how it can connect to classroom practices and also give teachers a space to begin what can only be considered a long and engaging discussion about bringing new media into the secondary classroom. The point of the book is not to prescribe "cut-n-paste" activities for teachers to integrate into their classrooms but to really grapple with serious technological and communicative changes that deeply affect how and what students learn in school. This book is first and foremost a philosophical discussion regarding education in the 21st century.

There is a tendency among classroom teachers to argue, "Just tell me how to weave these technologies into my curriculum. I don't have the time to analyze and understand technological and communicative change." Here is the problem. We are acting as if these technologies are neutral, somehow just inconsequential tools to be used to further instruction when in fact these technologies are used as socio-cultural forms and connected to larger cultural contexts (Buckingham, 2007). Buckingham argues digital media

> provide new ways of mediating and representing the world and of communicating. . . . The problem with most educational uses of such media is that they continue to be regarded as merely instrumental means of delivering information—in effect, as neutral tools or "teaching aides." (p. 145)

Thus, it is expected that readers of this book are not solely looking for activities to insert into their curriculum or new *tools* to assist instruction. It isn't as easy as *insert technology, out comes student learning*. Instead, my hope is that teachers will commit themselves to understanding the numerous ways youth are participating and learning with new media and, at the same time, how new media are essentially altering our understanding of learning, literacy, and knowledge.

REFERENCES AND HELPFUL RESOURCES

Baron, N. (2008). *Always on: Language in an online and mobile world.* New York: Oxford University Press.

Buckingham, D. (2007). *Beyond technology: Children's learning in the age of digital culture.* Cambridge, England: Polity Press.

Burbules, N., & Callister, T. (2000). *Watch IT: The risks and promises of information technologies for education.* Boulder, CO: Westview Press.

Ito, M., Horst, H. A., Bittanti, M., boyd, d., Herr-Stephenson, B., Lange, P. G., Pascoe, C., J., & Robinson, L. (with Baumer, S., Cody, R., Mahendran, D., Martínez, K., Perkel, D., Sims, C., & Tripp, L.). (2008). *Living and learning with new media: Summary findings from the Digital Youth Project.* The John D. and Catherine T. MacArthur Foundation Report on Digital Media and Learning. Download the report at http://digitalyouth.ischool.berkeley.edu/report

Jenkins, H. (with Clinton, K., Purushotma, R., Robison, A., & Weigel, M.). (2006). *Confronting the challenges of participatory culture: Education for the 21st century.* The John D. and Catherine T. MacArthur Foundation. Retrieved August 18, 2007, from http://digitallearning.macfound.org.

MacArthur Foundation. Re-Imagining learning in the 21st century. http://tiny .cc/teachtech_1_2

Moll, L., Amanti, C., Neff, D., & Gonzalez, N. (1992). Funds of knowledge for teaching: Using a qualitative approach to connect homes and classrooms. *Theory Into Practice, 31(2),* 132–141.

Pew Research Center. (2010). *Millennials: A portrait of generation next. Confident. Connected. Open to Change.* (P. Taylor & S. Keeter, Eds.). Retrieved March 24, 2010, from http://pewresearch.org/millennials.

Street, B. (1995). *Social literacies.* London: Longman.

Hanging Out With Friends

MySpace, Facebook, and Other Networked Publics

danah boyd and Jessica K. Parker

INTRODUCTION

Social network sites, sometimes referred to as SNS, like MySpace, Facebook, and Bebo provide American teenagers with an environment in which they can engage with many facets of American culture. For those who use them, social network sites have also become an important tool for socializing with friends and peers, developing support networks, and sharing cultural artifacts. Social network sites have altered the ways in which teens interact with each other and the culture around them. Adults need to understand these sites and the practices that take place on them if only to guide teens through the challenges they face in an increasingly mediated world. Adults, and especially educators, have a powerful role to play in helping to facilitate the cultural transition taking place—as the public and private aspects of our social lives converge teens enter a public culture that is networked and mediated at every level.

WHAT ARE SOCIAL NETWORK SITES?

Social networking sites are Web-based sites that allow individuals to (1) construct a public or semipublic profile within a bounded system, (2) articulate a list of other users with whom they share a connection, and (3) view and traverse their list of connections and those made by others within the system (boyd & Ellison, 2007). Like many others, we both adopted social network sites to connect with our friends. As an early adopter, danah joined most social networking sites before her friends did, but she made each social network site useful to her by convincing her friends to join. Jessica first signed up for Facebook because a friend uploaded her newborn baby's pictures to the site and she needed a Facebook account to access the photos. After joining, she ended up communicating with a number of other social contacts: high school and college friends she had not heard from in years, current friends she sees all the time, former high school students and even work colleagues. Like Jessica and danah, most people engage with social network sites to socialize with those they know, rekindle old relations, and develop emergent ones. Some people use social network sites to meet new people but such networking is rare especially among teens. Although teens spend a great deal of time on social network sites, they are primarily interacting with peers who are part of their extended network.

Because of their unique properties, social network sites have prompted changes in how teens interact socially and share information about their lives. Today's teens are growing up in a society with a different sense of public and private—a public profile is very different than a name and address appearing in a phone book; social network site comments are very different from a note confiscated by a teacher; and photos uploaded to media-sharing sites are different from a homemade scrapbook.

Although teens are embracing this change, most adults are panicking. Out of fear, schools often ban social network sites. Confused by these new social technologies, some educators have resigned themselves to play ostrich by burying their heads in the sands of incomprehension and unfamiliarity in the hopes that this phenomenon will disappear. These educators are missing an ideal opportunity to help their students. Instead of rejecting or ignoring new forms of social media and friendship-driven practices, educators must learn to understand and embrace the new technologies that continue to emerge. Not all teachers may understand these systems, but this presents an ideal opportunity for such teachers to learn from their students while simultaneously guiding them through uncharted cultural waters. To begin, teachers must first understand how social network sites are constructed, what teens do on them, and why they matter.

WHAT HAPPENS ON SOCIAL NETWORK SITES?

Three most important social network site features for teachers to understand are profiles, *friends* lists, and comments. When new users create accounts on social network sites, they are asked to create a profile. Profiles are a form of self-expression, a way of writing oneself into being in the digital environment. While we are accustomed to accessorizing our bodies when we go out in public, there are no bodies online. Instead users must explicitly create their presence through the construction of a profile that demonstrates their tastes, values, and identity. Profiles can be enriched with the use of text, images, video, audio, links, quizzes, games, and surveys.

THE MAIN FEATURES OF SOCIAL NETWORK SITES

1. Profiles
2. Friends lists
3. Comments

Figure 2.1   Jessica's Facebook Profile

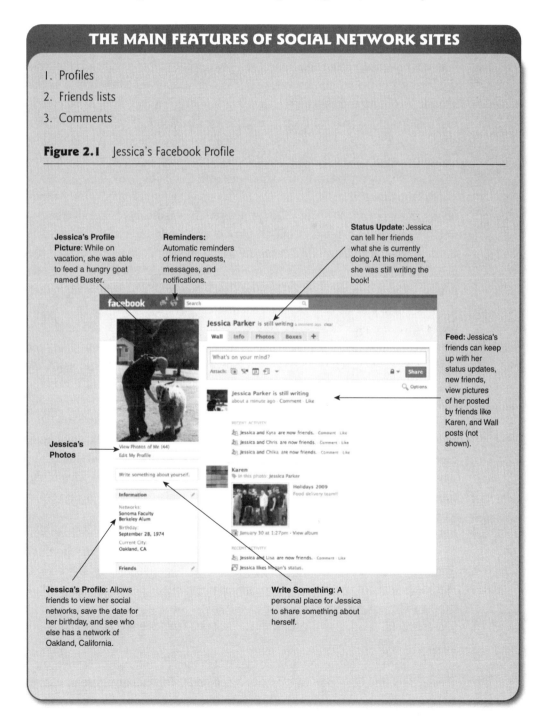

Jessica's Profile Picture: While on vacation, she was able to feed a hungry goat named Buster.

Reminders: Automatic reminders of friend requests, messages, and notifications.

Status Update: Jessica can tell her friends what she is currently doing. At this moment, she was still writing the book!

Feed: Jessica's friends can keep up with her status updates, new friends, view pictures of her posted by friends like Karen, and Wall posts (not shown).

Jessica's Photos

Jessica's Profile: Allows friends to view her social networks, save the date for her birthday, and see who else has a network of Oakland, California.

Write Something: A personal place for Jessica to share something about herself.

Many teens are quite creative with their profiles, investing extensive time into creating a complex form of self-expression. Such profiles are a contemporary equivalent to the highly decorated bedroom wall or locker. Most adults take a more simplistic approach, updating their content and photos occasionally.

The profile page also offers a place to update one's status. These status updates are about sharing information with friends: it's a way to create a personal account of one's daily interactions, emotional state, and much more. There are no right or wrong approaches to updating one's status. It can take the form of personal comments, politics opinions, humorous slants, or just mundane observations. The status update is simultaneously a form of self-expression and a way to keep connected with friends. Figure 2.1 demonstrates a status update from Jessica's profile page—she was trying to gain sympathy from friends by sharing that she was still busy writing this book!

The second key feature on social network sites is the *friends* list. The most important thing to know about *friends* lists is that what constitutes a friend on a social network site is not the same as what constitutes a friend in everyday life. A *friends* list is a public display of mutually agreed upon connections. Most commonly, one person invites the other to be their friend; this prompts a friend request, which can either be accepted or denied. A list of a person's *friends* is displayed on their profile. While someone may wish to only include their closest and dearest friends as *friends*, saying no to a friend request from an acquaintance or colleague is about as awkward as it gets. As a result, most teens—and adults—accept friend requests from everyone that they know, even if they are not especially close. No adult wants to negotiate the office after having rejected their boss's request and no teen wants to face their peers at school after having rejected them.

Just because two people are friends on a social network site does not mean that they interact that often. Still, a broad *friends* list does have meaning. How individuals frame themselves on the site is shaped by whom they think they are interacting with. A person's list of *friends* signals who they imagine to be a potential part of their social circle on the site. In other words *friends* lists are the "imagined audience." While social network sites allow users to adjust privacy settings to only make their profiles visible to that narrow group of *friends*, they also allow users to make their profiles more broadly visible. Yet, just because a teen's profile is "public" does not mean that they expect all people across all space and all time to view it. Their hope is that anyone who should be part of their social world on the site might have access and engage with them; all others should stay out.

The third key feature is variably called *testimonials*, *comments*, and *the wall*. This is a section on a person's profile where their *friends* can write messages to them. Those messages are then viewable by anyone else who can see that person's profile. Comments are essentially distributed public bulletin boards, akin to the white boards that sometimes appear in colleges on the doors of dorm rooms. Teens use these to converse with their friends and peers. While there are other available channels of communication, teens generally prioritize the comments section unless the conversation has embarrassing or personal overtones. Their attitude is essentially, "public by default, private when necessary." The value of comments is less about their communicative efficacy and more about the always-on connections that are consistently reaffirmed through these interactions.

The three core features of social network sites—*profiles*, *friends*, and *comments*—are combined to support hanging out, exchanging ideas, and communicating with one another.

WHY ARE SOCIAL NETWORK SITES IMPORTANT FOR TODAY'S STUDENTS?

Research suggests that the informal social learning provided by the social network system is required for maturation—understanding one's community, learning to communicate with others, working through status issues, building and maintaining friendships and working through personal values are all processes our students should experience (boyd, 2008). As adults, we sometimes underestimate these processes because, traditionally, they happened so naturally. Yet today's youth culture lacks the same opportunities for social interaction as we did. Their lives are much more structured and restricted. They have less mobility and freedom to wander around. We grew up with some equivalent of "get out of the house, be home by dark." That is no longer the dominant mantra. We hung around before and after school just to hang out with friends; this is no longer allowed in most schools. We had tremendous free time to get together with friends; they are involved in many more activities and their time is much more structured. While curfew laws, loitering laws, and shoplifting fears were already in place when we were growing up, they are much more extensive today. When teens gather in public places, they are assumed to be up to no good. The culture of fear that is pervasive today means that teens rarely interact with adults who don't hold power over them. Additionally this fear means that parents are wary of letting kids leave their line of sight. Social network sites like MySpace, Facebook, and Bebo create a youth space, as Christo Sims argues below, to "redefine the social possibilities of time spent in the home, beyond family, beyond planned sociability, and toward unplanned peer-based social activity."

STORIES FROM THE FIELD

This Is Not a Second Life

By Christo Sims, Doctoral Candidate at U.C. Berkeley

In many ways, Lynn Milvert's* use of digital media resembles that of a stereotypical 15-year-old girl growing up in suburban America. She spends hours each day in her music-filled room, multitasking between social networking sites, multiple instant messaging applications, and maybe even a little homework. But Lynn is not a suburban girl—Lynn lives in the upper foothills of California's Sierra-Nevada mountain range where she has been homeschooled since sixth grade, largely with a group of other kids from her church.

Lynn's particular form of homeschooling is not conducted alone with a parent as tutor but instead with a group of roughly 20 kids who share a tutor and even attend "class" together for three hours three times a week. Lynn's class consists of both boys and girls, ranging in age from 12 to 22. She considers everyone in the group to be friends with everyone else in the group. As a social structure, the group is remarkably dense and persistent. Its basic structural form has not changed since Lynn was a young child. As Lynn puts it, "Most of us have known each other all our lives."

Her family's participation in the local First Baptist church reinforces the group's durable structure. While the homeschool program is technically administered by a separate organization, many kids belong to both groups. The church, in turn, sponsors opportunities beyond school for the homeschooled students to get together in social settings. Every Friday the church youth group organizes a social event. Out-of-town trips are planned for roughly one weekend a month. And every Sunday afternoon the youth group holds its own session after the regular service.

In addition to the homeschool program and her church, Lynn's family comprises the other main social structure in her life. Lynn's father grew up next door to where they now live. He built their current house on a portion of what used to be a family ranch. Lynn's grandparents, aunt, uncle, and cousin all live within walking distance. This closeness affords frequent family-based social time for Lynn. At least once a week Lynn's family tries to have meals with members of the extended family. Almost daily Lynn goes to her grandparents to watch satellite TV. And during the summer she babysits her infant cousin between roughly 9 a.m. and 5 p.m. four days a week.

These interwoven social structures—family, church, school—frame Lynn's participation with digital media. Like many teenagers, her favorite digital technology is a social networking site. But unlike most teenagers, she chose Bebo instead of MySpace or Facebook. She perceives it as "safer." And unlike some teens, she doesn't use social networking and instant messaging to build new relationships. Instead she uses them to participate in her existing peer group. Her friends on Bebo match her densely interconnected friends from school and church almost exactly.

Contrasting the dense structure of Lynn's social network is the geographical dispersion of homes in her neighborhood. Being an "up-the-hill" family means much greater distance between homes; it is usually not possible to walk or bike to the house of a friend. This is particularly true in the snowy winter months. Without a driver's license Lynn's collocated social activity with peers either requires routine, formalized group activities such as school, sports practice, work, and church, or convincing a parent, or other older person to transport them to a common location. In both scenarios spontaneous collocated peer gatherings are difficult to achieve.

These constraints lead Lynn to spend a good deal of time at home. As a social space defined by her parents, home has been a place for family and occasionally planned socializing with friends. On the Internet, Lynn finds ways to redefine the social possibilities of time spent in the home, beyond family, beyond planned sociability, and toward unplanned peer-based social activity. This technological reach out of the home is not directed toward distant, unfamiliar, or dangerous worlds on the Internet; rather, it hones toward a well-established group of friends. This dense friend group places each individual member in a uniquely central position, a position that contrasts with the geographic dispersion of their homes and neighborhoods, a position in stark relief with their marginal relation to the community that organizes around the public high school down the hill. It is an inversion of geographic and social isolation, a counterpoint to their perception of being situated "in the middle of nowhere."

Christo Sims's vignette was originally published online in November 2006 on the Digital Youth Web site, the online home of the "Kids' Informal Learning with Digital Media" Project (http://digitalyouth.ischool.berkeley.edu/node/58).

*Please note that the names of individuals mentioned in this article are pseudonyms and were designed to protect the privacy of the research participants.

NETWORKED PUBLICS

Social network sites are networked publics. A ***networked public*** is both the space constructed through networked technologies and the people who are connected by those technologies. Networked publics are spaces that share many of the same properties as unmediated publics like parks, cafes, malls, or parking lots. People use both types of space to gather with others for a variety of different purposes. Yet networked publics have four unique properties that affect what takes place. These properties are what make hanging out on a social network site different than sitting around at a café.

Four Unique Properties of Social Network Sites

1. Persistence: What you say sticks around. This is great for ***asynchronous communication*** but not so great when your boss finds the anticapitalism rant you wrote in 1994.

2. Searchability: With the flick of a few keystrokes, people can easily be found. The same features that let your former high school classmates find you also let your mother-in-law track everything you're doing.

3. Replicability: You can copy digital content from one place and paste it into another place without any loss in quality. This allows information to flow far and wide, which is great when that information is news, but not so great when that information is gossip.

4. Scalability: Physical spaces have limitations to how many people can be present. Networked publics do not. This combined with persistence and replicability means that interactions can scale in visibility to tremendous levels. Of course, just because millions of people can read something does not mean that they will. Likewise, just because something is intended for a small audience doesn't mean it'll stay that way.

These four properties are also magnified by dynamics of networked publics. Invisible audiences are the norm in networked publics. In person we can usually sense who has access to our conversations. In networked publics our audiences are invisible. Not only can we not see when people are lurking, we are also unable to predict future audiences.

Additionally, users must develop an acute sense of context when engaging in networked publics. Context is not a given in any situation, but teens are typically socialized into public life by adults who help them understand how to interpret social cues and develop a sense of context. Social network sites present an entirely new cultural environment and teens must learn how to negotiate the contexts there. While teens may choose to share information based on their understanding of a particular social context, this might be all wrong. Their content might be misinterpreted or taken out of context entirely. Teens must struggle to negotiate the different properties of networked publics in order to present themselves in a way that can be understood. The Internet lacks walls. Conversations spread and contexts collapse. Learning how to navigate this is an essential part of growing up in a mediated culture (boyd, 2009).

If social networking sites have unique properties and teens' online hangouts lack walls, how do educators support teen engagement in social network sites? We do not pretend to have all the answers, but we do have some concrete advice for teachers. For one, recognize that teens like Lynn want to hang out with their friends in teen spaces. Currently online spaces are the primary public spaces for teens to gather and this is one of the reasons why we see the blurring of public and private realms of life. When danah talked to teens, they consistently reported that they would rather socialize with peers in physical spaces without constant parental oversight. Since this is not an option for some and that they may have more access to networked publics than to public spaces, social network sites like Facebook and MySpace are often important alternatives.

Bits and Bytes of Research: An Additional Perspective

Bits and Bytes of Research is a sidebar designed to further our understanding of a topic. In this instance, C. J. Pascoe discusses friendship-driven practices of gay, lesbian, bisexual, transgendered, and queer teens and their use of social networking sites and other digital technology.

Safe Spaces to Connect: GLBTQ Teens and New Media

By C. J. Pascoe, Sociologist

On a fairly regular basis we hear about the dangers new media pose to kids—online bullying, getting involved with inappropriate significant others, and sexualized online content. What I found in talking to gay, lesbian, bisexual, transgendered, and queer (GLBTQ) teens is another side of the story about new media and youth. The teens I spoke with told me that new media can actually tap GLBTQ teens into communities they previously did not have access to and that this technological reach has allowed them to participate in the sort of sexual and romantic sphere that other teens might take for granted.

Like their straight counterparts, GLBTQ teens used new media to flirt, maintain relationships, and break up with significant others. Because GLBTQ teens have a harder time engaging in these romance cultures offline, digital media and, in particular, social network sites and cell phones provide a much more important resource for GLBTQ teens than for straight teens and allow them to build community, make supportive friends, and find romantic partners. Through using new media technologies many GLBTQ teens create mediated communities not easily accessible in their immediate physical environment. New media allows gay teens to form social groups, make friendships, and date much like straight teens do. However, this newfound independence and sexual and social liberation also renders some of these teens vulnerable to predatory practices by adults. But, for the teens I talk to, the benefits of enhancing their community through new media practices outweigh the negative experiences they've had.

Using new media, GLBTQ teens seek resources in terms of information and friends. One of my respondents, Adam, told me that to get answers to his questions or find support around issues of sexual identity he often went to the sexuality section of a teen-help Web site. Other teens joined online message boards, and others use social network sites to look up other GLBTQ teens who were going to be members of their freshman college class.

(Continued)

(Continued)

GLBTQ teens forge and sustain relationships online that would be difficult to access offline. The Internet can put gay teens in touch with other teens so that they can have the romantic flirting experiences that their heterosexual counterparts presumably find more readily in offline contexts. Robert told me that he was so frustrated about not finding other guys to date in his offline social groups that he wrote a Facebook note about his difficulties dating as a gay teen. Robert told me that a friend set him up on a blind date with Matt as a direct result of "my desperate note on Facebook!" Matt and Robert were introduced through Facebook, and after the initial set up, Robert giddily told me, "We've been texting the past few days a lot, he is really good looking, and a jock, believe it or not, but we seem to really have hit it off, I hope for the best." The two had a very sweet day picked for their first date: Valentine's Day.

For all the opportunities new media provides to create community for gay teens, it also puts them at risk as they seek this community. Robert, for instance, told me that an older man online had approached him in an inappropriate way. Instead of getting experience in often public and socially acceptable ways through structured rituals of heterosexuality, gay teens often have to find their own way. On the one hand the Internet is an invaluable lifeline, but on the other, it renders them more vulnerable to situations such as this one.

New media is an important tool for GLBTQ teens. It allows them to meet other teens like them for friendship or dating and affords them a level of independence as it does for straight teens to carry on relationships outside of the purview of their parents if need be. It also exposes them to some online dangers as they seek information about nonnormative romantic/sexual teen relationships.

Even though these online spaces may appear foreign from our adult perspective, teens are engaging in basically the same activities as we did when we were young. They are simply hanging out online instead of in malls, parking lots, and arcades. Second, although negotiating friendship and peer status may appear trivial, these skills are essential to a collaborative work culture. Learning how to navigate social norms and properly engage in impression management are also necessarily skills for adult life. These must be developed during the adolescent years and teachers should support the informal environments that make this learning possible.

Third, the Internet mirrors and magnifies all aspects of social life; if a student's online behavior is troubling, chances are that their offline behavior is also troubling. It only looks like more teens are engaged in risky or troublesome behaviors because the Internet makes such behaviors more visible than the classroom. It is usually easier to blame and ban the technology than address the underlying psychosocial problems, but this does not solve the problem. Social network sites provide a fantastic opportunity to intervene as a caring adult, not as a teacher or parent intent on punishing. In fact, the technology makes it easier for educators to find students who are in need of guidance. When all is said and done, most students like Lynn use social network sites to engage in relatively mundane activities. The rest desperately need your help.

Finally, remember that opening up dialogue is the best way to bridge divisions. Over the years, dozens of parenting guides have hit the market with so-called rules to keeping students safe. These adultcentric approaches tend to dismiss or seek to control teen practices. Alienating your students is counterproductive. When it comes to safety, the best technique is to start a conversation. What can protect our students is open and honest dialogue concerning the uncertainty of living in a culture shaped by networked publics. We don't know what these mean with regard to our public and private lives, and we would be fools to suggest that the future will be like the past. Our students are developing a sense of what this world might mean faster than we are. We have a responsibility to guide them and learn from them. To guide them, we cannot offer answers, but we can start a dialogue about advantages, disadvantages, and consequences. Before we can initiate this dialogue though, we need to think through how we understand socially appropriate behavior in specific contexts. We need to be cognizant of how specific spaces can shape our social interactions: our classroom, our homes, a BBQ with friends. The ethical concerns presented by social network sites are the "stuff" of teaching and educators are aptly prepared to initiate open and trusting conversations with students. Log on to YouTube and watch Henry Jenkins discuss his views on digital media and how schools usually handle the issue of MySpace (http://tiny.cc/teachtech_2_1).

A TEACHER'S PERSPECTIVE

How I Got 798 Friends

By Rick Ayers, High School Teacher

I have 253 friends on MySpace and 545 on Facebook. I got on MySpace and Facebook simply as another avenue of communication with my students. I started in 2005 when I was teaching high school in Berkeley, California. We are in an era of digital communication which is swamping traditional modes of connection and too often teachers find such contact to be a distraction if not downright subversive. Until 10 years ago, many teachers found computers and the Internet to be simply an irritant, the domain of lazy writing, sloppy research, and dangerous temptations. My feeling is that if this is where the students are, we should be there. I don't say this without some reservations.

(Continued)

(Continued)

Sometimes young people want to maintain a space that is their own, without the bumbling presence of the elders. Slang, graffiti, social networks are all erecting barriers to keep our judgmental eyes out. So an elder going onto such a space risks appearing as a transgressor, kind of like the dad barging in on the daughter's slumber party with a tray of healthy snacks. So why do I want to go into something set up to keep us out? Simply because it is where my base of students are. It is more effective than e-mail contact (kids often change addresses) and allows me to make announcements. When a former student was killed at Tuskegee, friends from across the country were able to connect, express sorrow, and plan gatherings quickly through Facebook. My wife, who is a college counselor at Berkeley High, has set up a Facebook account and creates groups of students at each grade level. She can then send out announcements, reminders, and advice— as well as answer questions—in a space that is informal, comfortable, and pretty constant for her students.

After setting up a Facebook or MySpace profile, it's important to be modest and low key. You have to step out tentatively at first and see if you are welcomed. I seldom *friend* students (I let them friend me) and even less often do I initiate a message, and I never do a wall post. I have connected with many former students in my school and use those contacts for the most effective way to put out announcements concerning reunions. If I get a friend request from a student who is not in our school or who I don't know well, I don't respond. An older person should not be aggressively contacting students or chatting them up.

I approach social networking sites like I approach teaching: with a fascination for the discourse and the literacy and the culture and the interests that students bring to the classroom. I don't view them as walking deficits, bubbling over with things they are *not*. Rather, students are creative, powerful, and wise in ways we must pay attention to tap into. Humbly entering a space that they have constructed is an important way I position myself as a mentor/coach/teacher. Certainly I do more of the learning in this space, and they do more of the teaching.

GETTING STARTED ON YOUR OWN PROFILE

In order to ask inquisitive questions, teachers need hands-on experience with social network sites. Here are four steps to get you started: (1) *Create a profile* on one social networking site that is popular in your school. This gives you a chance to learn the system and make a profile that represents you. Use your own profile and your own experiences to introduce conversations in the classroom—this way they will know you are online and that you too have to work to figure out what is appropriate. (2) *Keep your profile public and responsible,* but not overtly teacher-heavy! Add your favorite song, some photos of the family or your cat. Write about your hobbies, your favorite movie or book. Post blog entries (see Chapter 5) about how you came to determine what to include and exclude on your profile. Students can read about your own experiences in handling these issues, even though not all students will read your blog, you are setting a standard. (3) *Do not search for your students' profiles!* Reread Rick Ayers' blurb if you are tempted. If students *friend* you, say yes. This is a sign that they respect you. If they leave a comment, make sure to reciprocate. If something concerns you, privately ask why they chose to put a particular item up on their profile. Ask inquisitively, not critically— show that you care, not that you can reprimand. And (4) *the more present you are online, the more opportunity you have to influence the norms.* You can be a responsible example for students to emulate, but your job is not to enforce rules or condemn students' practices.

PEDAGOGICAL IMPLICATIONS AND CLASSROOM PRACTICES

As educators, we have the opportunity to directly engage with students about their actions on social networking sites. This *direct* engagement though should be thought of as a conversation, not a lecture or an assertion of power. Rick Ayers discusses how students "want to maintain a space that is their own" and if educators lecture *at* students about their space, we lose a chance to connect with students and help them create norms and reflect on how different online actions will be interpreted. By conversing with students, especially groups of students in an informal setting, we can allow them to consider their relationships with social networks and mediated public life. Here are some of the questions danah has used to help teens think about the ethics of online engagement:

1. Technically I have access to your profile. Should I look at it? Why or why not?

2. What do you think are the do's and don'ts for having a profile?

3. Who do you think looks at your profile? How would you feel if your mother, grandmother, coach, or future boss looked at your profile? Why? What do you think they would think of you based on your profile alone?

4. Pretend you were at a birthday party and a girl you barely knew took pictures of you that you know will get you into trouble, even though you did nothing wrong. She posted them to her profile. How does that make you feel? (When you asked her to take them down, she told you to lighten up. What next?)

5. Two of your friends are fighting. One posts an instant message conversation to her profile that makes the other look really bad. Now people are talking behind that girl's back. You doubt that this conversation really happened. What do you do?

These questions can foster a dialogue around online behavior and allow students to reflect on their experiences with social networking sites. It is important for educators to approach these types of conversations with an open mind and without condescension because, often, there are no right or wrong answers. Remember, forbidding participation on social network sites is not the answer; students will find ways to participate when adults are not looking. Our job is to create an informal setting in which to foster dialogue and ask inquisitive questions.

Social network sites are popular because teens are using the Internet to carve out a youth space and engage in informal learning with their peers even if it has to happen in mediated environments when face-to-face encounters are not viable. Just as book learning is important for our students, we need to broaden our definition of learning to include social experiences that are vital to maturation.

Here are some of our ideas for integrating social network issues into the curricula:

- Media literacy curriculum is a wonderful place to discuss the cultural transition of private and public space and online behavior
- History classes offer a site in which to discuss how social practices such as communication have changed over time
- Many popular novels and plays discuss public life and private matters. Try using themes from literature, especially teen favorites, to start conversations concerning social networking sites
- Health curriculum also provides a space in which to talk about online safety and experiences with public-private issues
- Homeroom, advisory, and leadership classes provide settings to discuss social experiences and the ethics of online engagement
- School publications like the school newspaper and classroom e-zines are places to bring up social network issues
- Peer advisors or facilitators provide a great way for older teens to teach their younger peers in small, informal groups about social network sites
- Use the group functions of social networking sites to have students run their own peer-based discussions regarding their social experiences on these network publics

Log onto our Web site (www.teachingtechsavvykids.com) and give us your ideas or explain how your school handles these issues.

A COUNSELOR'S PERSPECTIVE

Escalating Emotions: Social Network Sites and Youth

By Ann Lauriks, Middle School Counselor

As social network sites become more commonplace in our adult world, they have already become the norm in adolescents' lives. For the students I work with, social network sites are not only an avenue for communication and socialization, but they also provide a forum for self-expression. Thus, Facebook and MySpace are interactive worlds where adolescents communicate ideas, explore their own identity, develop and enhance their social skills, and demonstrate their sense of self on a daily basis.

As a middle school counselor, much of my focus is aimed at helping adolescents recognize their emotions and develop effective interpersonal skills. Developmentally, adolescence is a time of exploration. For teens, learning how to negotiate feelings and relationships can be hard. As a result, primary feelings like fear, rejection, sadness, jealousy, frustration, guilt, or disappointment can be exhibited instead through anger, which is a more tolerable feeling to manage at such a tender age. Instead of expressing their primary feelings, teens tend to react with anger, and serious miscommunication can then impact and compromise friendships. My role often becomes one of helping adolescents negotiate their feelings and communicate them clearly in an effort toward conflict resolution. Because of the increased use of social network sites, technology often plays a role in escalating conflicts among close friends and peers. In certain instances conflicts can become magnified with a few online posts. A primary example of this effect is when a conflict over potato chips eventually led to verbal threats.

Stephanie and Carla were eighth-grade students who circulated in the same peer group. One school day during snack break, Stephanie sat enjoying her potato chips and socializing with her friends without conflict. Carla then approached Stephanie and asked if she could have some of her chips. Stephanie opted not to share with Carla, leaving Carla feeling rejected. Struggling to identify her true emotions, Carla reacted impulsively in anger. She initially responded by speaking negatively about Stephanie to their peer group while at school. Once at home, Carla continued to vent her anger and posted derogatory comments about Stephanie online. Stephanie noted these postings and felt attacked, hurt, and embarrassed. Like Carla, Stephanie responded out of anger and retaliated by posting similarly negative comments. As their interactions continued, each girl enhanced the magnitude of her verbal attacks until Carla threatened Stephanie's safety.

(Continued)

(Continued)

I learned about the escalation when Stephanie was unable to concentrate in school the following day. She was fearful that Carla was going to follow through with her threats and came to me for assistance. In an effort to help the girls understand their feelings and communicate them clearly, I met individually with both Stephanie and Carla and helped them each identify their primary emotions and how acting on the secondary emotion of anger only perpetuated and intensified their conflict. I then brought the girls together for conflict mediation where they were able to address their feelings face-to-face. Within 30 minutes, the girls were laughing and had apologized for their words, acknowledging that indeed their emotions did get out of hand and that they had reacted mainly out of anger.

This is a classic case of adolescent miscommunication. While it is common for teens to react with anger, technology can intensify the situation. Several elements concerning social network sites are important to consider. First, the lack of face-to-face communication removes the ability of the speaker to observe the impact of her words on the listener, making it easier for one to speak more harshly. In the case of Carla and Stephanie, I believe that the lack of face-to-face interaction allowed both girls' angry online responses to escalate into what Stephanie perceived to be a serious threat from Carla. Second, the audience of the cyber world lies in the fact that it is endless. Essentially any comments posted, pleasant or not, are potentially public and beyond anyone's control; as danah suggested, there is the issue of an invisible audience, so it is easy for one person to take a private conflict and open it for all their friends to see and add to. Third, while the feelings of the adolescent may later shift, what they originally post online sticks. As adolescents learn to negotiate their feelings, it is vital that they understand the impact of their self-expressions online. As they progress through the normal process of exploration and experimentation with their identities, they may say or do things in the moment that will not necessarily match their feelings in a month or even a week. But as they continue to grow and try on different personas online, what they say or do online can be difficult to escape.

It is imperative that adolescents understand the pros of social network sites as well as the risks. Teens need to be aware of the ramifications of online postings: their duration, their impact, and their consequences. It is the responsibility of educators, administrators, and counselors to discuss these issues with adolescents. Electronic communication is such an important aspect of an adolescent's life, this conversation is not a one-time event; it is an ongoing process that needs to be developmentally appropriate. In my work with students, the most useful discussions are ones where adolescents feel heard. I always try to engage them in a conversation with open-ended questions and end up doing more listening than talking.

Here are some helpful tips for adults to share with students:

- Writing is a great way to vent one's emotions, but you do not always need to post what you write. Try writing something down when you are angry and then take a break and try to focus on other things.

  o Discuss with students that they might not be able to erase what they posted online!

- Would the comments you post online change in anyway if you were physically talking to the person? Would you use the same words? Would the level of conflict be the same?

  o Have students share instances in which there were miscommunications between friends and discuss how they mended these situations.
  o Have students evaluate reasons why online conflicts can escalate more rapidly than face-to-face conflicts.

- If an incident does arise, find a person you trust and talk to them about what you are feeling. It is usually safer to have a conversation with a caring adult, school counselor, or a good friend rather than immediately go online and post one's feelings.

  o Remind students that what they write sticks and will be accessible by an infinite amount of viewers. Once you post online, you can lose control of your words and their intended impact.

- Educators can also share their teenage experiences with students and talk about how miscommunication occurred, especially if a written note or a phone call (or some other form of communication our students are privy to) magnified the instance.

  o See if it is possible to compare and contrast how written notes or telephones magnified the situation in the same manner in which social network sites can.
  o Adults can normalize the challenge in identifying primary feelings and acting on those rather than allowing the secondary emotion of anger to guide actions. Share healthy ways to express feelings of anger and ask students to also discuss what they have done in the past to express feelings of anger.

AN ACTIVITY FOR TEACHERS

danah has provided an interesting vignette for teachers to read about a high school student named Mary who went shopping for a dress for homecoming. Read through this vignette and see how Mary's shopping strategies compare to your own. The goal of this activity is to identify and understand some of the key differences (and potential similarities) between the common social practices of kids and those of adults. Keep in mind that, for now, we are intentionally focusing on everyday practices and interests and avoiding a discussion specific to school-based practices such as studying, homework, and note taking.

Student Purchasing Practices

By danah boyd

I had just finished giving a talk about youth culture to a room full of professionals who worked in the retail industry when a woman raised her hand to tell me a story. It was homecoming season and her daughter Mary was going to go to homecoming for the first time. What fascinated this mother was that her daughter's approach to shopping was completely different from her own.

Using Google and a variety of online shopping sites, Mary researched dresses online, getting a sense for what styles she liked and reading information about what was considered stylish that year. Next, Mary and her friends went to the local department store as a small group, toting along their digital cameras (even though they're banned). They tried on the dresses, taking pictures of each other in the ones that fit. Upon returning home, Mary uploaded the photos to her Facebook and asked her broader group of friends to comment on which they liked the best. Based on this feedback, she decided which dress to purchase but didn't tell anyone because she wanted her choice to be a surprise. Rather than returning to the store, Mary purchased the same dress online at a cheaper price based on the information on the tag that she had written down when she initially saw the dress. She went for the cheaper option because her mother had given her a set budget for homecoming shopping; this allowed her to spend the rest on accessories.

Mary's mother was completely flabbergasted by the way in which her daughter moved seamlessly between the digital and physical worlds to consume clothing. More confusing to this mother, a professional in retail, was the way in which her daughter viewed her steps as completely natural. In telling this story, Mary's mother was perplexed by the technology choices made by her daughter. Yet, most likely, Mary saw her steps in a practical way: research, test out, get feedback, purchase. Her choices were to maximize her options, make a choice that would be socially accepted, and purchase the dress at the cheapest price. Her steps were not about maximizing technology but about using it to optimize what she did care about.

Technology alters the way that Mary shops, but it also alters the way in which she socializes with her friends. Like many teens, Mary sees shopping and socializing with friends as inherently intertwined. While she can take her friends with her when she shops, technology allows her to connect the two in a much more complex way.

After reading danah's vignette, what was your initial reaction to Mary's use of technology for shopping and socializing? Think back to one of your first purchases for an important occasion, what strategies did you use to find the right look? What are some of the obvious similarities and differences? As an adult, have you adopted some of the same technological techniques as Mary or were you just as surprised by Mary's strategies as her mother?

Take What You Learned Into the Classroom

Now, take what you have learned about Mary and her shopping strategies into your own classroom and ask students how they use technology to socialize and research meaningful items in their own lives. Music is a topic danah and I think will elicit rich responses from students. (You could also include other topics such as movies or television shows.) Try asking these questions:

1. Who are your favorite musical inspirations, e.g., singers, bands, DJs, producers, or American Idol winners?

2. Where did you first hear about them?

3. How do you learn more about them?

4. What are some of the things you do if you are a fan of a particular performer?

5. How do you listen to your music? What kinds of technology allow you to listen to music?

6. How do you purchase music? Or if there is a way to get music without paying for it, describe this process.

7. How do you share music?

8. How do you know when new music is going to be released?

9. Describe ways to include your favorite songs or performers in your daily life, e.g., ring tones or MySpace page.

By bringing these questions into the classroom, you have taken on the role of teacher-researcher and now have an opportunity to understand how your students' practices concerning popular culture compare to your own experiences when you were their age. Being a teacher-researcher in this area can assist you in understanding your students' relationships to technology and can arm you with insight into their out-of-school lives and interests.

We also feel your students should engage in some of their own research regarding music—with their parents, guardians, older family members, older friends, or even other teachers. Why should you always be the one researching their behavior? After you and your students have discussed their responses to the questions, have your students ask their elders the same questions you asked them, making sure students question them about their musical experiences as kids.

When students return to class with these responses, have a discussion concerning the similarities and differences between the students' own answers and those they collected. Both danah and I think there will be interesting parallels between *then* and *now*, and here are just some similarities that might appear across age groups:

Then	Now
Making a "mixed tape"	Making a "play list"
Recording music off the radio	Downloading music off the Internet
Using a synthesizer to make songs	Using software to make beats
Learning The Electric Slide, the Macarena or The Running Man from friends or music videos	Learning Crank Dat from YouTube or playing the video game Dance Dance Revolution
Listening to a Sony Walkman	Listening to an iPod or MP3 player
Having air guitar contests	Playing the video game Guitar Hero
Putting posters of favorite artists on your bedroom wall	Using a favorite song as a ring tone or as one's MySpace song

This portion of the activity should hopefully give you and your students some common ground for strengthening your intergenerational relationships around new media.

Profile Creation

Creating social network profiles can be a wonderful way for students to gain a better understanding of specific characters, historical figures, famous mathematicians and scientists, important locations, or even different species. This does not mean that students actually join Facebook as Martin Luther King Jr. or Eleanor Roosevelt. Plain paper and colored pens can do the trick if computers with Word, PowerPoint, or Publisher are not available or you do not have online access to free applications such as Ning (http://www.ning.com) or Google Groups (http://groups.google.com/).

In order to develop a profile for people, it is important for students to have an understanding of their lives whether this includes actually researching their lives or gaining deep knowledge of fictional characters.

With this knowledge students can make arguments for the construction of profiles, interactions, and postings: What would be Amelia

Earhart's favorite song or Eleanor Roosevelt's profile picture? Who would Harriet Tubman invite to be her friend or what would be Abraham Lincoln's hobbies and interests? What would Martin Luther King's blog from the Birmingham jail contain? Who would Scout from *To Kill a Mockingbird* poke and why? What would Harry Potter's friend list look like? What kind of dialogue would Sir Isaac Newton and Tyrannosaurus Rex have on their walls? Would Malcolm X have joined a Facebook group for nonviolence? What would be Albert Einstein's favorite quote on his page? What would Gandhi be doing right now on Facebook? What types of activities would Cesar Chavez organize on MySpace?

Not only would this type of activity really engage students and get them thinking about people, places, or dinosaurs and their historical contexts but it would also give the teacher an opportunity to have students analyze appropriate behavior in networked publics and what it says about someone who is networked. How do we understand people in networks and how do their networks give us insight into their identity?

SHARE YOUR INSIGHTS, STORIES AND EXPERIENCES!

As educators, it is important to rely on colleagues for support, ideas, and even friendship. We have created a Web site (www.teachingtech-savvykids.com) just for the purpose of bringing educators together to connect, share, and support one another. This online community forum is an opportunity for you to continue discussing issues concerning new media, collaborative and interactive sites, and the interpretation and evaluation of information. From this online community can come a rich and diverse space in which to upload, download, and discuss ideas, general activities, or even content-based activities and pose questions.

We want to hear from you. Join our community of teachers and post your responses to this chapter. Here are some questions to address:

1. At your school, how have teachers or administrators dealt with ethical issues or initiated discussions with students concerning social network sites?

2. Which design features of social network sites, e.g., *profiles*, *friends*, *status update*, or *comments*, might lend themselves to specific classroom activities? Why or why not?

3. Ann Lauriks, the middle school counselor, described her experiences with students as one of helping them negotiate their feelings and communicate them clearly in an effort toward conflict resolution. What happens to students who do not have access to school

counselors? Are teachers prepared to help students negotiate their feelings and communicate clearly, especially when the conflict may have occurred online?

4. danah boyd described in her Student Purchasing Practices how much times have changed when it comes to the Internet and shopping experiences. What are some of the other ways that "times have changed" when it comes to young people?

Feel free to pose your own questions on the online community forum.

REFERENCES AND HELPFUL RESOURCES

Bibliography of social networking site research: http://www.danah.org/SNSResearch.html

boyd, d. (2007). Information access in a networked world. Talk presented to Pearson Publishing, Palo Alto, California, November 2. http://www.danah.org/papers/talks/Pearson2007.html

boyd, d. (2008). Why youth heart social network sites: The role of networked publics in teenage social life. In D. Buckingham (Ed.), *Youth, identity, and digital media* (pp. 119–142). The John D. and Catherine T. MacArthur Foundation Series on Digital Media and Learning. Cambridge, MA: The MIT Press.

boyd, d. m., & Ellison, N. B. (2007). Social network sites: Definition, history, and scholarship. *Journal of Computer-Mediated Communication, 13*(1), article 11. http://jcmc.indiana.edu/v0113/issue1/boyd.ellison.html

boyd, d. (2009). Do you see what I see?: Visibility of practices through social media. *Supernova* and *Le Web*. San Francisco and Paris, 1 and 10 December. http://www.danah.org/papers/talks/2009/SuperonovaLeWeb.html

boyd, d. (n.d.) Best of Apophenia, danah's blog: http://www.zephoria.org/thoughts/bestof.html

boyd, d. (n.d.) danah's research publications: http://www.danah.org/papers/

Davies, J., & Merchant, G. (2009). *Web 2.0 for schools: Learning and social participation.* New York: Peter Lang Publishing.

Digital Youth Research: Kids' Informal Learning with Digital Media: http://digitalyouth.ischool.berkeley.edu/

Facebook: http://www.facebook.com

Google Groups: http://groups.google.com/

Jenkins, H. (with Clinton, K., Purushotma, R., Robison, A., & Weigel, M.) (2006). *Confronting the challenges of participatory culture: Education for the 21st century.* The John D. and Catherine T. MacArthur Foundation. Retrieved August 18, 2007 from http://digitallearning.macfound.org.

MySpace: http://www.myspace.com

Ning: http://www.ning.com

Watkins, S. C. (2009). *The young and the digital: What the migration to social network sites, games, and anytime, anywhere media means for our future.* Boston, MA: Beacon Press.

YouTube

Creating, Connecting, and Learning Through Video

Patricia G. Lange and Jessica K. Parker

INTRODUCTION

This chapter continues the discussion of networked public culture through an analysis of YouTube, another site where kids hang out these days. YouTube, a media-sharing site, enables people to upload, share, and view digital content and has become another social space for kids and teens to pursue creative interests such as watching, making, and critiquing videos. But with participation in a networked public comes a need for students to take responsibility for their actions and representations, and that is one of the reasons why intergenerational relationships are so important. We conclude with suggestions for how YouTube, or more generally, video creation and sharing can play a role in educational settings.

ONLINE MEDIA SHARING AND YOUTUBE

YouTube, which was founded in February 2005, is a video-sharing Web site where people can upload, share, and view videos. (Visit http://www .youtube.com/.) Many people enjoy watching videos on YouTube, which has a very wide range of content, from corporate sponsored works to more personal forms. Many people associate YouTube with humor and shock value, but it actually contains a variety of videos and facilitates a range of different types of social relationships and uses. Jessica uses YouTube for social and personal purposes such as viewing family videos of her nieces and nephews who live across the United States and sharing silly videos via e-mail with her friends. Other people not only watch videos on YouTube but also enjoy **posting** videos. Patricia actually posts her own video blogs that cover topics of potential interest to other scholars conducting research on YouTube and to anthropologists studying media. In addition, Patricia's video blog also includes more personal and fun videos on topics such as public art and sculpture.

COMMON MISCONCEPTIONS OF YOUTUBE

Many people associate YouTube with funny, shocking, or news worthy videos made hastily by amateurs. But the site has many dimensions, and it looks quite different depending upon one's entry and exit points. People who use YouTube to watch the occasional video will experience the site in a far different way from those who see it as a social network site. For the former group, YouTube simply offers a convenient viewing platform. For the latter group, YouTube enables people to connect socially with people around the world who share a similar passion for making media or for connecting on important issues. People may be surprised to learn that many of the people Patricia interviewed:

- Easily spend hours at a time on the site
- Seek out videos in personal networks
- Check for new videos and comments on a daily basis
- See it as crucial to have their own account on the site so that they can access more intensive forms of media-driven sharing and participation
- Extensively post text comments and ratings to videos
- Post and promote their own videos
- Feature *other* people's videos on their own account pages to give the videos or the people or ideas contained within them more visibility
- Receive advice, emotional encouragement, and technical support from people they meet on YouTube

A SOCIAL SPACE

FEATURES OF YOUTUBE

A person's first introduction to YouTube is often through a link that a colleague, friend, or family member wishes to share. For instance, it might be a funny video or a news item or even a video that has received many views—since it is easy to see the number of times an uploaded video has been accessed. This act of sending someone an e-mail with a link to a video is much more than watching videos. It offers a way to socialize with other people and maintain a connection that allows people to come together through the sharing and oftentimes discussion of a video. One of

YouTube's strengths is that anyone can watch videos. While some people are happy to just watch videos, others enjoy having access to more features such as uploading, commenting on, ranking, or even making videos in response to other YouTubers' videos.

In order to upload a video or to "broadcast yourself" as YouTube's motto suggests, a user must establish an account on the site. With an account, a user is given a "channel page" and their uploaded videos are present on this page. It is like a MySpace profile page in that it includes the person's YouTube name. It also contains data that YouTube tracks, such as the sum total of views that all of the person's videos have received and information people choose to post about themselves such as their hobbies and goals. Currently having an account on YouTube is free, although people must submit a short form that includes a valid e-mail address to join the site and upload videos.

Patricia has her own YouTube channel called *AnthroVlog*. As a way to familiarize yourself with YouTube, visit Patricia's channel, read the description of her channel, and watch a few of her videos (http://www.youtube.com/user/AnthroVlog).

Figure 3.1   Patricia's AnthroVlog

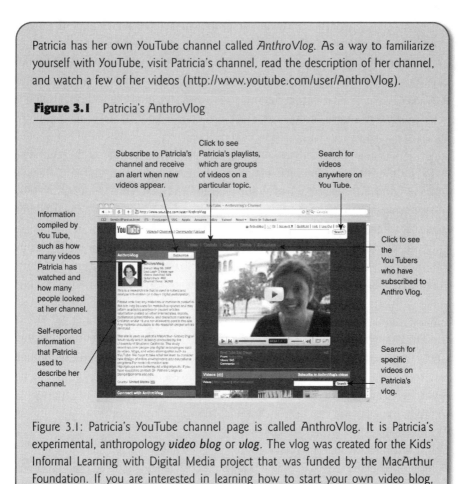

Figure 3.1: Patricia's YouTube channel page is called AnthroVlog. It is Patricia's experimental, anthropology *video blog* or *vlog*. The vlog was created for the Kids' Informal Learning with Digital Media project that was funded by the MacArthur Foundation. If you are interested in learning how to start your own video blog,

(Continued)

(Continued)

Patricia recommends *Secrets of Video Blogging* (2006). Also visit the Freevlog Web site at http://www.freevlog.org; it was created by two of the coauthors of the *Secrets of Video Blogging.*

There are a number of places on YouTube to find answers to your questions and videos that address your concerns.

- For how-to articles on creating and managing an account or watching and uploading videos, visit http://www.google.com/support/youtube/
- There is also a "help" link which will take you to videos YouTubers have made offering tips and advice: http://www.youtube.com/user/YouTubeHelp
- Check out the community help forums to ask questions and share expertise: http://www.google.com/support/forum/p/youtube?hl=en

Many people who create an account on YouTube wish to do more than watch videos or even upload their own videos. Just like Patricia, they are interested in participating in a social space where it is possible to interact with video creators with similar interests by posting text comments or a video response. Having an account also enables viewers to accomplish a range of functions:

- Rating a video with a number of stars (ratings go from one star which means *Poor* to five stars which means *Awesome!*)
- ***Flagging*** inappropriate videos such as those that contain violent or copyrighted material
- Subscribing to particular video creators on YouTube. To subscribe to a video, a person with an account merely needs to hit the subscribe button on a video maker's channel page. After subscribing, the person will be alerted via e-mail whenever the video maker posts a new video to YouTube.

On Patricia's *AnthroVlog* page, notice the ratings of each of her videos. Click on an individual video and see if there are any text comments. What is the tone of these comments? Do you notice if Patricia (known as *AnthroVlog*) responds to individual comments? What can you surmise is Patricia's reasoning for responding to individual comments?

VIDEO COMMENTS: POSITIVE AND NEGATIVE ASPECTS

It is well-known that having such an open and diverse set of YouTube viewers invites a range of reactions to one's carefully crafted and often very personal material. Needless to say, not all comments from viewers are positive and encouraging. Some people have experienced mean-spirited or hurtful criticism while others have experienced even more serious complications such as receiving physically threatening or harassing messages. Patricia found diverse reactions to criticisms and hurtful remarks (Lange, 2007a). In general younger people in her study felt more strongly about preserving what they saw as access to free speech even when remarks were hurtful or threatening (Lange, 2007b). They did not want to condone formal mechanisms that would prevent people from posting commentary except under certain conditions.

For example, youth did not respond well to the proposal that someone should not be able to post a text comment until they had participated on the site for a specific length of time and had built up the trust of the community. Struggling to find their own voices and maintain their freedom to participate, young people in Patricia's study were sensitive to any rules that could threaten their own ability to participate or respond to videos. Some of them even argued that literacy includes being able to handle and deal with such commentary.

YouTube has several features to address such problems. For instance, it implemented a rating system in which people with accounts can negatively rate a video or even a text comment that is hurtful, racist, or sexist. In addition, people with accounts can remove any comment on one of their own videos that they do not feel is appropriate. Another option is to set up one's own comment system so that the account owner can moderate all comments. This means that no comment will be posted until the moderator, who is the owner of the channel page, reads and approves it. This feature is especially useful for families and teachers who might not want all commentary to automatically be publicly posted without prior screening and approval.

Educators may be tempted to focus on the more visible, negative aspects of commenting on videos and fail to see or appreciate the excitement that kids (and adults) feel when they receive positive reactions to a meaningful video. Many kids report that people in their schools and neighborhoods are not particularly interested in video or in the technical aspects of making and editing them. Yet many of today's youth understand that making media is a way to participate in our mediated culture and some even aspire to become professional media makers. Posting a video on a site like YouTube that contains other video enthusiasts who can provide specific commentary or even knowledgeable encouragement can be extremely important. As one 15-year old boy that Patricia interviewed said,

> Even when you get one good comment (it) makes up for 50 mean comments, 'cause it's just the fact of knowing that someone else out there liked your videos and stuff, and it doesn't really matter about everyone else that's criticized you.

VIDEO RESPONSES

Now see if there are video responses to Patricia's videos on *AnthroVlog*. A video response—when people post their own video in response to someone else's video—is another interesting form of participation on YouTube. For instance, with Patricia's "Midwest Gathering" video, users posted additional footage from the Midwest YouTube meet-up as a video response. (A meet-up is an in-person gathering dedicated to YouTubers interested in hanging out and, in some cases, collaborating.) Additionally users can simply record a video of themselves talking into the camera and explaining what they liked or did not like about a particular video. Part of YouTube's appeal is this peer-based reciprocity in which a person, through comments or video, can provide critique, advice, or even simple encouragement to the original creator.

In a digital era, participatory cultures such as YouTube offer ways of engaging, relating, and commenting on one another's creations whereby peer-based sharing and reciprocity are the norm (Jenkins, 2009). These norms reinforce interest-driven practices such as making films or videos that are time-consuming, intensely motivating, and challenging. Are there ways to instill peer-based sharing and feedback as a classroom norm in order to engage students in content-area subjects?

GEEKING OUT WITH VIDEO

> *Shooting a movie is like a stagecoach ride in the Old West. At first you hope for a nice trip. Soon you just hope to reach your destination!*
>
> —Fictional director Ferrand in *Day for Night*
> (Truffaut, 1973), subtitles in English from French

Making videos can be a long and uncertain process that requires creators to adapt to their surroundings and improvise because of unforeseen circumstances. In a lot of instances, video making is a collaborative, socially reliant process with creators working with each other and their participants, e.g., actors and subjects. Thus it can be a "stagecoach ride," a long, bumpy, laborious and yet also engaging, creative, and powerful process starting from the small nugget of a video maker's idea and concluding with peer feedback and critique on a full-fledged video. Most importantly, a metaphorical stagecoach ride contains the stuff for geeking out. As Ito et al. (2008) describe:

> The ability to engage with media and technology in an intense, autonomous, and interest-driven way is a unique feature of

today's media environment. Particularly for kids with newer technology and high-speed Internet at home, the Internet can provide access to an immense amount of information related to their particular interests, and it can support various forms of "geeking out"—an intense commitment to or engagement with media or technology. . . . (Geeking out) is a mode of learning that is peer-driven, but focused on gaining deep knowledge and expertise in specific areas of interest. (p. 28)

Since video making can be an intense and unpredictable activity, YouTube provides an important peer-driven space for youth to geek out with digital video. They can improve their skills and deepen their knowledge. YouTube offers a network for kids (and adults) to join other YouTubers, share expertise, and participate in a community centered on digital video. Below, Ricardo describes how he geeked out in a high school devoted to media literacy and video production.

A STUDENT'S RETROSPECTIVE

Countless Hours of Freedom

By Ricardo Navarro, San Francisco State University Student

I was lucky enough to go to a high school that had a media program and media classes. Our film projects varied from silent 30-second films to fiction films and even documentaries. Sometimes teachers would work together and create projects that included multiple subjects and video production. Even though media class was for only 50 minutes per day and only five times a week, I would spend more time in that classroom than in any of the other classrooms put together.

When we had film projects at school I spent countless hours thinking about my film: day in and day out, in class, while walking home, eating, even while watching television. I always wanted to make the best film I could because each movie I made was going to be watched by my class or even the school. That's why I would always work really hard on each film assignment. When my movie screened at the school's film festival, my friends and I were sitting in the back and I just kept staring at the program to see when it would come on. I remember when the movie before my film started, in my head I was thinking, "What if no one likes it? What if no one gets my jokes?" By the time my friends noticed me, I was sweating bullets. As my movie was playing on the big screen, I was not even watching it. I was looking at the reaction of the audience. Luckily my peers loved it.

With filmmaking I have the freedom to do anything. I usually had to follow some guidelines or rules depending on the type of film I made and the books we

(Continued)

(Continued)

read. But even if 30 students were given a film assignment about a certain topic, we would not end up making the same film. When it comes to film everyone thinks differently, everyone feels differently, everyone understands differently. So one student might show their version of the assignment on screen in a completely different way and blow my mind because I had never thought of it in that way and still both films worked very well. That's what amazes me about film! No matter how many movies and scripts were made, there was always something new and different that would come out and still attract the audience's attention.

I loved working on all the stages of filmmaking: pre-production, production, post-production, and then the class screening. My favorite stage though was when I started out by brainstorming ideas. I would close my eyes and my movie would start rolling. I could see how my movie would come out, and even though none of my films were exactly how I imagined them in my head, most of them came close.

Patricia interviewed students outside of school who explained that they started making videos because they wanted to do something "just for fun," or they were messing around with friends—that is they began to tinker, explore, and extend their understanding and interest in making videos (Ito et al., 2010). Yet as they continued to make media, many kids began to recognize areas of improvement for their work and wanted to devote the time and energy needed to do so. Although some reported getting useful feedback from family and friends, most kids that Patricia spoke with felt they learned quite a bit by watching their own videos and recognizing mistakes and areas of technical and creative improvement. Once they had achieved a basic understanding about how to make and edit a video, some teens began experimenting with more complicated and advanced editing tools such as Final Cut Pro, a desktop-editing program. At this point, few friends and family in their local social spheres could provide meaningful technical or artistic assistance.

Many kids discussed with Patricia how their participation on YouTube allowed them to learn about crafting videos in a specific genre by watching videos from their favorite YouTubers. In some cases kids received feedback from other advanced amateurs about issues of audience and how to tailor their works to a larger population. For instance, YouTubers provided information on a new model of microphone that would improve sound quality or they made suggestions about how to make the overall message of the video more effective by editing a specific sequence of clips.

Although many kids enjoy making videos, once they achieve certain skills and target specific goals, they begin to describe their video making in ways that many adults would characterize as *work*. In other words, improving one's technical ability with video includes having patience, accessing online tutorials and information pages, and repeatedly redoing scenes on the computer until certain effects or goals are achieved. Many advanced amateurs described some of the difficulties and drawbacks of trying to make videos. These problems included coordinating with other teens' schedules to make and edit videos, learning to use complex editing software, and maximizing the quality of their videos. Kids often described devoting many hours to the making of a video but their motivation was often sustained by the fact that their project emerged from a "fun" inspirational idea.

STORIES FROM THE FIELD

Learning About Civic Engagement

By Patricia G. Lange, Anthropologist

Many kids use YouTube in different ways: for social reasons, as a serious hobby, or just to have fun. Adults tend to think of kids as making certain kinds of videos including personal, comedic, or more serious. Yet I found in my extensive study of YouTube that many kids across the United States who make entertaining and comedic videos often have an interest in documenting aspects of their personal lives or political opinions that they feel are important. Contemporary generations of kids do not segment their videos in the same way that adults do. Often adults tend to categorize kids as either having goal-oriented aspirations or are just messing around with video. But kids are increasingly carrying around cameras in their day-to-day activities in ways that enable them to act, think, and later reflect more deeply on what has happened to them by manipulating and sharing everyday, recorded images.

   The three teens briefly profiled below—Wendy, Frank, and Max*—offer particularly illustrative examples of the many different dimensions to kids' multifaceted contemporary video making on YouTube. All include in their body of work examples of videos that engage in wider topics of civic interest. These topics range from raising awareness about local issues to larger concerns about global conflict. What they have in common is an interest in using more personal forms of video making styles to participate politically in wider networked public spheres. They demonstrate that kids can and do use video to engage in important civic issues in their own way.

Documenting Neighborhood Problems: Wendy

Wendy, a teenage girl, enjoys making a video sitcom series with her friends. In her spare time she also volunteers for an organization that offers internships for kids to gain experience with community improvement projects. The organization is a

(Continued)

(Continued)

nonprofit group that works to improve the physical environment of underserved areas in a major metropolitan city. For this organization, Wendy and her friends elected to make a documentary about a local park in a nearby ethnic neighborhood that could be rebuilt. She visited other parks in the city and compared those facilities to the local park, which had fallen into disrepair. She next interviewed people from the community and asked them about their vision for a newly built local park.

Her investigative report showed that the facilities in the ethnic community lacked a number of features that other parks had. She juxtaposed her documented observations with remarks from people she interviewed, who offered suggestions for how the local park could be improved. Their suggestions included making the new park larger, using elements that reflected the culture of the local neighborhood, making the play structures and equipment safer and bringing them up to date, and keeping the park cleaner on a regular basis.

The documentary was well received both by viewers from the city as well as those within the organization which encouraged its development. Wendy said the organization requested that she make more documentaries in the future, which she plans to do. Wendy's experiences show that kids can and do make videos that are meant to engage in issues of broader civic interest and she is able to bring to bear aspects of video making she has learned in other genres into her documentary work. Although the focus of her work is generally on making comedic videos, the open-ended, do-it-yourself platform of YouTube also facilitates distribution of a wide range of genres and messages from individual video makers. Kids who are more familiar with appearing on camera may choose to take advantage of this kind of medium to circulate personal and political messages that resonate with a much wider civic sphere.

Raising Awareness About Internet Access: Frank

A teenager named Frank has a very eclectic channel on YouTube. His work cannot be pinned down to a single genre as he makes humorous videos, tutorials and analysis, and personal, diary forms of videos that express his views on different issues. One of his videos includes remarks about a political issue that is increasingly important in the United States' political climate. This is the issue of net neutrality. The Save the Internet organization defines net neutrality as ensuring that Internet providers, such as AT&T or Comcast do not "[block], [speed] up, or [slow] down Web content based on its source, ownership, or destination." The subject of net neutrality is hotly contested. Some corporations and Internet service providers reportedly want to be able to block certain political content, charge rates or slow down transmission of information based on specific criteria. Thus, individuals who cannot afford to pay additional charges for deluxe services may experience a slow down or blockage in their ability to transmit their messages online.

As evidenced in one of his videos on the subject, Frank strongly supports net neutrality. In his video he explains why he feels it is important as a way to protect free speech. He argues that without it, large media companies and service providers may have greater ability to control what we see. He expresses the concern that having an ability to discriminate in quality of service or charges for using online services could threaten to turn the Internet into more of a one-way medium controlled by corporations and governmental bodies. He argues that this has happened with radio and newspapers. He traces through potential political ramifications of having corporate- and government-controlled Internet infrastructures that could restrict important forms of information dissemination. He expresses concern, for instance, that future news dissemination may be even more biased than is seen today.

In contrast to Wendy's approach, Frank does not go on location nor does he use advanced editing and montage techniques with dramatically contrasting images to make his point. Frank simply faces the camera and argues his case. In many ways the structure of his videos directly illustrate one of his most basic points. He is able to communicate his personal views and political messages in his preferred way without being judged on the basis of arbitrary or controversial criteria such as technical quality or political content. His videos illustrate a point made by video blogging pioneer Ryanne Hodson (2007), who argues that making and distributing videos about one's point of view is a form of activism (for more information see "Video Blogging and Activism" on *AnthroVlog*). Notably, Frank mentions in his video that he was very influenced by another video on net neutrality which made points that he thought were important enough to pass on to his viewers. A communicative chain results in which Frank views messages through video and then transmits political messages that are important to him. Having his own platform enables him to raise awareness and participate in the public sphere. As he mentions in his video, he is a teenager who will soon be able to vote. His video becomes an important part of his emerging engagement with larger issues of civic interest.

Participating in Global Political Debates: Max

Max is a 14-year-old boy who has had success on YouTube with his comedic videos. In one particularly successful video, he spontaneously captured his mother singing a song as they hung out on the beach. Wearing her headphones and closing her eyes, she was unaware that people around them had started to watch her and laugh. Media companies picked up the comedic video and Max says it aired on television shows such as *Good Morning America*.

Max wishes to be a filmmaker in the future and most of his videos orient around comedic themes. Yet Max also has extended family from the Middle East and he has used his video making talents to express his concern for them. In one political video that he made, he juxtaposes disturbing photographs of events in Palestine. As the images are displayed, the theme song to *Schindler's List* plays in the background.

(Continued)

(Continued)

Schindler's List is a film about the Jewish Holocaust. This juxtaposition compares Palestinian experiences to those that people suffered during the Holocaust. During the two-year period since it was posted, the video received over 200 comments that express a range of reactions. Some people expressed support for Max's political views, while others expressed opposition. Although Max has the ability to remove oppositional comments, he left them on the page, including the following comment which takes issue with how he presented his message:

> There are two sides to every story, this is very sympathetically produced in favour of Palestine. I think you should stop and look at the whole picture. I sympathise with both sides, but not all muslims are terrorists, just like all Palestinians don't blow up buses[*sic*].

Another comment expressed support for Max's choice in tackling an issue which for many people is controversial. This commenter said:

> Good for you: having the courage to put out an unpopular point of view. most folks seem not to be able to tolerate things that conflict with their Walmart, McDonald's, and Pepsi culture—which inhibits and discourages difference of opinion, debate, and intellectuality. good for you. [*sic*]

These comments reflect the potential that exists for some people to use YouTube and other video sharing sites to stimulate dialogue about contentious, emotional, and important issues. While it is true that many of the comments address detailed aspects of the content, some of the comments convey more general gratitude for Max's ability to take a position and stimulate discussion about human responses to war.

These three teens initially became concerned about a particular issue for very personal reasons. By having an ability to create videos and distribute them on YouTube, their personal concerns about important civic topics stimulated discourse and raised awareness among a much wider networked public.

*Please note that the names of individuals mentioned in this article are pseudonyms and were designed to protect the privacy of the research participants.

PEDAGOGICAL IMPLICATIONS AND CLASSROOM PRACTICES

The vignettes of Wendy, Frank, and Max in Patricia's Story from the Field have crucial implications for educators. Not only were the youth interested in important topics but also through their own initiative they created videos on these subjects and uploaded them to YouTube to add their voice to ongoing civic discussions. Patricia's research-based vignette presented three key insights for teachers interested in engaging students, utilizing digital media and promoting a community of learners:

1. Provide ways for students to pursue personal or interest-based topics

2. Offer assignments which incorporate media production

3. Provide a space for students to receive peer and adult feedback (not just from a teacher)

Interest-Based Topics

It is important to try to incorporate students' choices throughout one's curriculum. Whether it means choosing a novel to read or determining the topic for a research project, incorporating space for students to pursue interest-based subjects within an academic discipline is essential. Not only can this jumpstart student motivation, it can also offer opportunities for students to explore issues that are emotionally and intellectually appealing to them. Additionally, interest-based topics can provide incentives to nurture relationships beyond the boundaries of school. Schools can create opportunities for students to participate in local internships, community service, and other volunteer work with organizations and companies that support student interests and career goals. This can provide "real world" experiences that can be shared with peers.

Media Production in School

Before Jessica and Patricia dive into this section, we wanted to start with a caveat: Whenever teachers incorporate media production or any form of educational technology into their curriculum, it is imperative that they differentiate between a tool and a task (Beatham, 2008–2009). It is not enough to incorporate media production into a unit plan or into class projects. The tools of technology, such as media production, are not the means to an end. They are means to a specific set of tasks, and teachers and students must remain aware that the task of a unit or a project is not the same as the tools used to support the task.

Let's use Patricia's examples of Wendy, Frank, and Max to explore this further. Wendy was interested in community improvement projects and wanted to demonstrate why a local park should be rebuilt. She used documentary video making as a way to capture actual footage of the park, compared it to other better maintained parks in the city, and then interviewed community members about their vision for a newly rebuilt park. Wendy did not start her community improvement project with the notion, "I want to make a documentary video and now I need to find an issue." Rather she started with something she was interested in—making a case for revitalizing a local park—and Wendy and her friends decided the genre of documentary would be a wonderful way to present factual information about the dilapidated park and connect it to the hopes and dreams of local community members. Wendy and her friends employed the tools of documentary forms to complete the task of improving community parks. The same can be said of Frank and Max who were interested in civic issues such as Internet access and political debates about the Middle East. They employed video as a tool for discussing issues that were important to them, and YouTube offered a public space in which to raise awareness, create conversation, and actively participate in democracy.

A TEACHER'S PERSPECTIVE

Why Integrate Media Production Into the Curriculum?

By Philip Halpern, Ninth Grade English/Media Teacher

Multimedia production is sexy. Students are drawn to it because they recognize it is an opportunity for self-expression in a language they know well. Production represents a chance for them to participate in the "conversation," to communicate with an audience using words and images. Not that they haven't been invited to communicate with an audience before—students write their first essay early in elementary school—but for most kids, a multimedia project is often the first time they have been invited to use words *and* images to tell a story or make a point. It's important work for students because producing multimedia makes them media literate, capable of navigating the media-saturated world in which we live.

The best way I've found to help high school students become media literate is to have them produce media themselves. Currently I teach a ninth grade course called Introduction to Communication Technology (ICT). Over the course of a school year, students produce still images, fictional and documentary videos and podcasts, and they study several genres of film. In so doing, they shift from being passive consumers of media to being critical-thinking, analytical participants in the world of media. In other words, they become media literate. Media literacy is not the only benefit for students though. The work they do in ICT helps them in terms of their academic success, their relationship with others, and their sense of themselves.

Fiction and nonfiction video production are all about students telling a story. The video production process helps students develop their rhetorical skills by requiring them to identify what "statements," whether a particular comment in an interview or an especially revealing shot in a fictional piece, are clearest and most compelling. They must be attentive to these concerns through all phases of the process. Each decision they make has consequences; whom they choose to interview, where they place a camera, what lines they ask an actor to speak. Students soon realize that they have a range of choices and that each choice will contribute to their overall objective to a greater or lesser extent. This awareness strengthens their work in their other classes, and with help from teachers, kids can transfer the awareness between disciplines.

Students' Relationships With Peers

The documentary video production unit in my ICT class illustrates another important benefit of this kind of work. It is very rare for a person to produce a video alone. In my classes, students always work with at least one other person and usually they work in groups of three. We collaborate on the composition of production teams. First we identify a list of possible documentary topics. Then we review the values to which our small school subscribes, like diversity and a commitment to community. After that we agree to guidelines for each group like gender balance and racial-ethnic diversity. Finally, students list three of the documentary topics in order of preference. I go home with their preferences and create groups that conform to the guidelines we've set. This process leads to a balance that allows students to focus on a topic that is of interest to them while working in a group that brings with it its own set of challenges; students often report that interpersonal relationships are as challenging as the video production process itself. I'm always glad to hear this because I believe that one of the most important benefits of video production is students' improved ability to collaborate with people from different backgrounds.

Students' Sense of Self

A significant number of my students have mixed or negative opinions of themselves as students. Video production allows students who have struggled in school to receive praise from their teacher, respect and admiration from their classmates, and good grades in a challenging class. In the context of a small school that values multiple forms of intelligence, ICT is a playing field that devalues competition, encourages collaboration, and offers opportunities for every kid to shine. Granted, on the first day of class there is a preparedness gap, with some kids having already produced videos while others have no production experience at all. In my experience this gap is not enormous and it actually creates an opportunity for media-savvy students to step into the role of teacher

(Continued)

(Continued)

and assist their peers. This collaborative effort allows the kids who haven't had prior experience to quickly gain the skills needed to participate as equals with their classmates.

I don't expect teachers to develop their own ICT class, but incorporating media production into any academic class has amazing benefits. Invite your students to take a journey with you into media production through something as simple as storyboarding or as complex as video production. I guarantee it will be an enjoyable and rewarding experience.

For teachers interested in incorporating media production into their curriculum, Philip Halpern detailed some important issues to further understand and explore.

- The creative process of media production is just as important as the final product. In the process of producing a video, there are a range of choices to be made and each decision has a consequence. This process can be challenging and also very fulfilling.
- Collaboration is an important aspect of video making. Schools tend to favor individual activities whereby students work on their homework by themselves, they take tests by themselves, and their grades are based on their own achievements. Video making can be a time to promote group engagements and work collectively to complete a challenging project.
- Phil also described the excitement in being "invited" to participate in a larger conversation; meaning that students may be motivated to engage in a common goal and then share their work with an audience made up of teachers and peers.
- Video making can provide a space for students who have mixed or negative feelings about themselves as students to create a new academic narrative. In most instances media production is something students have not had in school.

SOME MEDIA PRODUCTION ACTIVITIES

Video Projects

- *Digital Storytelling:* a way to create a story using pictures, music, and voice-over narration. Visit the Center for Digital Storytelling: http://www.storycenter.org/

- *Report the News:* a way for students to summarize important aspects of class experiments, research projects, or daily activities at school through a mainstream genre.
- *Public Service Announcement (PSA):* a way for students to address an issue connected to the public good. It is also feasible to have students create a fictional PSA. Jessica conducted research at a high school in which an integrated English, history, and media class had students read Huxley's *Brave New World.* Students then were asked, "Imagine that you now work for the Department of Propaganda. It is your job to produce a PSA that will reinforce the values already taught through hypnopaedia, Huxley's version of brainwashing, and take it one step further. You will add the power of imagery to our messages. Remember that our goal is a happy, stable, efficient society." The requirements for the PSA included a length of one to two minutes, a theme and at least one slogan from the book, and the use of powerful words and dynamic images as the peer- and teacher-based audience "must want to watch it over and over."
- *Class Video Page:* a way for teachers and students to create a public page on a video-sharing site such as YouTube or some other site, according to the class's needs. Decide on a particular theme and post videos related to that theme, such as issues of environmental sustainability. If the instructor wishes the page to go public, then students might see how or whether their video sparks larger discourse about the particular issue. Of course certain literacy and security concerns would need to be discussed, such as knowing what information or images students should avoid in their videos (such as identifying information about their houses). It is important to help students understand what kinds of images are less safe; some kids that Patricia talked to regretted putting certain sexually themed or other videos of themselves that future employers may see.

   In terms of concerns about negative commentary, there are many ways to control the comment responses. For instance, when a video is uploaded, the moderator or owner of the channel page can set the comments so that they must be approved before they are publicly posted. This minimizes opportunities for comments that are not appropriate for the classroom discourse. Videos could also be posted and shared with friends, family, and other members of the school to raise awareness and promote a wider range of reactions and perspectives. In a way these practices change the model of the instructor to that of a facilitator in which students might connect with other resources and experts pertinent to their area of interest.

- *Personal Video Essay:* a way for students to explore a personal issue that provokes emotion in them. The Center for Social Media offers suggestions about how to incorporate video to produce social documentaries in educational settings (http://tiny.cc/teachtech_3_1). Students can employ several different techniques in their essays, including speaking their own thoughts into the camera. They might also interview people or narrate their observations while showing images. They can juxtapose personal or public media photographs or images or include video-recorded images of public places, such as their neighborhoods to highlight a problem. The idea behind such an essay is to enable students to focus on an issue of importance to them and to gain a more intuitive understanding for how media helps shape and transmit particular messages (http://www.centerforsocialmedia .org/resources/).

Text-Based Projects

- *Print Advertisement, e.g., billboard or ad in a magazine:* a way to persuade an audience to support a specific product or cause. This can be done with old-fashioned pencil and paper or even with a computer program such as Adobe Photoshop Elements (http://www.adobe .com/products/).
- *Textbook Entry:* a way for students to organize an historical or fictional event and grapple with issues such as objectivity and bias. From history to science, this activity can contain text describing an event, first person accounts, photos or art accompanying the written word, or even brief videos and references linked to the entry. Students will need assistance with writing in a particular discipline: documenting a historical event such as an inauguration is very different from writing about a scientific experiment.

If one of the fears of teachers in implementing media production is, "I don't know how to teach this software program" or "I don't know how to use this media device," then utilize the knowledge of the classroom: Who knows how to do what? Is there an opportunity for students to step up in a technological role and assist the teacher and his or her peers? Is there a parent, a teacher's assistant, or another teacher who brings with them specific knowledge of media production? Is there a local organization that can volunteer their time and share their understanding of media production? Teachers are not expected to be teaching experts and technological experts within a community of learners. No one knows everything about technology; that is why networked publics are so popular: our digital era is about collective intelligence in which many brains are better than one! Even though this shift in thinking challenges our notions of authority and expertise within a classroom, it opens up the possibility to create a community of learners made up of both teachers and students working together for a common goal.

Yet with a boisterous culture of media production comes a need for responsibility, and this responsibility lies on both the shoulders of students and teachers. With ethical issues at the forefront of the creation, publication, and distribution of media, adults have a responsibility to guide students and learn from them. Jenkins (2006) discusses the importance of teaching media literacy precisely because of the ethical challenges students face in a participatory culture. Jenkins explains: "One important goal of media education should be to encourage young people to become more reflective about the ethical choices they make as participants and communicators and the impact they have on others" (p. 17).

For instance, the *personal video essay* described above incorporates the interviewing and videotaping of certain subjects. This brings up a number of issues for consideration. There are legal and ethical issues with regard to who should be photographed and under what circumstances. Capturing footage at public transportation centers such as airports and train stations may present problems. Additionally, student media makers must also negotiate personal relationships with their subjects, make decisions, and take responsibility for how they represent their subjects in their videos. If students use copyrighted materials, then distribution issues should be taken into consideration. These are all pertinent issues that must be discussed with students. Media participation in any form is both agentive and constraining (Silverstone, 2007), and as educators we must support the development of intergenerational relationships whereby a number of adults can help youth navigate the dual terrain of participation and responsibility.

CREATE SPACE FOR FEEDBACK FROM PEERS AND ADULTS

There are numerous ways to provide space in the curriculum for students to receive feedback from peers or adults. In order to do this, teachers might wish to rethink the traditional classroom model with *one* teacher assessing student work. Newer models of teaching suggest opening the process up to larger audiences based on peers and caring adults. By creating a community of learners, students can invest in their assignments in a collaborative manner rather than through the punitive routine of grading in which one authority figure is their only source of feedback. Grading is not discarded in this vision. Rather peer feedback and critique are activities that can complement traditional grading and work to foster a classroom community based upon collaboration and reciprocity.

With media productions in particular, having a class or grade level video screening or a schoolwide video festival can provide a wonderful venue for peers and families to view student work and foster informal and formal avenues for feedback. A class screening is also a time to reinforce the polysemic nature of texts—having multiple interpretations—and collective meaning making. As Ricardo wrote earlier in this chapter, "Everyone thinks differently, everyone feels differently, everyone understands differently" when it comes to making media. A class screening can provide space for students to engage in a social and collective search for meaning. It can reinforce for the media makers, teachers, and students the importance of placing one's creative productions in front of an audience.

Additionally, offering a class contest (with or without small prizes) for the top three print advertisements or textbook entries in which teachers and students from other classes or subject areas, alumni, administrators, or parents and community members make up the judging panel is another way for students to see their work as viewed by a larger community and receive feedback. Bringing in multiage tutors from upper grades or even college students is another way to establish intergenerational or multiage relationships based on a widening of resources and networks. Collaborating with after-school organizations can also provide spaces outside of school for students to continue their educational endeavors with media. Establishing online partnerships with sister schools is also a way to encourage feedback from different sources. Remember, throughout the process of producing media, from a simple brainstorming session to a completed project (whether this is print based or multimedia based), there are always occasions to include peer feedback and critique.

This is not an exhaustive list of the types of activities that can foster peer feedback and critique, but one of the most important points of this section is the fact that students want to create work that is for an authentic audience who may share similar interests, career goals, social networks, and civic concerns. Giving and receiving feedback from peers is an essential characteristic of new media environments since it offers another avenue in which to participate in our mediated world. Teachers know that students are more likely to engage in classroom culture when they feel their interests and efforts are appreciated.

Bits and Bytes: An Additional Perspective

Bits and Bytes of Research is a sidebar designed to further our understanding of a topic. In this instance, Heather A. Horst discusses interactions among kids and parents around technology.

Interactions With Media at Home

By Heather A. Horst, Anthropologist

As a sociocultural anthropologist on the Kids' Informal Learning with Digital Media project, I focused upon one of the primary informal learning environments in young people's lives—the home and family. Like other researchers on this project, I found that the ways parents tried to cope with the changing media environment varied in fascinating and often unexpected ways.

In the middle class Silicon Valley households where I carried out my research, parents' experiences with new media and technology in the workplace influenced their ability to talk about some of the sites their kids participated in online and, at times, discuss with their kids how to evaluate the credibility of information on particular sites. It was also easier for parents to support their kids' use of digital media production software by purchasing microphones and video cameras. Yet as a project we also found that parents and kids who were less economically well-off or technically proficient also came together around new media. For example, in Dan Perkel's studies he found that 10-year-old Miguel in the San Francisco Bay area had fond memories of playing video games with his dad, uncle, and cousins before his parents were separated. Lisa Tripp, who carried out research in urban Los Angeles, talked to a single mother about spending time on the computer with her son in middle school by helping him find words and information. Other researchers such as Katynka Martinez and Becky Herr-Stephenson, who studied immigrant families of Central American and Mexican descent in Los Angeles, discussed how some kids taught their parents to send e-mails and upload photos from the shared family digital camera. Others helped their parents with English. In many cases, such as in Latino/a families, older cousins played a key role as mentors.

While we tend to focus upon new media, we found that different types of media (*old* and *new*) played a part in these intergenerational interactions. Television continued to be a gathering point for families: in middle class Silicon Valley, television shows and movies were often mediated by Netflix queues and TiVos, while we saw traditional broadcast television in many of the Los Angeles families who lived in studio apartments. In other words, while we commonly hear the tensions between kids and parents, such as parents being "clueless" or incompetent in dealing with the norms and literacies of online peer culture, we also chronicled many instances of parents and kids coming together around new media. These acts became moments for cross-generational communication as well as

(Continued)

(Continued)

expressions of family identity. The challenge for parents, educators, and administrators centers around ways to understand and mobilize the positive cross-generational dynamics we encountered to enhance young people's learning in and through new media.

Implications for Teachers

- Ask (and even chronicle) how your students and their parents or guardians come together around new media. This will not only give you insight into your students' digital media habits but could potentially lead to parents and guardians coming into the class to share their knowledge and help with media projects.
- Also give students an opportunity to share instances in which they taught their parents or guardians about media and discuss times when they learned from their elders. This offers a space to celebrate intergenerational learning and allows students to view themselves as teachers rather than simply learners.
- Family reading nights and family math nights are both popular practices at elementary and middle schools to create cross-generational learning activities. Is there a need or desire to implement a family media night? What would this look like?
- For more information on the Kids' Informal Learning with Digital Media project visit http://digitalyouth.ischool.berkeley.edu/.

BANNING YOUTUBE

Similar to the concerns raised in the previous chapter around MySpace and Facebook, YouTube is an open system and anyone can view a person's YouTube page, whether or not the viewer has an account. Unless a video is marked as private for only certain individuals to see, a video is open for viewing to the world. It is possible to mark a video on YouTube as private such that only people in a person's designated YouTube friend network may view a video. But the problem with such a feature is that, as currently implemented, it requires viewers to have an account and friend the video's creator. Yet not everyone wants to have an account to access these features.

Many people respond to these concerns by banning YouTube entirely in homes and classrooms. Yet given that media plays such a large role in our lives, another approach is to engage in more hands-on and open discussions about what it means to post videos online, especially since such practices are becoming more and more common ways for kids to network. Shutting down such options for kids complicates their ability to learn about media and to develop social networking skills that inform their sense of self and support their creative interests. Kids, like adults, network with extended groups of friends and associates by exchanging media that helps keeps channels of communication active and ongoing.

For these and other reasons, some educators have been concerned about using YouTube in classrooms. Other scholars argue that avoiding use of media over concerns about potential copyright issues is detrimental to literacy education. They believe that it is a mistake to ignore opportunities for creative personal expression, especially in an era in which making media is an ordinary part of personal creativity and social life. And as Marlo Warburton explains below, banning YouTube makes showing clips in class difficult.

A TEACHER'S PERSPECTIVE

Why I Teach YouTube

By Marlo Warburton, Eighth Grade Algebra Teacher

Conjure up in your mind the classic 1970s song "I Will Survive" by Gloria Gaynor. Now insert these lyrics to the same tune: "At first I was afraid, what could the answer be? It said given this position find velocity." This is the beginning of "I Will Derive," one of my favorite "teacher finds" on YouTube (uploaded by MindofMatthew on May 8, 2008, http://www.youtube.com/watch?v=P9dpTTpjymE).

Most people go to YouTube for entertainment, to see cats flushing toilets, pageant beauties flubbing interviews, and comedians performing spoofs. I use YouTube to teach. Because I only have 45 minutes a day to teach Algebra, I need to be efficient with time. Most days, my students start the period with a five-problem warm-up. To mix things up, I sometimes start class with a quick video instead. The content ranges from parabolas to littering to beatboxing, depending on whether my objective is teaching math, promoting positive behavior, or simply sharing an interesting experience with my students. I know teenagers will work hard in classes they find engaging. I use videos to grab students' attention and create excitement about my class. That excitement leads to math learning.

Most of the video clips I use come from YouTube. I search for "quadratic formula" and quickly find a two-year-old who sings the formula to the tune of "Pop Goes the Weasel." I search for "y=mx+b" and find a "lope-intercept rap" performed by a charismatic high school teacher. There's also a news clip about Algebra as the civil rights issue of today, an animation series about a superhero called Math Girl, an Abbott and Costello argument about division, a dog who "does math" by tapping her paw, and Lindsay Lohan competing as a mathlete in *Mean Girls*. Any one of these videos is a shot in the arm to the start of my math class. I use a video to generate student interest, and then I run with it for the rest of the period.

(Continued)

(Continued)

But not all of the videos I show are math themed. Sometimes I show clips of break dancers, "mad" scientists, opera singers, or athletes to entertain and inspire students to follow creative pursuits. We ooh, ahh, and laugh together, forgetting who said what about whom in the halls before class and focusing instead on a positive shared experience. Teenagers can be prickly at times, and these fun moments help me maintain an upbeat classroom climate that is conducive to learning. For Anti-Bullying Week, I selected five of YouTube's 50,000 videos about bullying. I chose videos from Sweden, Canada, England, and the United States. Two of them were animated, one starred several famous celebrities, one had high-tech special effects, and one featured a popular song. The videos set the stage for class discussions in which students demonstrated compassion for the characters in the videos and shared their similar experiences. I believe our conversations created a classroom environment in which students felt more open and safe.

Unfortunately, teaching with YouTube is not without its issues. First, I have to be ultracareful about previewing videos before showing them to students. I don't expect to encounter vulgarities in algebra videos, but sometimes they are there. Second, to find a video I do want to show in class I have to filter through many videos I don't want. This is time consuming. Third and most problematic, the computers in my school are blocked from accessing YouTube at all. I'm barred from using it, and so are my students. I am forced to search YouTube and download videos on my slow home computer. It's inconvenient but worth it to see my students enjoying "I Will Derive."

Help! YouTube is banned at my school. What do I do now?

A number of parents and teachers report that YouTube is banned at their schools for a variety of reasons, including children's security, emotional well-being, and technical concerns. We wish we had an easy answer to this situation. Even when teachers welcome the idea of trying to connect with students by engaging with the media and messages that kids make on their own, schools often have policies blocking on-campus access to the site. The reasons for such blockages are not always made explicit through school policy.

One approach might be to engage in broader community dialogue with the school to understand what the specific concerns are and talk about ways to address those specific concerns in order to continue to engage with media in productive ways. In some cases the solution may be to avoid using YouTube—but to find other platforms and mechanisms for bringing student-driven media into the classroom setting. It might be helpful to see if there is a way to allow teachers access to YouTube in certain classrooms. If YouTube is not banned, is it possible to establish "rules of YouTube conduct" with students in order to discuss some of the ethical concerns of online viewing and lay down ground rules for student viewing? Creating rules of conduct with students—or at least including student input—can be an excellent way to allow students to participate in the process, improve online self-presentation skills, and help build a community based on trust.

Here are some potential suggestions that address specific concerns:

Concern	*Kids do not pay attention in class when YouTube is used on the campus.*
Potential Approach	Teachers do need to be vigilant about media use during class. Part of multimedia literacy includes teaching kids about appropriate behaviors in terms of using media in a classroom setting. Having this dialogue and interaction in school is important for helping kids gain the technical and participatory skills needed to handle use of increasingly available media.
Concern	*Kids put inappropriate things about themselves or the school on YouTube.*
Potential Approach	Kids do not stop putting things on YouTube because it is banned in the classroom. Teachers report that bringing material on YouTube into the classroom is advantageous because it helps teachers engage in honest discussions about why certain material is posted and whether the right choices are being made. Teachers have noted that it can be advantageous to have access to things that kids are making in their daily routine.
Concern	*YouTube is too broad and enables anyone around the world to interact with kids and post harmful comments to their work.*
Potential Approach	Kids can often be upset at the kind of comments posted on their videos. As social media becomes broader and more globally connected, having the skills to address these concerns will be important. Teachers can set up classroom accounts on YouTube that moderate comments so that students never see inappropriate or hurtful feedback through the moderated account. Also teaching multimedia literacy skills means giving students an understanding about the risks of interacting with unknown persons and providing personal information. With a teacher-moderated account, only videos that a teacher approves will be posted from this account. Such a model does not prevent students from posting to their own account. But the in-classroom dialogue that occurs should include important information about safety and avoiding the posting of explicit or inappropriate content to be accessed by the general public.
Concern	*YouTube contains inappropriate material.*
Potential Approach	YouTube does have a mechanism for removing unwanted material, and enables people to flag videos that are inappropriate. One option might be to use other sites that are more specialized or have less of a reputation for containing inappropriate material. Teachers might also be curators who select only certain material for viewing in the classroom. They can download the videos on YouTube and show them in class. School administrators should be made aware that banning these kinds of resources makes it more difficult for teachers to show legitimate material in the classroom such as news, art, and important speeches.

(Continued)

(Continued)

Concern	*The school's IT department says posting video files will not work because they are too big and will strain the school's network.*
Potential Approach	This concern breaks into two parts. The first is the concern about having a large local server to host the videos. However this is not usually a problem because there are many sites on the Web that will host videos. An example is WordPress. For local collaborative sharing and comment exchange, a school can establish a wiki on a modest computer system, while the actual videos are stored elsewhere. Kids can watch password-protected videos on the school wiki or on a video blog site and interact with other students either at the school or within a delineated network of schools. However, such methods for using password-protected online video exchanges restrict distribution of videos to a limited group of students and participants. The second concern is that transferring the video files will slow down the school's Internet connection. Although uncompressed video files are large, videos formatted for the Web are compressed and the file sizes are actually much smaller, mitigating this concern. In addition, uploads tend to be infrequent, and schools can stagger the timing of video uploads. As the Internet becomes increasingly important to professional and social life, broadband and other higher speed networks are becoming far more widespread in educational settings.

Whatever the method used, it is important to remember that kids already have a very wide access to materials online. Blocking certain sites at schools does not ensure that kids are not exposed to these sites and issues. Teachers report that such blocking policies can complicate teachers' abilities to help discuss and navigate these concerns in a more frank and productive manner in a formal school setting. Media literacy skills include much more than reading the messages in images or even being able to manipulate software to publish one's own message. An increasingly crucial component of such skills involves helping kids understand how to examine and evaluate content and discuss guidelines for appropriate and productive video-mediated participation in online, social, and pedagogical settings.

SHARE YOUR INSIGHTS, STORIES, AND EXPERIENCES!

Patricia and Jessica do not have all the answers for integrating media production and sharing into the classroom! We would love to hear from you. Log onto our Web site at www.teachingtechsavvykids.com and post your answers to these prompts or pose questions of your own:

1. From a teaching perspective, if access to technology is limited, how can media production such as making videos be integrated in the classroom?

2. From a technological perspective, what are some of the obstacles to incorporating media and video production, e.g., purchasing hardware, teaching software programs, and lab time and how can teachers and administrators work around these obstacles?

3. Larry Cuban (1986), a professor emeritus at Stanford University, describes how instructional technology is historically deemed a panacea for educational ills. The technology itself is thought to bring an aura of modernity and innovativeness to the classroom but usually ends up unused and covered with cobwebs in the back corner of a classroom. Are there concerns that history may repeat itself with media production and YouTube? If so, how do educators come to terms with the relationship between teaching and technology?

4. David Buckingham (2003), a well-known and respected media educator, notes that media production is "not an end in itself" but "must be accompanied by systematic reflection and self-evaluation" (p. 84). What would systematic reflection and self-evaluation look like in a middle school or high school setting?

REFERENCES AND HELPFUL RESOURCES

Beatham, M. (2008–2009). Tools of inquiry: Separating tool and task to promote true learning. *Journal of Educational Technology Systems, 37*(1), 61–70.

Buckingham, D. (2003). *Media education: Literacy, learning, and contemporary culture.* Cambridge, England: Polity Press.

Carrington, V., and Robinson, M. (2009). *Digital literacies: Social learning and classroom practices.* Thousand Oaks, CA: Sage.

Center for Social Media: http://www.centerforsocialmedia.org

Creative Commons: http://creativecommons.org/

Cuban, L. (1986). *Teachers and machines: The classroom use of technology since 1920.* New York: Teachers College Press.

Digital Ethnography at Kansas State University: http://mediatedcultures.net/youtube.htm

Hodson, R. (2007). Video Blogging and Activism. Retrieved December 8, 2007 from http://www.youtube.com/watch?v=1aB2FmeWUdw

Ito, M., Horst, H., Bittanti, M., boyd, d., Herr-Stephenson, B., Lange, P. G., et al. (2008). *Living and learning with new media: Summary of findings from the digital youth project.* The John D. and Catherine T. MacArthur Foundation. Retrieved December 15, 2008 from http://digitalyouth.ischool.berkeley.edu

Ito, M., Baumer, S., Bittani, M., boyd, d., Cody, R., Herr-Stephenson, B., Horst, H. A., Lange, P. A., Mahendran, D., Martinez, K., Pascoe, C. J., Perkel D., Robinson, L., Sims, C., & Tripp, L. (2010). *Hanging out, messing around, geeking out: Living and learning with new media.* Cambridge: MIT Press.

Jenkins, H. (2009). What happened before YouTube. In J. Burgess, & J. Green. (Eds.), *YouTube: Online video and participatory culture* (pp. 109–125). Cambridge, MA: Polity Press.

Jenkins, H. (with Clinton, K., Purushotma, R., Robison, A., & Weigel, M.). (2006). *Confronting the challenges of participatory culture: Education for the 21st century.* The John D. and Catherine T. MacArthur Foundation. Retrieved August 18, 2007 from http://digitallearning.macfound.org. Download the white paper at

http://www.newmedialiteracies.org/files/working/NMLWhitePaper.pdf

Lange, P. G. (2007a). Searching for the 'You' in 'YouTube': An analysis of online response ability. In *National Association of Practicing Anthropology Proceedings of the Ethnographic Praxis in Industry Conference 2007* (pp. 31–45). Berkeley: University of California Press. http://www.patriciaglange.org/page3/page.html

Lange, P. G. (2007b). *Commenting on comments: Investigating responses to antagonism on YouTube.* Presented at the annual conference of the Society for Applied Anthropology, Tampa, FL. http://sfaapodcasts.files.wordpress.com/2007/04/update-apr-17-lange-sfaa-paper-2007.pdf

Silverstone, R. (2007). *Media and morality: On the rise of the mediapolis.* Cambridge, England: Polity Press.

The Institute for Multimedia Literacy (IML) at the University of Southern California: http://iml.usc.edu/index.php/resources-articles/2008/09/07/a-pedagogy-for-original-synners/

Truffaut, F. (Director). (1973). *Day for night* or *La nuit Américaine* [Motion picture]. France. Warner Bros. Pictures.

Verdi, M., Hodson, R., Weynand, D., & Craig, S. (2006). *Secrets of video blogging.* Berkeley, CA: Peachpit Press. (Also visit Ryanne and Michael's Web site at http://www.freevlog.org.)

VoiceThread: http://voicethread.com/#home

Wordpress: http://wordpress.com

YouTube: http://www.youtube.com/user/YouTubeHelp

YouTube Education: http://www.youtube.com/education?b=1

Wikipedia

The Online Encyclopedia Based on Collaborative Knowledge

Jessica K. Parker

Wikipedia can be a great tool for learning and researching information. However, like all sources, not everything in Wikipedia is accurate, comprehensive, or unbiased.

—Wikipedia: Researching with Wikipedia

INTRODUCTION

This chapter is devoted to discussing how digital media allows for the sharing of information and the distribution of knowledge by analyzing Wikipedia, the online, collaborative encyclopedia that is setting the precedent for reference material in the digital epoch. With millions and millions of articles in numerous languages, Wikipedia is an amazing resource for all teachers, both personally and professionally. Wikipedia not only challenges our understanding of traditional resources such as encyclopedias and almanacs or any material that publishes practical information on particular subjects, but it also highlights how important it is to be able to comprehend, interpret and evaluate information in this Internet age. I hope this will be the start of many career Wikipedians!

WHAT IN THE WORLD IS WIKIPEDIA?

It seems like every time I tried to look for something through Google's **search engine**, I ended up being directed to a Web page in Wikipedia. The problem: what in the world is Wikipedia? The answer to this question lies in understanding the words *wiki* and *pedia*. A **wiki**, a term borrowed from the Hawaiian language meaning quick, is a special type of Web site that uses unique software that allows users to edit the content as they see fit. The word *pedia* is borrowed from encyclopedia. Wikipedia, then, is a quick and easy, online, collaborative encyclopedia in which users can create new articles and edit and discuss existing articles. The operative word in the previous sentence is collaborative. Wikipedia is a prime example of the power in collaborative knowledge: it is a user-generated, user-edited and user-maintained site. That means each article is open to anyone interested in contributing to the creation of content. This is different to most Web sites in which a webmaster, an individual or corporation in charge of running the site, determines the content and style of each page on the site. With Wikipedia, its content is interactive and the style supports its collaborative characteristics. Wikipedia is unlike any other encyclopedia we have ever seen.

Professor Laura Robinson (personal communication, December 7, 2007) explained to me that even if you are not familiar with Wikipedia's design of peer-to-peer sharing, you might have experience with some other user-generated and user-maintained sites. Two popular examples include eBay, a user-generated reputation system in which to buy and sell merchandise, and Craigslist, a location-specific online site featuring free classified ads and forums on various topics. These sites, including Wikipedia, are based on collaborative content sharing in which anyone can add to the site.

Wikipedia is run by the Wikimedia Foundation, a nonprofit organization dedicated to a number of wiki-based projects which promote the "development and distribution of free, multilingual content." Examples of other sister wiki projects include Wiktionary, Wikinews, Wikibooks, and Wikimedia Commons. At the time this book went to press, one of Wikipedia's goals is to give a "free and accurate encyclopedia" to everyone, and its motto is "The free encyclopedia that anyone can edit."

MYTH: Technology is complicated and scary, and I have missed so much that it will take forever to try and learn it.

REALITY: Today's technology is frequently user-friendly (but not necessarily easy to learn). I run into teachers who often underestimate how long it will take them to understand a new technology or software application. They usually give themselves five minutes and then quit out of frustration. Here lies the problem. Today's students have a different mindset: they play with the technology and will "fail" over and over again until they have mastered it. Don't get frustrated and give up in five minutes. Give yourself ample time to play with the technology and allow yourself to fail over and over again. And ask yourself: Are there ways to harness this "willingness to fail" in an educational setting? Post your opinion on our Web site!

UTOPIAN IDEALS OF PARTICIPATION

The creators of Wikipedia support the utopian ideals of democratic participation and collaboration and new media has made this ideal an online reality. Instead of a select few writing and vetted reference materials, Wikipedia has offered an invitation to all who are interested to help create such material. In practice, these utopian ideals present themselves throughout the Wikipedia site. Let's visit the Wikipedia Web site and focus on two such examples: the discussion and history tabs (see Figure 4.1).

Figure 4.1 Wikipedia Tabs

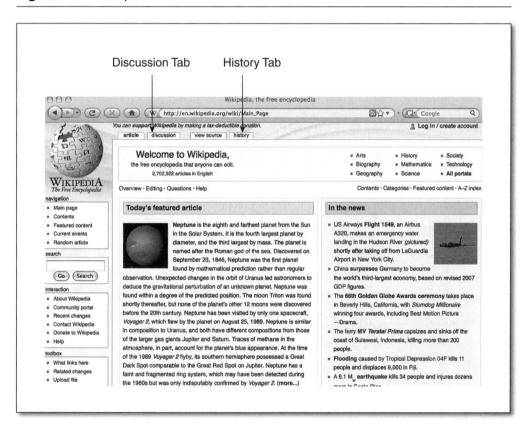

Activity

Go to Wikipedia's main page and see if these tabs are still in the same location. If they are, what about these locations seem to work? Are they easy to find? If they have changed, why do you think this happened? How is the new location different from the location I have shown?

Let's use a real example to explain the purpose of the discussion and history tabs. Search for *teacher* in Wikipedia. Read or skim the article. What is your general impression? Is the content accurate? Do all the sections of the entry cover important aspects of being a teacher? Whether or not you find this particular article satisfactory, you have the power to pull back the "curtain" and see first-hand the historical development of the page and its different iterations by using the tabs above the entry.

Click on the discussion tab for the teacher article and it will take you to a page where you can discuss how the article has been edited. How we define someone who is a teacher and what type of photograph accurately portrays a teacher are two questions that might not have a "correct" answer. Thus, the discussion tab is meant to allow you to understand the previous and current conversations concerning the teacher article. It may be that the information one wants to insert was already edited out for a number of reasons and this saves time and energy. From the standpoint of collaborative knowledge, everyone has access to the discussion tab and can view the questions, concerns and insights Wikipedians have shared. Additionally, the educational value of this aspect is enormous; not only does it bring to our attention the construction of media (and the representation of a teacher) but also our ability to change it.

Now let's look at the history tab in the teacher article. This page gives you the actual changes made to the teacher article and even stores old versions of the text. Additionally, there is a record of every edit, the date and time the edit was made, and the username who made the edit and their edit summary. The changes are presented in reverse-chronological order and you can compare an old version with a current version. The history tab is another example in which Wikipedians are urged to, as Wikipedia's founder Jimmy Wales, said, "Imagine a world in which every single human being can freely share in the sum of all knowledge" (http://tiny.cc/teachtech_4_1). In theory and in practice, Wikipedia is dedicated to the ideals of democratic participation and the distribution of collaborative knowledge.

FUN FACTS ABOUT WIKIPEDIA

- It is created by volunteers
- It is multilingual and it can translate pages for you
- It can be updated quickly as news and other events unfold as opposed to waiting for the new edition of the printed encyclopedia to be published
- It is constantly expanding
- It is a powerful resource for sharing information
- In terms of reference material, it is extraordinary

- It has challenged notions of authority and the role of experts
- It has challenged notions of knowledge production and distribution

Make sure to check out Wikipedia's own list of insights:
"Ten things you may not know about Wikipedia" at http://tiny.cc/teachtech_4_2

Figure 4.2 Ten Things You May Not Know About Wikipedia

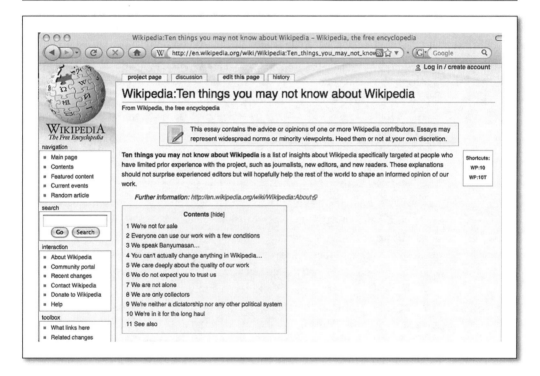

(Continued)

regular basis for homework and for pleasure. An avid information consumer, Milo reads daily, uses the library approximately once per month, and consults traditional encyclopedias once per week on average. He eschews online TV sites in preference to online newspaper and news sites that he visits at least once per week. In addition Milo uses Wikipedia and search engines at least three to four times per week. He has constant access to both on- and offline resources and sources of information.

Throughout high school Milo reports using Wikipedia for leisure and for school research. A Wikipedian since 2003, Milo is a self-taught early adopter who considers himself a faithful adherent to the Wikipedian community. During our interview, he describes his status clearly, "I found it *before* it was cool." When asked, "How often do you use Wikipedia?" Milo explains that at present he "only" visits the site three to four times per week. However he hastens to explain that this is a substantial change from a long period of time in which he consulted Wikipedia several times per day. Milo's family substantiates this shift in use; during our interview his mother explained that Milo was so "hooked" on Wikipedia that they were forced to "unplug the computer!"

When asked about how he started using Wikipedia, Milo explains that he found it though a Google search. He describes his first reaction to the site, "I thought it was pretty cool." Milo's fascination with the site is part of a larger understanding of technology use as potential entertainment. As he explains, "I discovered that you could push 'random page' and spend time . . . finding gems." Milo describes his delight in reading articles from the "random page" selection as a form of casual entertainment that is the antidote to boredom: "Every time I was on Internet, I would get bored and go there." Milo explains that visiting "random pages" provides a type of break or pause: "I may as well take a little break and read about something else for awhile." For Milo, information on Wikipedia is serendipitous for both himself and his friends: "Most of my friends waste time on Wikipedia" through links that allow one to "meander off topic" and "drift off and read about hot sauce for a half hour." These respondents experience Wikipedia as a type of play.

When Milo first began using Wikipedia, he "didn't really understand what it was for a little while. . . . I thought it was some sort of referencing site. I didn't realize that anyone who wanted to could edit it. I hadn't taken the time to think about it." However as Milo spent more time on Wikipedia, his understanding of the site changed. Once Milo read the site's official introduction from its home page, he realized that the site was a flexible, user-generated content venue rather than a stable source of pre-vetted information. Interestingly, this is in large part due to the fact that many users like Milo come to Wikipedia from a Google search that takes them directly to entries within Wikipedia. Users are directed to embedded links that appear to be static pages. This path bypasses Wikipedia's home page where links may be found explaining the site's reliance on collaborative production.

Once Milo discovered that *anyone* can edit Wikipedia entries, he "understood that it wasn't the most reliable source of information." From that point onward, Milo reframed his understanding of Wikipedia as a valuable starting point: "What it is good for is getting the basic information about something." For example, for his history classes Milo regularly consults the site because, "it seems like people really geek out over wars." I asked Milo how he determines the reliability of the information he finds on Wikipedia. More specifically, he explains: "Wikipedia comes in very helpful . . . [to] see what the basic information is about." Knowing that Wikipedia is created by its own unpaid users who are not vetted by a third party, Milo believes that Wikipedia is written "in small portion . . . [by] everyone who looks at it . . . [and in] large portion . . . [by] geeks who spend all of their time doing it." For this reason, Milo states that, "Wikipedia doesn't work when the people writing the pages don't know all that much what they are talking about" or when the site is "vandalized" or when "people are trying to intentionally . . . post false information." In this way, Milo articulates a critical stance toward the information he finds on the site. Although he believes that Wikipedia is an excellent source of general information, he states the following caveat, "I think that most of the time the information is quite trustworthy, but there are enough exceptions that I could not say it's always true."

Laura Robinson's vignette was originally published online in May of 2007 on the Digital Youth Web site, the online home of the Kids' Informal Learning with Digital Media Project at http://digitalyouth.ischool.berkeley.edu/.

*Please note that the name mentioned in this article is a pseudonym and designed to protect the privacy of the research participant.

STRENGTHS AND WEAKNESSES OF WIKIPEDIA

It's Collaborative!

Wikipedia has devoted supporters, many of whom find its collaborative nature one of its main strengths. As users spend more time on Wikipedia, most realize that the site is a flexible, user-generated site that allows content to be added and edited with ease. Adding and editing content is not available on most Web sites, but the special wiki format allows Wikipedia users to read and write content as they see fit. As opposed to a traditional print encyclopedia that would offer a stable source of information, Wikipedia is always a work in progress and provides a community of learners who read and share their knowledge broadly. Our students are used to their work being read (usually) by an audience of one. Wikipedia's community of learners can potentially empower youths (and adults) to share their knowledge and feel connected to an online project that is beyond the confines of their classrooms.

Wikipedia also has its detractors, so it comes with no surprise that there is a contentious debate concerning the online encyclopedia. Its collaborative nature is also one of its main criticisms and Laura touched upon this with her case study of Milo: Wikipedia is viewed as an unreliable source since it does not go through the same channels of scrutiny as a traditional encyclopedia. It may not be fact-checked: it could be correct or full of errors. An important question to ask ourselves is if older print publications are always reliable and free of errors. And since all texts are constructed, aren't we always obligated to discuss and analyze issues of reliability and perspective?

Look at the Sheer Quantity of Articles!

According to Wikipedia's statistics page (http://en.wikipedia.org/wiki/Wikipedia:Statistics), "In the month of July 2006, Wikipedia grew by over 30 million words." Since an average person could read nearly 20 million words in a month (if they read 24-seven and did not sleep), Wikipedia claims it would take an average reader over two years to read every word and "by the time they were done, so much would have changed with the parts that they had already read that they would have to start over." Wikipedia's millions and millions of words means there are over three million articles in English for anyone to edit. Even though Wikipedia has millions of articles, and this number can increase by the minute or second, not every article is guaranteed for quality. Wikipedia even warns that older articles are more likely to be of higher quality than newer articles because, according to Wikipedia, these pages have been viewed and critiqued by more people over a longer period of time and tend to have had the kinks worked out.

The quote at the beginning of the chapter should remind us that Wikipedia has strength in numbers but may be limited in terms of accuracy and partiality: "Wikipedia can be a great tool for learning and researching information . . . (but) not everything in Wikipedia is accurate, comprehensive, or unbiased." According to Wikipedia, "All articles and other encyclopedic content must be written from a neutral point of view, representing fairly and without bias. . . . [This] policy requires that where multiple or conflicting perspectives exist within a topic each should be presented fairly." A question all educators should ask themselves is whether or not it is possible to write from a neutral point of view. Mark Glaser (2006) writing for MediaShift, a weblog that tracks how new media affects our society, suggests that "the search for a 'neutral point of view' mirrors the efforts of journalists to be objective, to show both sides without taking sides and remaining unbiased. But maybe this is impossible and unattainable, and perhaps misguided. Because if you open it up for anyone to edit, you're asking for anything but neutrality."

Students Love It (While Teachers Are Wary)

Students are some of the most vocal supporters of Wikipedia as described by the common comment on the Wikimedia blog, "Wikipedia got me through college!" They tend to find it easy to access and search, and the entries usually provide a coherent description of their searchable entity and frequently present links to other sources. Unfortunately, the main complaint from teachers across all grade levels, including college professors, is that students do not check the reliability of the source. "If it is printable, then it is a source!" is a motto for many students. The extensive use of Wikipedia on college campuses has caused such a stir that some departments have formally banned the citation of Wikipedia as a source for academic work, even as many instructors encourage it as a first step in the research process. In the past, many teachers would say to their students that they should avoid Wikipedia and that would be the end of the discussion. But there are valuable educational lessons that can be learned by discussing the nature of Wikipedia, even if your school does not allow Wikipedia to be cited as a source. I will address this in the pedagogical-implications section.

It's Transparent!

danah boyd (2007), the coauthor of Chapter 2, writes on her blog, "The key value of Wikipedia is its transparency. You can understand how a page is constructed, who is invested, what their other investments are. You can see when people disagree about content and how, in the discussion, the disagreement was resolved. None of our traditional print media makes such information available." For instance, a front-page article in *The New York Times* is a polished piece. The editors of the *Times* do not publish every draft of this front-page article nor do they make available to their readers conversations they have had with their reporters about the revision of the article. We as readers are not privy to how a paragraph was constructed, if a word was changed in the title or how all parties at the *Times* came to an agreement concerning the content of the newspaper article. In Wikipedia, the edited versions are available for everyone to see and review. Because of this, the user has access to content that most newspaper readers can only dream of experiencing.

danah boyd (2007) suggests that understanding Wikipedia means knowing how to:

1. Understand the assembly of data and information into publications
2. Interpret knowledge
3. Question purported truths and vet sources
4. Analyze apparent contradictions in facts
5. Productively contribute to the large body of collective knowledge

Dan Perkel, a doctoral candidate at the University of California, Berkeley's School of Information, takes a different stance concerning Wikipedia's "transparency" (personal communication, December 19, 2007). He explains that Wikipedia's transparency is not helpful if users do not understand the nature of the site. Due to its popularity and the large quantity of articles, Wikipedia is often one of the first sites to appear in the list of search results. If users click on this Wikipedia link, it is common for these users, such as Milo, to not really understand the purpose of the site. Interestingly, this is in large part due to the fact that many users come to Wikipedia from search engines like Google that take them directly to entries within Wikipedia. Users bypass Wikipedia's home page, an area that explains the function and collaborative design of the site and end up confused by an entry that asks the user to "edit" its content. According to Dan, Wikipedia is only transparent if users understand what they are looking at.

IT'S TIME TO PLAY!

Wikipedia 101 is designed for newcomers to Wikipedia. Haven't visited Wikipedia? Don't really understand what it is? Try the simple (and not so simple) activities below. Remember to adopt the youthful mentality of play.

Wikipedia 101

Just as our students are active innovators of digital media such as Wikipedia, it is also important for us, their teachers, to see what all the fuss is about. The following activities are for you to try. All you need is access to the Internet and some good old-fashioned curiosity.

- Since Wikipedia supports collaborative knowledge, find a friend or colleague who is also curious about Wikipedia and explore the site together. It might not be beneficial to partner up with a peer who is already a Wikipedian; they might move too fast, assume too much, and even hog the mouse and keyboard. Your best bet is to find another novice such as yourself and start exploring.
- The first thing to do is find and read the about page. A majority of sites have this type of link and it can provide important contextual information in order for you to get the lay of cyberland, so to speak.
- Visit "Today's Featured Article" on the main page: Allow yourself to get your bearings with this fun article.
- Click on "random article" and see where it takes you.
- Now you are ready to check out articles on topics you love and have taught over the years. See what is out there and see if these articles

are up-to-par or if they need some additional work. Also make sure to check out their history and discussion tabs.

- If you consider yourself brave (and since you are presumably an expert in your field), go forth and edit! As Wikipedia says, "Be bold, but remember to stay cool. You are judged wholly and solely on the quality of your contributions, not on your education or profession." You might even find that writing Wikipedia articles is more difficult than it may first seem.
- Once you have tried these activities, continue with the Expert Wikipedian section for another challenge below.

Expert Wikipedians

Are you already a Wikipedian and want to see what else is possible with a wiki? Then this section is for you. This section is designed for teachers who are familiar with Wikipedia but don't know what to do beyond editing entries. Here are some ideas.

- User/Designer Perspective: first, take the perspective of a user of Wikipedia and spend five minutes searching for topics, visiting the main page and the random page. Then, for the next five minutes, take the perspective of a *designer* of Wikipedia. Look at the layout of each wiki page: What are your eyes attracted to at first? Do you find it harder to find some links rather than others? If so, why do you think they designed it this way? If not, what about the design makes it easy for you to see the links?
- Taking both a user and a designer perspective is an important aspect of understanding digital media (and our traditional media as well). As a user, you make meaning of the site as you navigate through the pages; as a designer, you come to understand how the site was constructed with certain intentions in mind. If you plan to teach your students about Wikipedia (or any medium for that matter), these two perspectives will be essential components in their study.
- Create an account! Although you can access Wikipedia and edit articles, you cannot start new pages without first creating an account and logging in. Logging in also allows you to rename pages, upload images, edit semiprotected pages and create a user page.
- Run out of things to edit? Check out the community portal link on the main navigation bar. It takes you to a community bulletin board which lists new project pages that are seeking contributors, a podcast called WikiVoices discussion forums, and collaborations.

- Visit Wikipedia's sister projects: Wiktionary, Wikiversity, Wikinews, Wikibooks and Wikiquote! Also check out Wikimedia Commons, a media file repository for freely-licensed educational media content.

Just as Wikipedia is a collaborative entity, we also want to create a community of teachers who can share stories, insights, and knowledge with one another. Go to our Web site (www.teachingtechsavvykids.com) and tell us how you think you can use Wikipedia in your classroom!

PEDAGOGICAL IMPLICATIONS AND CLASSROOM PRACTICES

With some colleges banning Wikipedia, teachers are left wondering if they should do the same. The problem with this situation is that it seems to be an either-or question: Should teachers allow Wikipedia to be used as a source? This question directs the discussion toward *including* or *excluding* sources when, really, teachers should concern themselves with the *quality* of sources. From Wikipedia's standpoint, questions should be, when is it better to consult a traditional encyclopedia, when is it better to consult Wikipedia, and when do we consult both? Instead of focusing on a question that could potentially exclude Wikipedia (even though we know the students will use it anyway even if we do this), we can now be critical of all sources and determine which sources will help us find answers to a specific inquiry.

Consider the content standards for history for eleventh graders in the state of California. Standard 11.1 requires students to "analyze the significant events in the founding of the nation" and this includes "the ideological origins of the American Revolution." As teachers, we understand that the view from an American history textbook concerning the American Revolution might vary considerably from the view of a British textbook on the same subject. Yet the English Wikipedia entry has to report both of these two perspectives. Instead of excluding Wikipedia because it is not a vetted source like a textbook, imagine if teachers helped students to understand why these two views differed. Imagine a culture where information is collectively valued. The current digital era has convinced me that the trusted single source, e.g., printed encyclopedias, has given way to a multiplicity of sources. This means that students now more than ever need to understand how to interpret and evaluate information; being *literate* depends on it. As Paul Duguid (2007), an adjunct professor in the School of Information at U.C. Berkeley, states, "Questions of quality . . . are less about what single source to trust for everything than about when to trust a particular source for the question at hand."

MYTH: Because print encyclopedias are vetted by a small number of professionals, they are error free and are usually the best reference material for students to use.

REALITY: Printed encyclopedias are not magic bullets presented out of thin air; they are but one "constructed" reference item to be used in conjunction with other sources. The best researchers, whether they are working on their seventh-grade assignment or their master's thesis, have a number of resources for finding information and will switch from printed reference material to Wikipedia and other online sources to primary source documents and back again in order to find what they are looking for. The goal of a researcher is to explore possibilities, not to search for the "right" answer since the right answer depends on context (see paragraph above concerning American Revolution).

CLASSROOM ACTIVITIES

As educators, we want our students to be engaged in our curriculum and take responsibility for their learning process. One way to accomplish this is to involve students in discussions about new media and have activities that provide engaging, student-centered learning opportunities. In today's digital age, educators must engage with students' changing media knowledge and, most important, recognize how students' experiences are (probably) fundamentally different from their own. This could entail involving students in discussions about Wikipedia, even if one's school does not condone it as a valid source; not only does this suggest to students that their educators are aware of their changing media knowledge, but more important, they are willing to engage in conversations and become more transparent in the making of their rules and regulations.

Promote Discussion

Have a discussion with your students regarding Wikipedia:

- Who uses it? How many times a week? Why? What do they like about it?
- Then share your personal insights and concerns about the Web site
- Pose the questions: Is it reliable? How do they know this? Additionally, you could ask: Are older print sources always reliable and free of errors?
- Share with your students Milo's story from the Stories From the Field section, and discuss his experiences with Wikipedia as a site and a source. Ask students if Milo's story is similar or different to

their own or have your students write their own Stories From the Field in which they discuss their experiences with Wikipedia

- Wikipedia is an ideal site to learn how to interpret information. As a class, make a checklist of ways to know that an entry is reliable. In my experience, students will rise to the challenge if we include them in creating academic norms. Some good questions to pose include: How many checks are needed to make an entry reliable? Is there ever an entry that is completely reliable? Is every perspective, fact, or issue always included? The same questions could be asked of our traditional print materials.

- For educators interested in how to teach better Web searching skills, Google for Educators (http://www.google.com/educators/index.html) has put together through their Google Certified Teachers program lessons and resources on this important subject. Lessons and resources include understanding search engines and search techniques and strategies (http://www.google.com/educators/ p_websearch.html).

EVALUATING WIKIPEDIA ENTRIES: A CHECKLIST

By Phoebe Ayers, U.C. Davis Librarian

If you and your students are going to use Wikipedia, here are some tips from Phoebe Ayers, a physical sciences and engineering librarian at the University of California, Davis, and co-author of *How Wikipedia Works* (2008). Download her one-page handout on our Web site.

☑ Look at the article quality:

- Does the writing read well? Is the topic clearly explained?
- Are there any citations, references, or outside links? Are there citations to print sources as well as online sources? Are individual statements referenced with footnotes within the text?

☑ Look at the page edit history: click on the history tab at the top of the article to see a record of all changes that have been made to the article

- Was the article recently created? When was it last edited? Older articles have likely been seen by more people.

☑ Check the article's discussion page, if one exists: click the discussion tab at the top of the article

- Are there discussions about the validity of the article? Are questions raised about the article?
- Does the article topic appear to be controversial or otherwise under debate?

☑ Check the templates at the top of the article if any exist:

- Is the article tagged with a common clean-up template, such as

  o "*To meet* Wikipedia's quality standards, this article or section may require cleanup."
  o "This article or section does not cite its references or sources."
  o "Some information in this article or section has not been verified and may not be reliable."
  o "This article or section may contain original research or unverified claims."

- If so, at least one Wikipedia editor thought that the article had problems that should be addressed by other editors, and the article may not be reliable.

Adopt a Wikipedia Entry

As a class or in small groups, adopt an entry in need of help or start a new entry all together, e.g., your school, your town, a topic from class, or a reference to popular culture. Make sure to pick something that is interesting to a majority of the participants. Brainstorm on the board about what everyone knows about the topic. If you want to get competitive, have two different classes write a new entry on the same topic. Have parents and administrators pick the winning entry and upload it to Wikipedia. The team that doesn't win can always chronicle their thoughts in the discussion section and make edits of their own. No vandalism though and make sure to read through the notability guidelines and standards that all editors should follow. Read "How to Edit a Page" (http://tiny.cc/teachtech_4_3).

Wikis for Educators

Now that you have been introduced to Wikipedia, go visit other wikis for educators! Using a Google search engine, type "wiki for educators" and see what is out there. There are too many to chronicle in this chapter, so see what appeals to you and what you think works!

I recommend Wikispaces (http://wikispaces.com). Make sure to take a tour. At the time of this printing, Wikispaces was giving away free sites to educators. Also, refer to Will Richardson's *Blogs, Wikis, Podcasts, and Other Powerful Web Tools for Classrooms* (2006) if you desire more information on this exciting topic.

Brent Freccia, a history teacher, has created WikiFreccia using Wikispaces for his syllabi, daily homework schedules, and contact information. The wiki allows him to update the site daily. He can even limit the access of the site to only his students and their parents, and this protects the site from public viewing (see Figure 4.3).

Figure 4.3 WikiFreccia

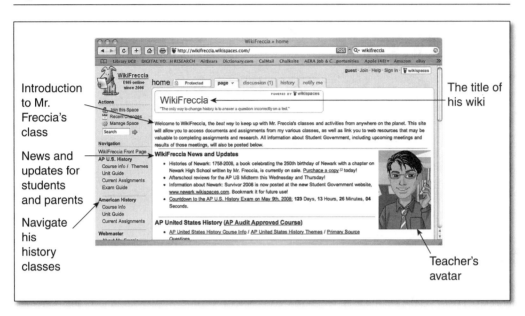

Introduction to Mr. Freccia's class

News and updates for students and parents

Navigate his history classes

The title of his wiki

Teacher's avatar

Educators such as English teacher David Conlay have also used this resource as a place to publish unit plans and activities and even student projects (see Figure 4.4). Students can upload their work whether it is a written report, a scanned art project, or even short movie clips.

Figure 4.4 Atticus Factor

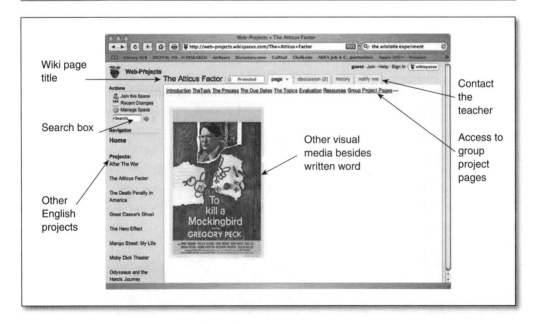

Wiki page title

Search box

Other English projects

Other visual media besides written word

Contact the teacher

Access to group project pages

Wikispaces can also be used for vocabulary lists, slang dictionaries, class notes, research projects, test preparation and study guides, student presentations, and even unit plans for parents or students. Make sure to use your wiki to its fullest potential by including students and parents in the design and content construction.

To sign up for your own Wikispace, type in http://wikispaces.com/site/for/teachers and follow the instructions. Remember to think beyond the written word; wikis can include photographs, video clips, art, music, and much more. Additionally, Wikispaces provides "private" wikis in case you only want specific students, teachers, parents, or administrators to have editing access.

SHARE YOUR INSIGHTS, STORIES, AND EXPERIENCES!

We don't claim to have all the answers. We want to hear from you. Join our community of teachers and post your answers to some of these questions:

1. What has been your experience with Wikipedia?

2. Describe any benefits or drawbacks to using Wikipedia in class.

3. What about Wikipedia's (or the wiki) design might lend itself to your classroom?

4. If schools don't have access to the Internet, how can teachers integrate the characteristics of Wikipedia into their classroom activities?

5. Where do you stand on the Wikipedian philosophy that the more people edit a page, the better it will be? And how does this philosophy compare to the practice of encyclopedias being written by a selected few?

6. Gunther Kress (2003), a professor of English education, argues that there are currently two major shifts taking place in terms of literacy. First, there is a broad shift from the dominance of writing to the new dominance of the image. Second, there is a shift from the dominance of the book to the dominance of the screen. If this is the case, what are some of the ways educators can or have adapted to these major shifts within the classroom?

Feel free to ask your own questions of the online teaching community.

REFERENCES AND HELPFUL RESOURCES

Ayers, P., Matthew, C., Yates, B., & Klein, S. J. (2008). *How Wikipedia works.* San Francisco: No Starch Press.

boyd, d. (2007). Information Access in a Networked World. Talk presented to Pearson Publishing. Palo Alto, CA: November 2. http://www.danah.org/papers/talks/Pearson2007.html

Carrington, V., & Robinson, M. (2009). *Digital literacies: Social learning and classroom practices.* Thousand Oaks, CA: Sage.

Digital Youth Research: Kids' Informal Learning with Digital Media. http://digitalyouth.ischool.berkeley.edu/

Duguid, P. (2007) Limits of self-organization: Peer production and "laws of quality." *First Monday, 11*(10). Retrieved November 22, 2007 from http://www.uic.edu/htbin/cgiwrap/bin/ojs/index.php/fm/

Glaser, M. (2006, April 17). *Is there a neutral view on George W. Bush?* Retrieved January 17, 2009, from http://www.pbs.org/mediashift/2006/04/wikipedia_biasis_there_a_neutr.html

Kress, G. (2003). *Literacy in the New Media Age.* London: Routledge.

Pew Research Center. (2007, April 24). *Wikipedia: When in doubt, multitudes seek it out.* Retrieved January 11, 2009, from http://pewresearch.org/pubs/460/wikipedia

Richardson, W. (2006). *Blogs, wikis, podcasts, and other powerful web tools for classrooms.* Thousand Oaks, CA: Corwin.

Wikimedia Commons: http://commons.wikimedia.org/wiki/Main_Page

Wikimedia Foundation: http://wikimediafoundation.org

Wikipedia's Statistics page: http://en.wikipedia.org/wiki/Wikipedia:Statistics

Wikispaces for Teachers: http://wikispaces.com/site/for/teachers

Role-Playing

Writing and Performing Beyond the Classroom

**Becky Herr-Stephenson
and Jessica K. Parker**

INTRODUCTION

In this chapter we discuss how students are using three role-playing activities to explore informal storytelling, meet new people and craft a sense of themselves as writers, performers, and gamers. Unfortunately in the popular media, online role-playing is usually presented as something for students to avoid, and writing about mainstream fictional characters can sometimes be viewed as obsessive and childish. These "stranger danger" and "childish" discourses are just one side of the coin and this chapter will highlight how aspects of role-playing, such as the interactive and collaborative storytelling aspects, can appeal to teachers and their students.

WRITING AND PERFORMABLE PRACTICES

One concern regularly expressed by adults about young people's use of technology is that technology replaces other types of activities—such as reading and writing—that are highly valued in schools. Additionally, educators, employers, and parents alike have lamented the communication practices kids and teens use in their everyday lives—such as writing informal e-mails, blog posts, status updates, or **tweets** to keep up with friends and abbreviating words for ease of texting on one's mobile phone. It seems that the ways in which schools teach students to communicate and expect students to communicate and the ways in which students actually use media and technology to connect to one another are at odds. Instead of perpetuating this divide, educators can pull from the written and performable practices of role-playing to engage students. In this chapter, we will discuss different examples of online role-playing, including

- **Role-playing games,** sometimes referred to as RPGs, in which players take on a role or character through which they define their actions in a game
- **Role-playing Web sites** in which participants write as a specific character
- **Fan fiction Web sites** in which participants write stories about characters from a literary canon

ONLINE ROLE-PLAYING GAMES

In role-playing games, participants become characters in a *game world* and collaboratively attempt to accomplish specific goals within a particular setting. The board game *Dungeons and Dragons* is a classic example of a role-playing game that has been around since the 1970s. Similarly, online role-playing games are sites for players to act out characters and work on specific tasks. Players can maneuver their characters to start quests, to initiate combat, to train, and to become more powerful and sophisticated characters as the game progresses. For instance, *World of Warcraft* is a *massively multiplayer online role-playing game (MMORPG)* that currently boasts over 11 million players worldwide. Players create characters through which they will explore and participate within the game world. During gameplay, players band together to complete quests and fight monsters.

> **MYTH:** Role-playing activities are forms of child's play and should not be condoned for older adolescents.
>
> **REALITY:** Professor Henry Jenkins (2006a) and his co-authors suggest role-playing is a fundamental new literacy skill. They argue that playing or writing about a character can offer one the capability to understand issues from multiple viewpoints, to digest information, and to problem solve.

Role-playing games of all kinds offer players an immersive and intensely social experience that, for many players, is a key part of the games' draw. Many role-playing games follow in the footsteps of *Dungeons and Dragons* and are set in medieval times and incorporate fantasy elements, such as nonhuman characters and magical abilities. In most cases, the lore of the game is deep and intricately connected to gameplay. The work of understanding and exploring the unique settings found in role-playing games can spark creativity and encourage flexible thinking in young people.

When Jessica hears the term role-playing games, she automatically envisions a game set in medieval times. This is probably due to the influence of J. R. R. Tolkien, whose ring trilogy led to a board game called *Dungeons and Dragons*, considered by most to be the oldest and most popular role-playing game. With the advent of computers and then the Internet, these games led to online role-playing games, which is why so many of them seem medieval in setting.

A TEACHER'S RETROSPECTIVE

Adventures With Role-Playing Games

By Andy Maul, Educator

Role-playing games such as *Dungeons and Dragons* often seem to carry a certain stigma: They are often thought to be the province of nerds, and others on the peripheries of normal social conduct. They carry an image of Tolkienesque swords and sorcery, branding them a bit uncool by the standards of some. And . . . all right, I'll admit it: I was a bit of a nerd growing up. Still am, in some ways. But I think I turned out pretty well, and looking back on my experiences with role-playing games, I must say they were a constant delight, that enriched my life in a number of ways.

At first RPGs (role-playing games as those in the know call them) mainly provided a way for me to interact with other people like me: introverted, bright, and perhaps a bit weird, or original, to be more kind. They also appealed to my very active imagination: My friends and I would create worlds together, populating them with as many beautiful and horrible and just bizarre things as we could come up with, and we would weave stories in those worlds. For at their heart, role-playing games are simply interactive storytelling: One of us would take the role of world-builder while the others would take on the roles of specific characters in the story, much like a director and his actors on the stage. Noncoincidentally, role-playing games would lead me to a love of both theater and creative writing in later life.

The stories we shaped were reflections of our own worlds but vastly exaggerated. As I first came to understand the tragedies of world politics, our villains became despotic rulers, and later cunning manipulators. As I was first introduced to the horrors of middle-school romance, beautiful (and sometimes terrible) heroines took stage. When I was young, the characters I played were mostly idealized

(Continued)

(Continued)

versions of myself, but as I aged I became interested in a wider variety of heroes; sometimes, it was the characters least like me who were the most fun to play, as they allowed me to take on a dramatically different perspective. This, I believe, had a profound impact on the way I was able to view human interaction. While I have by no means mastered the art of perspective-taking, I do think role-playing games gave me a broader view of people's motivations and personalities.

Online gaming has taken this all to a new level. In a game such as *World of Warcraft* I take on a specific role, and I need to understand how my character's abilities work so that I am able to use them effectively in pursuit of my goals. For especially challenging missions I need to team up with friends, who play different characters—and then I need to understand not only my abilities *and* their abilities but also how they interact and how we can effectively be more than the sum of our parts.

In addition to the strategic element of *World of Warcraft*, there's also the acting-storytelling element. I find myself acting out improvisational scenes, fully in character, with other gamers—many of whom I don't know. The actual players I'm interacting with could be anywhere or anyone and this lends an additional thrill to the shared world we're creating. Sometimes I might bond with other players enough to learn more about them, and through this I've made friends literally all around the globe even if I haven't met most of them in person.

In addition to how many happy memories they've given me, I do think role-playing games have enriched my life. Telling stories interactively, acting out characters, thinking strategically and cooperatively, and connecting with others around the world has been thrilling and unexpectedly educational. I do regret that many kids will shy away from these types of games in the rather harsh social environment of primary and secondary school because I do think role-playing games can hold interest in value for a wider range of people than so-called nerds. In fact my wife—the very antithesis of a nerd—has recently found absolute delight in the *World of Warcraft*, as foreign as it must have seemed to her at first. Now it's she who asks if we can game together, taking on our roles as heroes and saving the world from whatever happens to be threatening it today. Nerdy? Perhaps. But somehow role-playing games are bringing me just as much joy and fulfillment today as they did the first time I heard of elves and dragons and I suspect, in some form, they always will.

Andy's literate experiences with role-playing games such as *Dungeons and Dragons* are important to analyze. He explained how, with friends, they collaboratively produced creative stories and developed and acted out characters. Not only did these experiences help Andy learn how to construct a narrative, but he also credited these experiences with fostering his love of theater and creative writing and with an ability to consider and empathize with different perspectives. Being literate in school in a number of subject areas requires that students appreciate different genres, work together in groups, and be able to think strategically to solve problems. Fleischer, Wright, and Barnes (2007) add that *Dungeons and Dragons* gamers cultivate "traditional print literacies such as story writing, vocabulary building mathematics, map reading" and that participation supports "enthusiasm for reading both fiction and nonfiction texts" (pp. 156–7). Additionally, the authors argue that online computer games, such as *World of Warcraft*, continue to reinforce and inspire print-based literacies through the reading and writing of supplemental material. Adults who ignore these literate practices end up dismissing role-playing games and the potential of these games to support school-based literacy practices.

Role-playing is a beneficial educational activity that should be utilized with students of all ages. Here's why. Our sense of self-identity is not based on a one-sided relationship with the world. That is I cannot define myself purely in relation to myself—I am always interacting with the outside world, especially with family, friends, colleagues, students, and parents. For teens, it is essential to understand and reflect on how one's sense of identity is constantly adjusting to how one appears to others. Using role-playing activities in classrooms can make this process, which is often naturalized and left unquestioned, highly visible. Because the characters in role-play activities are separate from students' own identities, it may be easier for students to do this kind of critical and reflective work, practice that can later be applied to understanding their own identities and relationships in the "real" world.

For instance, to play Romeo in Shakespeare's play *Romeo and Juliet*, students must understand the character of Romeo: his family, his background, his desires, and his strengths and flaws as a friend and a lover. This kind of reflection involves hypothesis testing, that is it grants the performer a chance to think about what could happen with Romeo as well as what he would hope will happen with his relationship with Juliet. This resonates with Andy Maul's experiences with *Dungeons and Dragons* in which he had to understand his character's abilities and those of the other characters in order to effectively play the game. Additionally, taking an active role in playing a character also allows students to manipulate their fictional world and appeals to the imagination. These experiences can be very empowering for students.

ROLE-PLAYING THROUGH WRITING

In addition to their role-playing roots in games such as *Dungeons and Dragons*, MMORPGs such as *World of Warcraft* and *Everquest* have emerged from a tradition of role-playing games specific to online communities. These communities, called **multiuser dungeons (MUDs),** emerged in the very early days of the Internet (before it was the World Wide Web), and provided players with a virtual space for social interaction based on textual commands and descriptions. Much of this interaction made its ways into later versions of online role-playing games. Textual role play in which participants write as specific characters also persists in online communities. Some of these role-playing sites are popular among kids, as these sites usually offer a skeleton of a story and role players then take on the task of writing the story through the interactions of their characters. With the help of other role players, the story then grows into a sophisticated, detailed work of imagination written by numerous authors, not just one. This is a chance for participants to develop favorite characters off of the paper and breathe life into him or her, as one role-playing site suggests.

Some text-based role-playing sites are based in fantasy worlds constructed from scratch by the participants. Others offer up characters from popular media for players to "claim." For example, on the popular online journal site Live Journal, one can find role-playing communities based on *Star Wars, Harry Potter, Twilight,* and various **anime** series. Panfandom role-playing sites, which incorporate elements from a number of series, are also gaining popularity. Like fan fiction (discussed later in this chapter), text-based role-playing is an interest-driven practice that offers young writers an opportunity to play with preexisting characters and story elements, reworking, remixing, and extending the stories in meaningful and creative ways. What makes role-playing sites different from fan fiction is that multiple players author them.

Just like MMORPGs and offline role-playing games, text-based role-playing sites are intensely social experiences for participants. For young writers, role-playing Web sites can be said to offer a "third place." C. J. Pascoe defines a "third place" as a place other than home or school where teens can hang out. With role-playing Web sites, teens virtually "hang out" around the writing of stories—*their* own fictional stories in which they write the characters into being through the construction of their personalities, their likes and dislikes, and even their underlying psyche. Essentially these Web sites become places in which kids can connect with people who are also interested in fiction writing, gain feedback on their written work, and enjoy being creative. Now we turn to a specific example from C. J. Pascoe, who describes the interest-driven experiences of a teenager named Clarissa on a role-playing Web site.

STORIES FROM THE FIELD

You Have Another World to Create

Teens and Online Role-Playing Web Sites

By C. J. Pascoe, Sociologist

As I was reading *The New York Times*, an article about teenagers' use of public libraries as hangout spots caught my eye. In it, experts bemoaned the growing lack of "third places," in other words, places which weren't home or school, where teens could engage in a time honored tradition of American adolescence, hanging out. Indeed as we perceive that our streets grow more dangerous, as suburban family life increasingly takes place in atomized homes, and the amount of public spaces decline, public or quasipublic places where teens can socialize appear infrequently. In talking to teens about their technology use, it seems that the Internet offers a form of this third place. While not a physical space, for those teens who have access to the Internet, in a variety of ways, from the ubiquitous MySpace to online game sites, it provides a form of a third space, a semipublic place for teens to hang out. As with many teen hangouts, adults are nervous about teens' activities when they are online. But most of the teens I've talked to about their Internet practices tell me that their online activities look a lot like their offline lives. They chat with their friends, flirt, find the latest "cool" site, watch videos, play games, and download music.

Clarissa*, a 17-year-old growing up in a working class suburb of San Francisco, is one of the many teens who uses the Internet as a third place. Like most of the teens I talk to, Clarissa checks her MySpace site daily, looking for messages from her friends, updating pictures or adding other content. Clarissa's primary hangout site is not MySpace though. She is an avid online role player and spends most of her time on her favorite site, Faraway Lands*, with her two best friends, also role players. Their online role-playing is not about murder and mayhem but about trying out varieties of selves, informal storytelling, meeting new people and crafting a sense of themselves as writers. On this site they can hang out in a manner that isn't always possible in any sort of constructive way in their physical community, one plagued by problems of crime and gangs.

Clarissa describes Faraway Lands as a "really nice quality, good, inviting, comfortable, fun place to be." She finds it to be a community of supportive friends who have high writing standards and creativity. Members must write intricate character applications to join the site. These character applications are essentially 25,000 word descriptions of a given character, its race, its history, and its location. For Clarissa, an aspiring writer and filmmaker, this site allows her to use "words like clay to create whatever stories suit your fancy." She finds the community to be a "nurturing" one, in which she is "able to fully develop intricate personalities and plots that in computer games, sports, and academics are simply not possible."

(Continued)

(Continued)

Faraway Lands is a text-based site where members weave long and detailed tales about their characters' quests and adventures.

In this online hangout Clarissa has made many friends and transcended her local boundaries. While people of all ages are on this site, "most of the people that I've interacted with are in my age group. It's sort of cool 'cause they're far away and sort of fun." On Faraway Lands she is simultaneously in character and out of character as she hangs out and chats on an Internet relay channel. During these chats she has made friends all over the world, telling me, "I know a guy in Spain now and fun stuff like that." She and her friend from Spain are currently in the middle of planning a new role play in which his "evil" character tries to hire one of Clarissa's characters, Saloria, as an apprentice.

Faraway Lands also provides a forum in which Clarissa can be creative and hone her writing skills. She and her role-playing friends critique each other's writing and stories. She and a fellow role player from Oregon "had this sort of thing where we were reviewing each other's work all the time 'cause he just wanted all the input he could get." The creative aspect of this site is part of what drew Clarissa to Faraway Lands. "It's something I can do in my spare time, be creative and write and not have to be graded," because, "you know how in school you're creative but you're doing it for a grade so it doesn't really count?" In this digital hangout teens are not treated as problem-causing kids, but as legitimate players, artists, and writers. Unlike in school where teens live in a world of hierarchical relations—where they are graded, run the risk of getting in trouble, and must obey all sorts of status and age-oriented rules, in Faraway Lands Clarissa is evaluated on her creativity and artistic ability.

Clarissa's character, Saloria, received glowing reviews from the site's administrators, who must approve characters before members can engage in a role play. Clarissa shared her excitement with me about the feedback she received saying for Saloria she was awarded "two golden approvals. I was amazed 'cause I was just finishing her." Clarissa's stories involve themes of fantasy, triumph, and escape. Her character Saloria, for instance, grew up in a poor neighborhood and was raised by a "loving community" rather than a nuclear family. As a teen, Saloria leaves this community to seek her fortune in the wider world. However, she soon realizes that, as a single woman, the world is a dangerous place. Saloria then decides to live her life as a man, "because men have it better. So she spends her days as a man." During the day, as a man, Saloria performs "roadwork around the city. She's a happy go lucky charming young fellow." At night "she's a crazy lady who has fun." Clarissa drew on her real life experience to create Saloria. She recalled fondly stories of adventurous women. She "loved those women who would go on these voyages acting like they were boys for months, and months, and months. It was daring and crazy. And I was like, 'I want to do that. That would be fun.'" While this sort of adventuring is not feasible for Clarissa, her characters can live out these fantasies. She sums up Saloria's story by saying, "It just started with that, the freedom of being a boy." Through this particular role play, Clarissa grapples with intense issues of adolescent identity work and imagines her way out of some of the gendered expectations faced by teenage girls.

Faraway Lands is Clarissa's third place, a place where she can make friends, hang out, chat and write fantastical stories. It's both an escape from the physical world of school and an extension of her offline social life. Internet forums such as Faraway Lands offer places for teens to both hang out and create. Clarissa sums it up aptly: "This is just a nice little world that you can control and you can make your own drama. But you can do it in a creative in-depth storytelling fun way that's all artistic. You have another world to create. It's fun."

C. J. Pascoe's vignette was originally published online in January 2007 on the Digital Youth Web site, the online home of the Kids' Informal Learning with Digital Media project at http://digitalyouth.ischool.berkeley.edu/node/65.

*Please note that the names of individuals and any Web sites mentioned in this article are pseudonyms and were designed to protect the privacy of the research participants.

ACTIVE READING AND WRITING: *HARRY POTTER* FAN FICTION

Unlike Clarissa's role-playing Web site that offered her a chance to write her own characters into existence, fan-fiction Web sites provide a space where participants can write stories about characters from a canon. Becky studied *Harry Potter* fans and found two highly popular practices among these fans (particularly female fans) who were reading and writing fan fiction. Fan fiction (often simply called *fic*) is a type of creative writing that uses characters, settings, and plots from established canons, such as other books, television shows, or films. The *Harry Potter* **fandom** has been a major force in putting online fan fiction on the radar of mainstream culture due to its large size and technological savvy. With hundreds of thousands of stories posted in various online communities, *Harry Potter* fans have access to an immense amount of text to read in addition to the seven books in the series.

As part of her research for the Kids' Informal Learning with Digital Media project, Becky spent a year hanging out with other Harry Potter fans in various on and offline spaces, spending time on large fan sites like Mugglenet.com and Leakynews.com, reading fan fiction on archives such as Fanfiction.net, interviewing fans she met at local events, and attending conferences such as Enlightening 2007, a weekend-long conference for kids and their parents held in Philadelphia in July 2007. In addition, she had the opportunity to speak with several young women who were avid fan fiction readers and writers. One teen Becky interviewed, who chose the pseudonym ChoMalfoy, described the appeal of fan fiction in this way: "I've always loved to read. I used to go to the library like every other day when I was younger. But since I've discovered *Harry Potter*, it became easier to read online, and it's always good that you know exactly where to find the type of story you like . . . whereas in books, you don't have as many books of a certain genre you like at your ready disposal." Other fan fiction readers and writers Becky interviewed echoed this sentiment of personalization, choice, and convenience, along with the value of participating in a peer-based community of readers and writers.

There are a number of genres of fan fiction, ranging from "gen" (for general) fic, which tends to focus on extending the original text by creating new situations for the characters to explore. These new plots are (or at least attempt to be) consistent with the settings and characterizations found in the original text or canon. Other genres of fan fiction take more liberties with canonical texts, playing with the ways in which characters are portrayed or transporting characters to different settings. One popular type of *Harry Potter* fan fiction in this vein is "shipper fic," which focuses on one or more relationships between characters. Some of the relationships are canonical, meaning that they are consistent with those in the novels; others, however, posit romantic relationships that are not explicit in canon, allowing fan fiction readers and writers to play with characters and relationships in creative and meaningful ways.

A BEGINNER'S GUIDE TO FAN FICTION

Still unclear on what exactly fan fiction looks like? Consider, for example, the following prompts, which Becky developed to be representative of the types of stories one might find on a large fan fiction archive:

1. What if Harry Potter was not the one destined to save the wizarding world from evil? What if the "chosen one" was, in fact, Harry's precocious friend Hermione Granger? Or his shy, clumsy classmate Neville Longbottom? How would the story be different if Harry were not "the boy who lived?"

2. When Harry arrived at Hogwarts School, he was sorted into (assigned to) Gryffindor House, one of four houses (groups of students) at Hogwarts. Before Harry was sorted, there was a question of whether he should be placed in Gryffindor House, known for being the house of valiant and honorable wizards, or Slytherin House, the house with a longstanding association with wizards who used magic for evil instead of good. What would have happened if Harry had been assigned to Slytherin House instead of Gryffindor? Would he have become the same powerful, good wizard? Or would he have turned to dark magic?

3. Harry Potter and his nemesis Draco Malfoy have an intense rivalry. What if the reason behind their antagonism is actually romantic infatuation? How could they manage to carry on a secret relationship without the other students finding out that they are not the enemies they claim to be?

4. Hogwarts School does not exist. Instead, Harry Potter is a fourth grader in a typical elementary school in Los Angeles. As the year progresses Harry discovers that he has abilities that are quite different from those of his classmates. How does he deal with this discovery in the absence of other wizards? What happens when he uses magic (by accident or on purpose) in a school full of non-magical people?

The first two prompts are examples of the types of topics and questions addressed in gen fic. The characters and settings are consistent with the world that has been established by J.K. Rowling, although the fan fiction author can play with the scenario in order to investigate topics that she or he finds intriguing. Prompt number three is an example of shipper fic, in that it focuses on a romantic relationship between Harry and Draco (in this case, one that is not explicitly established in the canon materials). The fourth prompt is an example of what is often called "AU" or alternate universe fic. In this prompt, the characters and some of the plot elements are lifted out of the world crafted by Rowling and placed in a different world (often one that is familiar to the author).

Some fan fiction writers work from prompts (often called plot bunnies) generated in writing communities. Others come to the ideas for their stories on their own or through conversations with friends; reading other writers' fic is another fruitful place for generating ideas for new stories. Fan fiction can be an independent, private writing activity; however, what is different and exciting about fic, particularly in comparison to some more traditional forms of writing at school, is that it can be a shared activity that draws on students' shared (and highly valued) experiences with popular culture. As an interest-driven activity, fan fiction writing can be highly motivating, encouraging investment not only in the product of the activity but also in the social interactions essential to the writing process. Further, fan fiction has its own "built in" processes for review, feedback, critique, and revision—writing practices generally believed to produce better, more polished text, but that are often omitted from everyday writing in classrooms due to time, resources, or curricular demands.

In addition to providing a creative outlet for students, fan fiction can be seen as an opportunity for students to practice literary analysis. Although they are just examples, the prompts above give an idea of the type of complex, detailed, and hypothetical thinking fan fiction writers use in creating their stories. Prior knowledge of *Harry Potter* is needed to make sense of these questions and sophisticated analysis can come from grappling with the questions presented. This deep knowledge and interest in a topic mirrors what teachers try to promote in their classrooms.

Given the large amount of fan fiction circulating online and the variety of genres of fic out there, many large fan fiction archives, such as FanFiction.net and FictionAlley.org, allow readers to enter search parameters—such as publication date, genre, character, relationship, era, and rating—to help them quickly find the stories they seek. To this end, writers are encouraged to tag their entries when they publish a piece of fan fiction in addition to providing a descriptive title and synopsis. An alternative way of finding and sharing fan fiction is by joining fan fiction communities, such as those on the site Live Journal. Live Journal fan fiction communities tend to be smaller and more specific in genre and also tend to blend various genres of social participation between members. In addition to sharing text, many online communities encourage authors to use visual media, such as icons, graphics, and banners related to a particular piece of fan fiction to enhance and promote the text.

SOCIAL ASPECTS OF FAN FICTION COMMUNITIES

Feedback is an important part of fan fiction authorship and takes various forms during the process of writing and circulating fic. Many writers have a "beta reader," a trusted editor who reads works in progress and provides feedback on the story and on mechanical issues such as grammar and spelling. Some sites require that stories be beta-edited or "beta-ed" before they are posted in an effort to ensure the quality of the fic on the site. This prepublication feedback can be extremely influential on the structure of a story and can help a writer break through writer's block or assist in solving problems with the story's content. For example, a beta-reader may provide suggestions about plot or note when a character appears to be OOC (out of character), or acts in a way that is inconsistent with its canonical depiction.

With postpublication, both archive sites and journal sites facilitate sharing feedback between readers and writers in a manner similar to that seen on Clarissa's role-playing Web site, readers are encouraged to comment on published stories, leaving notes about what they liked in a story or suggestions for changes. Frequently this feedback is simply encouragement for the writer to continue writing, which, according to several of the fan fiction authors with whom Becky spoke, is often the most valuable kind of feedback because it indicates that the writer has an engaged audience. Particularly in smaller fan fiction communities, providing feedback can be a pathway to friendship or a way of reinforcing friendship. Reviewing a story can act as an introduction—a way to demonstrate that you would like to be friends with another writer in the community. Once friendships are established, providing feedback on friends' writing becomes an important means of "checking in" and maintaining contact with those friends.

The social aspects of fan fiction communities—feedback and friendship—are key to the value of reading and writing fan fiction. They are also the characteristics that differentiate the practices of writing and circulating fan fiction from the types of writing familiar to most students. Rather than writing in response to a prompt created by a teacher or a textbook or working to identify a predetermined answer, fan fiction writing engages with content that is salient to the student and draws upon the knowledge and energy of the students' peers. Since the writing is ungraded, fan fiction writers may feel comfortable taking more risks in this type of writing than in writing produced for school. In many cases, the feedback a writer receives from his or her audience is much more meaningful than a grade on a school essay.

MOTIVATING FACTORS OF ROLE-PLAYING

- Students choose the roles they are interested in playing
- There are many types of role-playing: costume play, live action role play, online role play boards, role-playing games, MMORPGs, and many more
- Students can have membership in a collaborative, online community
- The community can nurture an identity as an artist, writer, and participant through comments and critique
- Students are not graded! They receive feedback from peers on their ability to write/perform/play a character. In this sense, feedback is formative and (often) immediate
- There is a low risk of failure (if your style doesn't fit the site, you can always find another site to join)
- Mentorship from other members of the game can help participants develop style and skills for participation

---

PEDAGOGICAL IMPLICATIONS AND CLASSROOM PRACTICES

In C. J. Pascoe's Story From the Field, Clarissa described her online writing experiences as something she does in her spare time, where she can be "creative and write and not have to be graded." With regards to school, she states that her creativity doesn't really count since she is doing it for a grade. Additionally, Becky discussed how fan fiction writers she interviewed felt comfortable taking more risks with ungraded writing than with writing produced for school, and that in many cases, "the feedback a writer receives from his or her audience is much more meaningful than a grade on a school essay."

When Jessica was teaching high school English, she was obligated to teach her students traditional academic writing, usually five-paragraph essays and other derivatives, but she also felt compelled to nurture her students' sense of themselves as writers. Jessica found that some of her students were afraid of "academic writing" even though these same students were avid writers of journal entries, song lyrics, texts, and online posts. She searched for ways to include multiple genres of writing in her classroom in the hopes that students could view themselves holistically as writers and then, together, take them on a collective journey to understand and engage in academic writing. And this problem is not limited just to English teachers. Math teachers have to confront their students' fear of math and researchers in science education have long argued for the need for students to see themselves as a part of the scientific community in order to demonstrate deep science conceptual understanding. Diana J. Arya, a science educator, discusses below how to invite students in the discipline of a subject area, and for science, this includes taking on the roles of "question maker" and "data analyzer."

A TEACHER'S PERSPECTIVE

Breaking Through the Mystique of Science

Inviting Students Into the Roles of "Question Maker" and "Data Analyzer"

By Diana J. Arya, Science Educator

Many students believe science class can only be conquered by the smartest of the bunch, placing subjects like chemistry and physics on a mystical pedestal. A while back, I asked my students to draw a scientist. Almost all of these drawings were of old white men who wore lab coats and glasses. This view of science fuels one of the greatest misconceptions about scientific discovery and knowledge—that it has nothing to do with real life or people like themselves. Many teachers have tried to combat this debilitating belief by introducing scientific concepts within a familiar context. Professor and researcher Jay Lemke (1990) describes in his book, *Talking Science*, how a high school teacher introduces the concept of germ cell formation by engaging his class about a discussion of the 1950s cult movie *The Blob*. This initial discussion provides a space that invites all to actively participate in learning more about cell generation. I have witnessed and tried similar attempts for student engagement during my time as an urban middle school science teacher; my colleagues and I are not above donning costumes if we think it will be a useful hook for our students' focused attention. However, once the initial excitement of the hook wears off, many students revert to the standby belief that science is for the "brainiacs," and begin to doodle and daydream once more. Thus, the real questions are, how do I show my students that science is part of and relevant to their everyday lives? Or how can I convince them that science is not just for a few individuals, that we are all a part of the scientific community?

Unfortunately, the bulk of school science curricula present scientific knowledge as a collection of hard-set facts that somehow sprouted from the ground. While many classroom experiments resemble preplanned recipes, textbooks particularly fail to explicate the tentative, explorative nature of the scientific process (Bowker, 2005; Griffiths & Barman, 1995; Lederman, 1992; Niaz & Rodriguez, 2000; Popper, 1959). Thus, students see science as a collection of information rather than what it really is—an opportunity to ask questions about our world and to figure out a way to find an answer that may change over time. In his book, *Science in Action*, sociologist Latour (1987) explains how the "real science" of science is masked for those outside the community that engages in the discovery process. So our challenge as science teachers is to bring our students into the real science of science, which means knocking down the pedestal and eliciting questions that our students have about our world. The ultimate goal for me was to see my students draw themselves as scientists, and role-playing proved to be a powerful strategy for easing my students into the discovery process.

Just like trying on a lab coat, I asked my students to imagine that a friend of theirs showed them a rock that glowed. How would you try to learn more about this rock? I was impressed to hear their answers; several actually collected rocks and had much to tell. This is how I began the discussion of chemical reactants and radioactivity—through the discovery story of Marie Curie. Henri Becquerel showed Marie and her husband a rock he called uranium ore (also called pitchblende) that gives of a light bluish glow. Curie (1903) describes in her book, *Radioactive Substances*, how she came to understand the power that this glow represented and that it came from an element no one knew existed before—she called it radium. Curie's natural curiosity and creative problem solving provided a meaningful context for learning concepts like elements, reactants, and atomic weight. For the chemistry labs I threw out the curricular recipes and asked my students what they would want to know about some given substances and how they would go about finding out the answers to their questions. In the beginning, I asked them to pretend they were Marie and Pierre Curie, faced with the unknown. Once I made this change in my instruction, I saw it—students were becoming scientists.

Marie Curie is only one of many scientists through which students could learn about the process of discovery. African American chemist George Washington Carver was a familiar name to my students of color, but they had no idea how he came to understand the utility of the peanut nor did they have a clue about his countless discoveries and inventions that had nothing to do with the peanut. I love to read aloud one of his letters addressed to a colleague in which he explains how he discovered a way to make cost effective paint from using ordinary clay—a familiar context with practical implications. It made the brainstorming session of potential cost-effective discoveries, e.g., a cheaper substance to fuel a car, with a follow-up researching session an easy project to facilitate because everyone was

(Continued)

(Continued)

engaged and invested. George Washington Carver was no longer a distant, iconic symbol from the past; he was being reincarnated in my students, who all wanted to continue his love for discovery and learning about our world.

An important part of playing the role of scientists is the experience of perseverance. Discoveries do not usually happen easily, which can be discouraging. Most people do not know about the painstaking process of observation that led to Jane Goodall's discovery of tool use among primates, but she describes her experience in great detail within her book, *In the Shadow of Man* (1971). After reading about her trials and tribulations, I asked my students to imagine what she would do if she planned to study the wildlife in a nearby park. A great discussion ensued, involving spontaneous renderings of diagrams and charts that plotted out potential sites. Then came the day for the walking trip to the park—I was nervous. Would they take this as seriously as Goodall would? Yes, they did. Everyone was committed to absolute silence. A solid half-hour observation period with no talking, only looking, listening, and writing.

Asking my students to play the role of scientists helped me to begin the connection, and once the discovery process was familiar, there was evidence of students owning their own discoveries. I used the power of role-playing to buy each of my students a ticket into the world of science, and I hope they never leave it.

Deep Participatory Learning

Cynthia Lewis, a literacy educator, describes with her co-authors (Lewis, Enciso, & Moje, 2007) how deep, participatory learning involves "learning not only the stuff of a discipline—science content, for example—but also learning how to think and act something like a scientist, even if one does not enter the profession of science" (p. 19). Science teacher Diana Arya wanted her students to learn how to think and act like scientists and not conflate the discipline of science with only wearing white lab coats and glasses. For Diana, the discovery process is at the heart of being a scientist. In order to alter her students' view and engage them in deep, participatory learning, Diana relied on role-playing as a strategy for easing her students into the discovery process. By having students step into the shoes of famous scientists, they were able to engage in the discovery process through observation, questioning, researching, and writing.

It is extremely important for teachers to make explicit the practices within a discipline (or within a profession) such as science. Only through recognizing and enacting the practices of scientists can students come to understand how they are similar or different to other practices, say of an historian. These distinctions are essential, especially if students have a limited understanding of what scientists actually do and the real science of science, such as how failures within experiments can provide important insight and turning points, is not explicitly discussed. It is this meta-awareness that allows students to take on new identities and recognize science practice; role-playing can provide an initial activity into identity development and deep, participatory learning. By making explicit the practices of a discipline, Diana's students can come to see themselves as a science kind of people (Lewis et al., 2007).

Role-Playing and School

Becky and Jessica consider these two questions important for understanding the relationship between role-playing and school: "How can pedagogy help students take on different roles in their classrooms—roles as performers, scientists, engineers or writers?" And "If students are pursuing their own reading and writing interests outside of school, is there a means to meet them halfway and offer activities which allow students the freedom to choose their topics of interest?" The activities outlined below are designed to address these two questions and further our understanding of how role-playing can function as a powerful tool in our classrooms. Remember though that these activities, some old and some new, are not meant to be autonomous exercises void of connection to larger philosophical pedagogical practices. The goal is not to skim through this section and pick out activities that can be integrated in the classroom as soon as possible. The goal is to think through how new media environments have offered opportunities for students to engage as writers, readers, and performers, and then analyze, question, and broaden our own thinking regarding school-based definitions of writing, reading, and performing.

It is through such questioning that we can make important connections between new media and youth culture and pedagogical practices and a broadened definition of learning and literacy. As such, we have divided the classroom activities into two sections: (1) performance-based activities and (2) reading and writing activities. The performance-based activities fit nicely with the role-playing theme of this chapter, while the reading and writing activities are designed to broaden our notion of writing in the classroom and, even though they might not provide the opportunity to play a role, these activities can assist students with taking another perspective.

Performance-Based Activities

Performance-based activities are a means by which students can participate in the construction of a specific identity. To take on a role involves hypothesis testing. If I am performing as President Franklin D. Roosevelt during his last term in office, I have to think about FDR's physical appearance and emotional state: As FDR, what would I wear, how would I sit, would I feel and look healthy, how would I act in public and what kind of words would I have for Stalin or for Winston Churchill? This type of questioning and thought process is considered hypothesis testing, and it gives students a manner in which to learn more about their characters and also understand how they would act in specific settings and relate to other people.

Role-Playing

A number of tools and online sites can facilitate written role-playing. For example, chat applications such as Google Chat, online message boards such as a Yahoo! Group, or instant messaging (IM) applications such as AOL Instant Messenger can be used to generate and record text from role-play activities. Maryanne Berry discussed in the introductory chapter her students' use of e-mail journals and instant messaging to discuss novels in their English class. Why not have students become the characters of a novel through role-playing? In history class, students can take on the roles of historical figures during specific events. By conducting research on the time periods and their specific figures, they can weave in relevant background information and personality traits of their figures, add in interesting facts about the time period, and discuss their figures' influence and affiliations within the relevant era. Role-playing can be used across all disciplines and grade levels. Particularly with younger students, don't be afraid to invite unconventional characters into role-playing activities. Batman may be able to explain gravity just as well as Sir Isaac Newton.

- **Collaborative script writing**: As a group, work with your students to write a script that imagines how a historical event or great discovery came to be. What did viewers say to DaVinci when they first saw the Mona Lisa? If we had never seen them before, how might Dali's paintings be received by a modern-day museum audience? Use word processing software, an outlining tool (such as Omni Outliner), IM, or even Twitter to capture dialogue generated through a group discussion of the topic. Detail everyone's work in progress so the whole class can view their peers' insights and also contribute. See Glen Bledsoe's (2009) chapter in *Teaching the New Writing: Technology, Change, and Assessment in the 21st-Century Classroom* for a great example of this technique in action.
- **Meme activity:** Create (on your own or with your students) questions/ prompts for students to fill in (either as themselves or while taking on a role). For example, a recently popular **meme** on Facebook prompted users to list 5 things about themselves (ranging from the mundane to

the unique) and post it to their profile, revealing trivia to their friends and prompting friends to do the same. A similar meme could be used to encourage and structure a biography or family history project. Circulate on paper or on a classroom blog.

Reenactments

Reenactments of important events such as the Wall Street crash of 1929 or famous battles are also exciting ways to have students take on roles. As an introductory activity to the trench warfare of World War I on the Western Front, what better way to bring to life this type of combat but by turning a classroom into an elaborately constructed front (made out of desks) and having students simulate catapulting grenades with crumpled up paper. The middle of the room would be declared the deadly "No Man's Land," and after a brief reenactment, students and the teacher can discuss how aspects of their performance connected to conditions of trench warfare such as immobility, full exposure beyond the trench, static fighting lines, and defense-style combat. This activity allows teachers to start a unit or project with an interesting and an energetic twist and can be used throughout the unit as a point of reference for key concepts and conditions of trench warfare.

Read about history teacher Mike McGovern from Palo Alto, California, and how he takes his ninth grade world history reenactments to a new level (http://tiny.cc/teachtech_5_1).

Small groups of students, an entire class, or even students and invited alumni, or community members can engage in reenactments together. The possibilities are endless with this type of performance-based activity, and students and their teachers will be able to reflect upon the topic at hand while they express creativity. Additionally, reenactments, speeches, and other forms of dramatic performance can be recorded using audio recorders or video cameras and presented in mediated form.

- **Podcasting**: A podcast is a great way to audio record students doing a dramatic reading of a piece of literature, a scene from a play or a historical document or speech, or a fictional interview with important people (e.g., what would they say about today's . . .?). All students need is software such as Garage Band (Mac) or Audacity (PC) and an external microphone. If this is too much of a hassle, a digital audio recorder can also do the trick. Students can also create sound effects in the classroom during the performance, e.g., in the style of old radio dramas or consistent with an audience at the time, or add them electronically after recording. Upload your podcasts to a class blog, school Web site or wiki. (iTunes has "learn to podcast" podcasts for those interested in tutorials).

- **Digital video:** By videotaping performances, students can be encouraged to think about how to use video to tell a story in a particular way. For example, students can present a speech as "breaking news," using graphics and other conventions of news casting. Encourage students to be creative in thinking about different genres; what would a presidential speech look like as a music video? What if *Our Town* was rewritten as a teen comedy? Have a class screening of the student performances or upload them to a specific blog or website, or—with student-parent permission—put them on Teacher Tube.com to share with other educators.

Teachers: Go Forth, Collaborate, and Perform!

Make time to get together with the drama, dance, or music teacher and see if the two (or more) of you can create a fun and collaborative role-playing experience for students. Make sure to explain to your coteacher that you want to incorporate role play but keep the activity centered around your content area. If you can't find time to collaborate, it does not hurt to ask if they have any ideas for role-playing. And if you don't have access to a drama or music teacher, try calling up your local community theater, performers, or other organizations to see if they can collaborate on a content unit with you. Who knows? Maybe they have a production related to a complementary topic and a fieldtrip could be arranged. It is always wonderful to get students to the theater and possibly on a backstage tour. Or a local company of actors might even want to come to the classroom and help students with their performances. It never hurts to see what the local community can provide, just make sure to tell them that the role-playing activities are designed to learn more about a specific content area, that way the collaboration is both performance and content based. Read what Amy Crawford, an English teacher, did with her students and their local theater company.

A TEACHER'S PERSPECTIVE

The Play's the Thing

By Amy Crawford, High School English Teacher

"Hey Rafael," I said, as a quiet and generally apathetic boy ambled into my classroom after lunch. "I heard you saw your brother's performance of *Zorro in Hell* last night. Was it good?" Rafael's brother was in the Arts and Humanities Academy at Berkeley High, a small school that specializes in visual and performing arts. His brother's class, just like his own, had spent the past 10 Fridays working with a performing artist through the Berkeley Repertory Theater preparing to see Culture Clash's latest play and creating their own skits to perform for their school community.

"Yeah," he said, veering toward my desk. "*Now* I get it. We're supposed to *act,* like we are the character in the *play.* Like TV actors or something. *Right?*"

I paused, trying to make sense of what he was asking me. My face probably revealed my confusion because he filled the quiet with an explanation.

"Last night was the first time I ever saw a play. All this time I just thought we were supposed to be reading the lines, but my brother's class is acting. Is that what you've been trying to get us to do?"

"Yes!" I shouted. "Thanks for helping me get what wasn't working for our class." I made a mental note to ask how many students in the two classes had actually seen a play, and 10 minutes later was shocked to learn it was less than half. Aha! After weeks of frustration I understood the barrier my students were facing.

I teach in a small school within Berkeley High called Communication Arts and Science (CAS) where students learn to master an array of media technologies. Located in the heart of downtown, Berkeley High School is rich with community resources. One of the best connections is the Berkeley Repertory Theater. Three blocks from the high school, it has premiered a long list of outstanding shows, and features amazing artists, directors, and performers. Among the many shows I have taken classes to over the years, some highlights have included Tony Kushner's *Homebody, Kabul;* Culture Clash's revamp of Aristophanes' *The Birds;* and more recently *Zorro in Hell; Rhinoceros* by Eugene Ionesco; Danny Hoch's *Taking Over; Mother Courage* by Bertolt Brecht; and *Joe Turner's Come and Gone* by August Wilson. Each of these plays captured the imagination and interest of my diverse population of students.

CAS has always prioritized getting our students to see live theater. Every young person deserves a chance to see actors bringing great literature to life right before their eyes. You never know what will be the thing that turns a kid on, what will ignite a spark or open a door. Some students recognize in theater the power of self-expression; others may become lifelong theatergoers; others discover new ways to use language or movement; some simply experience what it means to be a respectful audience for live actors; and some discover within themselves a hidden talent. Rafael, uncovered his own talent and began to take risks that paid off academically and artistically. But perhaps the greatest gift from the Berkeley Rep was a boost in his confidence.

Six years ago CAS formally partnered with the Berkeley Repertory Theater, and with the help of an education grant, the theater has provided students from a variety of grade levels with free tickets and a guest artist to work with specific classes for 15 sessions. For six years one grade level of our students, through English classes, have participated in a series of workshops, and I have been that teacher for three of those years. As a partner teacher, my job is to work with the artist to help develop objectives that fit with the goals of my class, as well as a time frame and

(Continued)

(Continued)

sequence. I have worked with Hector and Ryan O'Donnell, and both director-actors found creative ways to connect my students with theater and reveal themselves through writing and performance.

It would be disingenuous to say that these partnerships are 100 percent effective for all students. Each year there are several students who ask, "Why do we have to do this?" And others approach me right before the performance and insist, "I will throw up if I have to get in front of this class. Please don't make me do this." Each year one student abstains, usually someone who shined during our prep work. But the rest face the challenge, their performances ranging from forgettable to amazing. Rafael's approached amazing. In just two days he was able to apply what he'd learned from watching his brother's class to his own character. Between the dress rehearsal and the performance he learned most of his lines and enthusiastically became his character. Rafael stunned and engaged his audience of classmates, and it was the first time I saw him openly connect with something in my class. In the years that followed I would observe his unbridled enthusiasm for filmmaking, but this was my first peek at his potential, and it inspired me and my belief in him. And that's what most kids need from their teachers—recognition for what they do well and a certainty that we believe in them.

Reading and Writing Activities

While writing fan fiction could be an engaging assignment to incorporate into the classroom, there is a danger in co-opting out of school practices that are important to young people by trying to force them to operate within the structure of the classroom. To this end, Becky does not recommend teachers try to require students to write fan fiction in the same way that they might engage in the practice outside of school. Instead, she highlights some of the "best practices" of fan fiction reading, writing, and sharing, and suggests ways that these practices can be applied in the classroom setting.

Active reading

- Regardless of content area, allow students to choose their own reading materials as frequently as possible. If a school or district requires specific texts, consider asking students to find supplementary reading on their own. If a textbook is the assigned reading, are there interesting historical events or periods mentioned that might be explored in other media? Create text sets for your students (or have students create their own text sets) that are thematically focused on a topic or concept and that represent a range of genres, media, and levels of reading difficulty. For instance, the topic of *flight* for a text set focal point could include books on Charles Lindbergh and how birds fly, a manual detailing a 747 airline, a flight Flickr gallery, and a video clip on hot air balloons. Films, graphic novels, Web sites, music, charts, maps, almanacs, encyclopedias, podcasts and Flickr photo streams are also great sources to explore and offer students access to a diversity of reading materials in addition to those they chose.

Flickr: A Photo-Sharing Network

Flickr is a great online tool for uploading, sharing, and organizing digital photographs. Teachers and students can create theme or concept galleries within Flickr, organize virtual fieldtrips, teach geography with the combination of Flickr and Google Earth, and develop their own photo streams (online slide shows). Visit http://www.flickr.com/ for more information. You do have to have a Yahoo! account to sign up for Flickr. Visit math teacher Adam Green's Flickr gallery that focuses on probability (http://tiny.cc/teachtech_5_2). (Please note that the gallery is intended for older students as it presents mature content.)

- Encourage students to talk about what they are reading, rather than just writing responses or essays on exams. If students are reading outside books, encourage them to share their impressions, favorite parts and questions with the class. Consider, however, that sharing this kind of reflection/information verbally in front of the class may be uncomfortable (or at least not interesting) to many of the students. Alternative ways of sharing include incorporating an online bulletin board (or a wooden one) where students can post notes, pictures, and drawings; a class Web site with a discussion forum; or even a notebook designated for sharing writing that is left in a common area of the classroom may offer more comfortable ways for students to participate.
- Model active reading for students! Often there is rarely time for teachers to share what they are reading; show students the books, magazines, Web sites or comics that you find interesting. Demonstrate that reading is part of lifelong learning, and talk about why you like them; don't be afraid to share this personal information and to be enthusiastic about the media you find compelling.

Active Writing

- Consider different formats for writing that are not common in the classroom but are likely familiar to students in their everyday encounters with media. For example, fan fiction writers often engage in "drabble" writing. Drabbles are 100 word stories written about a specific theme, often within a strict time frame (10 minutes, 20 minutes, one hour), and shared at a specific time or around a particular event. For example, holiday drabble challenges are common practices in some fan fiction communities. Captioning contests, movie reviews, memes such as those that ask students to list information about themselves or answer a series of questions, and collaborative writing projects are other interesting models that might be adapted to classroom assignments.

- Encourage students to share their writing with peers, rather than just turning it in to a teacher for grading. This requires additional planning on both the part of the teacher and the student, but can be very rewarding for students. Teachers might consider adopting the fan fiction practice of beta reading, in which a peer editor assists a writer with grammar, spelling, and style issues. Unlike the way peer editing is often done in the classroom, beta readers and writers establish enduring and reciprocal relationships based on shared interest (and often friendship), making the feedback process consistent and valuable to both reader and writer.

- With their permission, circulate your students' writing among the class and the larger school community. Create a class literary journal using easy blog publishing software like WordPress or Blogger (see blogging activity below). Students can upload and edit their writing, read and comment on others' writing at school and (if they have Internet access) at home. Pieces can also be printed out in order to circulate them on paper or archive them in the school library. Using blog software eliminates the need for expensive and time-intensive desktop publishing, as a large number of templates and styles are built in.

Blogging 101

From Jessica's research at a high school in Northern California, she found twelfth-grade students and their teachers contributing to an online **blog** designed for their combined English and history class. In the beginning of the school year, the blog asked respondents to answer general prompts, for example, "How have you changed since the ninth grade?" and this gave both teachers and students an opportunity to get to know each other. Students were very open and honest in their responses and appreciated the informal writing assignment and a chance to converse online with peers. Later in the year the blog prompts became specific to their English and history classes but still informal in nature. For instance, while reading *Brave New World*, one prompt asked, "Imagine you are an Alpha living in the *Brave New World*. What would you miss the most about your current life?" Although the students were not asked to write in terms of a character like Clarissa, they did have to imagine what it might be like to enter the lives of the characters from the novel and compare this fictional experience to their own.

Blogging is a great way to have students write to their peers (and their teachers, parents, administrators, or community members) in an informal manner. What is wonderful about blogging is that the students write to each other and not solely for the teacher. They can write in slang or in abbreviations. Teachers or students can design the prompts for the blog, since blogs are by nature a collaborative effort between writer, reader, and commenter.

It is important to note that teachers and students should view numerous blogs and get a feel for the different types of writing that go on in the blogosphere. Tech blogs are very different from entertainment blogs, which are very different from "mommy" blogs or political opinion blogs. This could provide an excellent opportunity to discuss issues of genre and audience and to give students a sense that different types of writing are valuable at different times and in different situations. Becky also encourages teachers to find examples of blogs that they like and ask students to read and comment on those blogs regularly. Once teachers create their own blog, they can add a blogroll, a list of recommended blogs usually placed in the side of a blog, so students can easily access sites of interest and also contribute their own ideas for hyperlinks. This is, of course, contingent on the status of the firewall at the school. Some teachers will not be able to do this because their network does not allow this.

There can be drawbacks to a classroom blog. Since a blog is valuable when a community shares it, it is possible that students will be reticent to participate and teachers may struggle with a lack of participation or even an inability to create a safe communal space in which to share opinions and reflections. Here are some important factors to remember when setting up a blogging community:

- Blogging is a reciprocal relationship in which a conversation takes place between students; prompts should be designed with this in mind. Additionally, blogs are not about the teacher grading the writing of individual students. Think of a blog as an extension of group work with teachers taking a back seat to the students who are leading one another through the topic at hand. Jessica suggests giving credit for blogging but not assigning specific grades and also allowing students to write in a manner they see fit. If students incorporate slang or abbreviations, just ask them to define their terms for the "older" people. This is a great way to tap into and honor youth culture.

- Remember, a blog is easy to start but hard to maintain. Teachers should tell students how often they will have to respond to a blog prompt: once a week or once a month? Here are some instances in which to use this resource: (a) if teachers cannot fully cover a subject and their students would want to continue discussing it on a blog; (b) if teachers are introducing a new unit and need a pre-reading activity; and (c) if teachers want students to bounce ideas off of each other (and then the teacher can bring up student-generated ideas during class), have students prepare questions for an upcoming guest speaker or even create a helpful study guide.

- A "prompt-reply" blog is not the only template teachers can employ. Why not try a blog for:

  o Small news announcements
  o Top 10 things one needs to know about
  o How to . . . (e.g., write a lab report, study for a geography quiz)
  o Editorial: A different slant on . . .
  o Critic's corner: Thoughts on a Text (e.g., novel or in-class reading)

Students want to be invested in their classroom activities and giving them authority over a prompt or a blog entry is a wonderful way for them to be agents in their academic lives. Ask students to create a prompt for a blog or design a "Top 10 things one needs to know about . . . . ." In these instances, students can take on the role of expert or moderator. A math teacher once told Jessica, "It is great to give students the space to show you what they are about," and blogs can be a site in which students can accomplish this.

- Remember too that blogs can contain media other than text. Photographs, scanned or digital artwork, podcasts, and links to other Web sites are common parts of blogs and part of what makes them a compelling multimedia format.
- Providing examples of an active blog community and having students submit their own examples can help to spark interest and participation in a classroom blog.

- Blogging sites such as WordPress also offer "private" blogs which make your blog a password protected site. Additionally, these sites also allow the owner or owners, i.e., administrator, of the blog to assign users a specific role and, hence, control their ability to publish, edit, and delete posts and comments and upload files and images.

For more information on blogs or setting up your own blogging site, read Will Richardson's (2006) *Blogs, Wikis, Podcasts, and Other Powerful Web Tools for Classrooms* and Beach et al. (2008) *Teaching Writing Using Blogs, Wikis, and other Digital Tools.* Also visit WordPress at http://wordpress.org or Blogger at https://www.blogger.com/start to get started on your own blog.

SHARE YOUR INSIGHTS, STORIES, AND EXPERIENCES!

Have great ideas or interesting activities for reading, writing, or performing in the classrooms? Visit our Web site at www.teachingtech-savvykids.com and share your insights. Also join our community forum by posting your responses to these prompts:

1. Becky Herr-Stephenson warns of the danger in co-opting out of school practices that are important to young people by forcing these practices to fit into the classroom curriculum. How do educators negotiate which out of school practices can work in the classroom and which might need to be altered in some form or another?

2. Role-playing activities are sometimes given the label of childish or immature. What do you think are the historical roots of these labels and how can educators work to promote a different understanding of role-playing practices?

3. Media educator Henry Jenkins (2006b) argues, "Bloggers are the minutemen of the digital revolution" (p. 179). Is his argument too extreme, right-on-the-money, or somewhere in between?

4. Have you ever participated in a collaborative writing project? A role-playing game or club? Do you play *World of Warcraft* or another MMORPG? Describe your experiences with role play. What do you get out of it? How did you get started? Why do you participate? Has the experience impacted other activities, such as the way you approach reading, writing, or even your teaching?

REFERENCES AND HELPFUL RESOURCES

Beach, R., Anson, C., Breuch, L., & Swiss, T. (2008). *Teaching writing using blogs, wikis, and other digital tools.* Norwood, MA: Christopher-Gordon Publishers. (Also visit the wiki designed to support the book: http://digitalwriting .pbworks.com/)

Black, R. (2008). *Adolescents and online fan fiction.* New York: Peter Lang Publishing.

Bledsoe, G. L. (2009). Collaborative digital writing: The art of writing together using technology. In A. Herrington, K. Hodgson, and C. Moran (Eds.) *Teaching the new writing: Technology, change, and assessment in the 21st-century classroom* (pp. 39–54). New York and Berkeley: Teachers College Press and National Writing Project.

Blogger: https://www.blogger.com/start

Bowker, G. C. (2005). *Memory practices in the sciences.* Cambridge: MIT Press.

Buckingham, D. (Ed.) (2007). *Youth, identity, and digital media.* The John D. and Catherine T. MacArthur Foundation Series on Digital Media and Learning. Boston: MIT Press.

Curie, M. (1903). *Radioactive substances.* London: Edwin John Davey.

Dyson, A. H. (2003). *The brothers and sisters learn to write: Popular literacies in childhood and school cultures.* New York: Teachers College Press.

Fan Fiction Archives: http://www.fanfiction.net, http://www.fictionalley.org, http://www.harrypotterfanfiction.com

Fleischer, S., Wright, S., & Barnes, M. (2007). Dungeons, dragons, and discretion: A gateway to gaming, technology, and literacy. In C. Selfe and G. Hawisher (Eds.), *Gaming lives in the twenty-first century: Literate connections* (pp. 143–160). New York: Palgrave Macmillan.

Goodall, J. (1971). *In the shadow of man.* Boston: Houghton Mifflin Publishing.

Griffiths, A. K., & Barman, C. R. (1995) High school students' views about the nature of science: Results from three countries. *School Science and Mathematics, 95,* 248–356.

Henry Jenkins' blog: *Confessions of an aca-fan* (http://henryjenkins.org). Search for Fan Fiction. (Both Becky and Jessica subscribe to this blog!)

Jenkins, H. (with Clinton, K., Purushotma, R., Robison, A., and Weigel, M.). (2006a). *Confronting the challenges of participatory culture: Education for the 21st century.* The John D. and Catherine T. MacArthur Foundation. Retrieved August 18, 2007, from http://digitallearning.macfound.org.

Jenkins, H. (2006b). *Fans, bloggers, and gamers: Media consumers in a digital age.* New York: NYU Press.

Latour, B. (1987). *Science in action.* Cambridge: Harvard University Press.

Lederman, N. G. (1992). Students' and teachers' conceptions about the nature of science: A review of the research. *Journal of Research in Science Teaching, 29,* 331–359.

Lemke, J. (1990). *Talking science: Language, learning, and values.* Westport, CT: Ablex Publishing.

Lewis, C., Enciso, P., & Moje, E. (2007). *Reframing sociocultural research on literacy: Identity, agency, and power.* Mahway, NJ: Lawrence Erlbaum.

Niaz, M., & Rodriguez, M. A. (2000). Teaching chemistry as rhetoric of conclusions or heuristic principles—A history and philosophy of science perspective. *Chemistry education: Research and practice in Europe, 1*(3), 315–322.

Popper, K. R. (1959). *The logic of scientific discovery.* London: Hutchinson.

Richardson, W. (2006). *Blogs, wikis, podcasts, and other powerful Web tools for classrooms.* Thousand Oaks, CA: Corwin.

Twitter: https://twitter.com/

WordPress: http://wordpress.org

Yahoo!: http://www.yahoo.com

Virtual Worlds

Designing, Playing, and Learning

Jessica K. Parker and Maryanne Berry

INTRODUCTION

This chapter presents new work exploring the potential of virtual worlds to impact the future of educational learning. Participation in virtual worlds allows users to form new kinds of communities. These communities are usually organized through peer-based learning—that is users enter a community and must rely on other users in order to function. From scientific exploration to bringing together different groups of students, participating in a community working toward a common goal is a motivating and engaging endeavor. As educators we should continue to investigate virtual environments in order to have a voice in the changing nature of learning in a digital age.

VIRTUAL WORLDS AND LEARNING

It is clear how engaged young people are with online activity, with video games and virtual worlds, but many of us wonder if this fascination is enhancing or detracting from learning? Researchers, designers, and educators have begun to study the practices of young people and to design educational programs that achieve the same high levels of engagement in virtual environments while also supporting academic outcomes. The work is challenging. Imagining how one might use a virtual environment for learning involves a conceptual shift in thinking. It involves shifting from the metaphor of the computer screen as the desktop to the computer screen as a portal. Through participation in virtual environments we are exploring how to form new kinds of communities, where shifting roles nurture the transformation of identities—to one's sense of self and one's sense of what is possible.

Virtual environments are places, accessible via the Internet, where people can discover, exchange, or share information, opinions, and ideas. A virtual environment might include a Web page of a political party or bookstore, a blog of a university course, a video game, or an online forum on the best places to eat in Miami. The newest and most advanced virtual environments and the ones we want to focus on throughout this chapter—known as **virtual worlds**—are immersive, accessible not only in text but also through the representation of a participant's self in the form of an avatar. Immersive environments include both virtual worlds such as *Second Life* where people meet for a multitude of serious and playful activities and games such as *World of Warcraft* that are designed with a specific purpose or objective in mind.

A virtual world offers opportunities for performing physical activities via the avatar. In an immersive world or game one's avatar might look and behave as one does in ordinary life as one strolls through a museum, gathers with others to attend a lecture, or dances at a concert. Some worlds offer opportunities to represent oneself as a medieval warrior, an intergalactic goddess, or a giant squid. Some allow one to lead a renegade army, conquer a nation, or build a church or palace. Regardless of the shape one takes or mission assumed, one might experience supernatural powers—flying, teleporting, or even morphing. Virtual worlds have already begun to transform the lives of individuals and shape the development of communities outside of schools and universities: musicians have held concerts, artists have set up galleries, and churches even have virtual worship services (Educause, 2008). Recently they have begun to shape classroom learning.

WHAT ARE VIRTUAL WORLDS?

By Rik Panganiban, Assistant Director of Online Leadership Program for Global Kids

Figure 6.1   Rik's Avatar

In a nutshell, virtual worlds are computer-generated, persistent, two- or three-dimensional, multi-user spaces, where people interact with each other and the environment through their avatars. Some examples of virtual worlds are *Second Life, Whyville, World of Warcraft*. These environments often mimic characteristics of the real world, including having land, water, space, gravity, buildings, and even weather. Different virtual worlds have different features and emphases, including the ability for users to communicate with each other using voice, to create objects and structures, to buy and sell goods and services, and to share video and audio content with each other. Although often compared to video games, virtual worlds aren't necessarily games with explicit ways of "winning" or points to accumulate.

A number of educational institutions are exploring the potential of virtual worlds as a new medium for education. Among the unique affordances of virtual worlds are their capacity to facilitate engaging and immersive experiences, the ability for educators and students to be distributed anywhere in the world, the sense of "presence" and verisimilitude, and the possibility of simulating phenomena and experiences that would be difficult or prohibitively expensive to do in the real world. RezEd.org is a great place to start for educators looking toward virtual worlds as a way to stimulate learning through disseminating best practices in the field, hosting themed discussions on subjects relevant to educators, and hosting relevant resources for practitioners in this space.

Any discussion of learning in virtual environments will necessarily involve a definition of learning and a measure for assessing progress or change. In recent research on virtual environments, the definition of one's learning included a wide range of outcomes: One study measured students' ability to recall historical information by flying through a virtual world (Foreman, Boyd-Davis, Moar, Korallo, & Chappell, 2007), another assessed the possibility of teaching science curriculum by having students solve the mystery of an illness that has struck the inhabitants of a virtual community (Nelson, 2007), and another explored a program that positions students as journalists who work together to create a newspaper reporting the events of a virtual town (Warren, Dondlinger, & Barab, 2008).

Since researchers have just begun to document and analyze these learning experiences, we are at the start of a long and complex conversation concerning virtual worlds. Throughout this chapter, we intend to discuss what researchers have discovered about virtual worlds and hope that educators will want to join us in this ongoing conversation.

MYTH: Kids are essentially becoming socially isolated, self-absorbed, and addicted to these fictitious worlds like *Second Life* and *World of Warcraft*. There are not any valuable skills to be practiced within these virtual realms.

REALITY: A staple of virtual worlds is its dynamic social space. Users engage in an interactive world whereby collaboration is appreciated and creativity is promoted. In fact, Rachel Cody Pfister has found that players in *Final Fantasy XI* rely on each another in order to learn how to play and ultimately succeed in the game. In essence, *Final Fantasy XI* supports a community of learners. Read Rachel's Story From the Field (below).

CHARACTERISTICS OF VIRTUAL WORLDS

A primary feature of virtual worlds such as *Second Life* is their generative nature. Users can create three-dimensional objects such as billboards and settings such as conference rooms that can be seen and used by other users. This type of environment lends itself to a number of different teaching methods: lecturing at an online conference, student-centered simulation, collaborative problem solving, role-playing, scenario building, and inquiry-based pedagogy to name a few. Additionally, learning within a virtual world is not limited to time or location. Learning in this environment can take place anytime and anywhere. Yet cost is an issue when discussing the purchasing of land in *Second Life* as is the creation of such educational environments since it requires specific skills. Even with the challenges of creating and maintaining a virtual world, the benefits at this time seem to outweigh the concerns.

STORIES FROM THE FIELD

Kalipea's Journey From Novice to Veteran in *Final Fantasy XI*

By Rachel Cody Pfister, Graduate Student at U.C. San Diego

Before *Final Fantasy XI (FFXI)*, Kalipea[*] did not fit the stereotypical image of a "gamer." Like most teens, she had played video games on consoles and even enjoyed some online flash games, but her interest in games was fairly casual and social. Despite this lack of experience, Kalipea began playing *Final Fantasy XI* and was immediately hooked. The game provided a virtual world in which she could play with her real-life friend as well as meet and form relationships with other players across the world. Kalipea lacked an extensive gaming background, but the player community provided her with teachers and mentors who helped her master the game. Collaboration was the norm for players in *Final Fantasy XI* and the key to advancement in the game. Kalipea thus found herself enmeshed in a peer-based learning community where teachers were friends and teammates, failure was a lesson on the path to success, and lessons were intertwined with hanging out and joking around.

Final Fantasy XI[1] is a massively multiplayer online role-playing game similar to *World of Warcraft* and *Everquest* in its game design. Players inhabit a virtual world where they can team up with other players to participate in hundreds of activities, including exploring the world, killing monsters, creating items, and fulfilling missions or quests. Players can form groups with each other to do activities, and they can create or join player-created communities called linkshells.

1. The official Web site for Final Fantasy provides a more detailed description of the game (http://tiny.cc/teachtech_6_1).

The social communities are an integral part to success in the game (see Figure 6.2). By design, *Final Fantasy XI* is a socially dependent game. The game provides little guidance on how to play, where to go, and how to succeed in tasks. Furthermore, nearly all activities in the game require a group of players, whether it be killing monsters or acquiring gear for characters to wear. As a result, players turn toward each other to learn to play the game and accomplish activities. The social and learning aspects become intertwined as players become students and teachers to one another, learning with and relying on each other to succeed in the game. These relationships and communities extend beyond the game as well, with players creating and using Web sites[2], guides, and messageboards[3] to communicate with and help each other.

Figure 6.2   Fighting Against Tiamat

Members: Members of a FFXI linkshell work together in a collaborative attempt to kill the dragon Tiamat. This linkshell spent several months researching the dragon and developing a strategy to kill her. In the end, it took over 36 players several hours to defeat her.

Turn-taking: Throughout the dragon fight, players may serve several different roles and rotate in and out of the fight as needed. They use the "looking for group" element of the game to help party leaders more easily rotate them back into groups.

Collaboration and strategy: Linkshell members use their knowledge of the dragon fight to strategically use the terrain around the dragon. This allows them to best fight the dragon and take little damage. Players collaborate by rotating their positions and their roles during the fight.

(Continued)

---

2. Players use numerous Web sites such as http://ffxi.allakhazam.com/ and http://ffxi.somepage.com/ to find information about aspects of the game, including gear, quests, missions, and monsters.

3. Killing Ifrit is a popular Web site with message boards that players use to chat with each other about aspects of the game (http://killingifrit.com).

(Continued)

Kalipea was introduced to this virtual world while staying at her friend's house one night. Her friend Keela had just purchased the game and told Kalipea to try it out. Twelve hours later, Kalipea was still playing the game and realized she should buy it. *Final Fantasy XI* was like an enhanced version of the instant messenger programs that Kalipea enjoyed using to chat with her friends. While playing a game, she was able to play with Keela and meet, talk to, and play with people from across the world.

The learning curve of *Final Fantasy XI* was steep though. The night she started playing, Kalipea had Keela's helping learning the basics of the game. Keela showed her how to create a character and do basic activities such as move throughout the world and kill monsters. Keela fell asleep as Kalipea continued to play though. Left to find her own way in the virtual world, Kalipea began chatting with the players she came across. Meeting new people was easy since new characters are "born" into major towns where new and veteran players chat, buy goods, and train their crafting skills. Kalipea soon found herself spending hours talking to other players and learning about new things in the game.

Kalipea revealed how easily the social and learning aspects of the game blend together when she described one of her early experiences:

I was just like running around outside; he came up to me and poked me or did some kind of funny emote[4] and I didn't understand what it was. I was like, "What are you doing? What did you just do?" And I would always type in *say*[5] 'cause I didn't know what a tell was, right?

So then he explained to me, he was like, "Oh, you should type tell or *talk* and then you can talk to just me." And he explained that to me so I thought that was kind of cool. And then we just talked for a while after that.

A simple gesture turned into a learning opportunity as the player taught Kalipea about a new social dimension of the game: private conversations. In his casual and friendly outreach to her, she also saw how players interact— playfully poking, doing silly gestures, and easily chatting with each other (see Figure 6.3).

---

4. *Emote* is a character action, such as waving or dancing

5. *Say* is a public chat channel that everybody in the vicinity is able to read.

Figure 6.3 Ryukossei Discusses Fishing

Meeting other players: Many players meet and form friendships with other players as they travel and participate in activities in Final Fantasy XI. Here, Ryukossei is going fishing with a linkshell member, Arkin. On the boat, he meets another player and chats about fishing and fishing gear.

Game elements: Players use game elements to help them better communicate and create a social world. Ryukossei and another player turn their characters towards each other while chatting, even though chat takes place in a textbox at the bottom of the screen.

Chat channels: Final Fantasy XI uses different color schemes to identify different chat channels. Ryukossei chats with another player in public chat, his party members in party chat, and his linkshell members simultaneously.

Learning to use the different chat channels was just the beginning of Kalipea's progression in *Final Fantasy XI*. She was introduced to the more complex aspects of the game as she made friends and advanced in the game. She joined groups with

(Continued)

(Continued)

other players, many of whom were more experienced, and was able to learn through the other players' examples of how to play in different roles and how to play within a group. Some players would even take on a mentor role with Kalipea, offering her tips on how to make her job easier (players pick a job for their character in the game, and the job determines what abilities and roles they perform, such as healing group members or attacking monsters). In one group, a player asked why Kalipea was taking so long to heal him (Kalipea's role in most groups is to heal other players and keep them from dying) and then taught her how to write macros, or scripts that allow a player to carry out a sequence of actions with one button. This made healing much easier and helped her become better at her job.

The learning process was not always easy, however. Over the course of her *Final Fantasy XI* career, Kalipea was a member of several different player-created communities called linkshells. She was good friends with most of her linkshell mates with whom she would do many linkshell activities, but the experience gap between her and some of the veterans sometimes became a problem. One linkshell mate often teased her for how she played her job, and another linkshell mate ridiculed her in front of the other linkshell members for not understanding some of the complexities of her gear.

Although stung, Kalipea used the teasing and ridiculing as opportunities to improve her performance and knowledge in the game. She turned to two linkshell members who shared the same job as hers (white mages) and who were well-respected by the rest of the linkshell for their performance and knowledge. Kalipea watched what the players did during linkshell activities and changed some of her own techniques to model them. She used their gear to create goals for herself on what she should acquire and sought their advice on how to improve her performance. Kalipea admitted that it was "kind of weird for me to look up to them" at first because both of the players were younger than her by several years. In *Final Fantasy XI*, however, experience and age do not necessarily correspond, and players of all ages can find themselves the students of other players younger and older.

By the time she quit playing *Final Fantasy XI*, Kalipea had spent over two years in the game and was helping newcomers learn to play. She showed them how to play different roles within a group, use macros, and choose gear. She was the one waving to novices in the starting towns, explaining *emotes* and private *tells*. She had moved from novice to veteran, completing the circle. Kalipea never quite abandoned the role of student—there is always something to learn with and from other players—but she was now also a teacher.

Figure 6.4   Collaborating to Complete a Mission

Players need to join groups with other players for most activities in FFXI. Collaborating and playing with others allows players to benefit from the experience and knowledge of their peers. Here, veteran players help a less experienced player, Arkin, complete a mission.

Usually, groups include players of several different jobs and roles. This allows players to complement each others strengths and abilities to ensure an efficient and successful group. In this group, for example, Wurlpin is a bard; he uses songs to strengthen party members and weaken monsters.

By playing within a group, players are able to defeat monsters that would otherwise kill them. Arkin has to kill Axesarion the Wanderer for a mission, a monster who is much stronger than him. Arkin's party members are all more experienced players and have already completed this mission. They help Arkin find the monster and provide strategies and help in killing it.

Design Elements of Final Fantasy XI

From the first moments of play, the design of *Final Fantasy XI* orients novices toward their peers to learn to play and succeed in the game. Players enjoy socializing, but the necessity of collaboration also means that players need one another to succeed in the game. *Final Fantasy XI* creates activities that require teamwork and thus rewards participants for working together and developing a shared division of labor. Each player has a role that is equally important and contributes to the success of the group (see Figure 6.4). This allows players like Kalipea, who are still learning the ropes of the game, to use their limited experiences and help their groups tackle problems. These seemingly small design elements foster an environment where players turn to each other for advice, work collaboratively to learn and advance in the game, and alternate between the roles of student and teacher depending on the task and context.

(Continued)

(Continued)

Classrooms may not have dragons for students to slay, but teachers can still incorporate many of the design elements of *Final Fantasy XI* into their classrooms to foster peer-based learning environments. These elements include designing activities and employing pedagogical practices that have students:

- Incorporate their own expertise in a given situation
- Work collaboratively
- Alternate roles between learner and teacher
- Work through situations that pose a challenge but are not impossible without much guidance from the teacher

Students in a classroom do not necessarily need to learn complicated techniques like writing macros, but they do come to us with certain kinds of expertise that can be utilized (see Moll, Amanti, Neff, & Gonzalez, 1992). In this regard, students can take on the role of teacher and collaboratively engage their peers in sharing information and experience to solve problems and succeed together. Just as Kalipea had multiple identities within *Final Fantasy XI*—as novice, veteran, mentor, and an ongoing learner—students should also find the classroom as another space to take on multiple identities.

*Please note that the names of individuals and online usernames mentioned in this article are pseudonyms and were designed to protect the privacy of the research participants.

STUDENT ENGAGEMENT AND LEARNING

Rachel Cody Pfister's piece speaks to the issue of collaborative learning through her profile of Kalipea, a student deeply engaged in *Final Fantasy XI*. Kalipea participates in a community of practice (Lave & Wenger, 1991) whose members are intent on improving skills and knowledge in order to enhance their experience of the game. As she becomes a more competent player, her role changes from learner to teacher of other newcomers. These social connections and shifts in identity are highly motivating for youth for it tends to promote and maintain a sense of membership and community dedicated to the game.

In addition to collaborative aspects of virtual worlds, there are also other issues that can motivate and engage students, especially in the classroom. The National Research Council Committee on Increasing High School Students' Engagement and Motivation to Learn (2004) recently reviewed current psychological research on motivation and studies of educational policies and practices of student engagement. Their publication, *Engaging Schools: Fostering High School Students' Motivation to Learn*, documents how students can learn and succeed in school when teachers and administrators focus on how a school's curriculum, instruction, organization, and broader community can enhance or discourage student engagement. Although they acknowledge that schools cannot control all the factors that affect students' academic engagement, the committee concluded that students should be engaged in authentic tasks that have meaning in the world outside of school, be provided complex, challenging and open-ended work, and allowed to use multiple resources and modalities, such as reading, writing, speaking, and drawing (pp. 66–68). Virtual worlds, like *Quest Atlantis* described below, offer kids access to the committee's recommendation.

What Does Your Virtual Self Look Like?

Excited about virtual environments? Totally mystified? Be brave and go ahead and create your own avatar in a virtual world.
Here are some options:

- *Second Life:* http://secondlife.com
  (Before you begin, make sure to download the quick start guide.)
- *Stardoll:* http://stardoll.com/en
- *Marvel Characters:* http://marvel.com/create_your_own_superhero
- *South Park Studios:* http://www.southparkstudios.com/avatar

---

The success of virtual worlds for learning depends upon the richness of the activities students perform. One of the greatest criticisms of contemporary schooling is that students are constructed as passive receptacles of knowledge (Freire, 1970). "Schools," Squire (2006) writes, "ask students to learn all at the same rate, in the same way, and at the same time. . . . Schools ask students to inhabit a limited and very particular set of identities as recipients of ideas and agendas prescribed for them; in contrast, games require players to be active participants in co-constructing their worlds and identities with designers" (p. 27). Squire, who references Shaffer's (2006) work, touts one benefit of engaging in immersive environments is that it allows students to construct epistemic frames, or strategies, for problem solving and students can learn to apply these frames to new situations they encounter. As educators we have to confront the fact that student identity and engagement may change only to the degree to which we change the conditions for learning. If schools are based on an assembly-line structure in which students all learn "at the same rate, in the same way, and at the same time," then we need to create learning environments that create opportunities for active and intense learning.

Let's look at a rich and powerful example of an educational game from the University of Indiana School of Education called *Quest Atlantis* that requires students to be active participants. Under the guidance of Professor Sasha Barab, *Quest Atlantis* was developed as a multiuser, interactive video game which allowed students aged 9–14 to investigate real-life problems and determine suitable action. In the example below, Professor Barab discusses how students take on the role of a scientific investigator in the virtual Taiga National Park: students enter the virtual world and learn about science inquiry, water quality concepts, and the challenges of balancing an ecosystem.

AN EDUCATOR'S CREATION

Quest Atlantis: A Game-Based Curriculum

By Sasha Barab, Professor at Indiana University

It is generally accepted that science learners should participate in hands-on experiments and explorations, not simply read textbooks or listen to lectures. Our game-based curriculum is a participatory framework that emphasizes action and reflection as central components to the learning process. This notion of an active learner engaged in real-world activities is central to the child-centered, experientially-focused, and inquiry-based learning environment of *Quest Atlantis*. We believe that there is an intimate and necessary relationship between actual experience and education.

More generally, games, more than any other form of curricula, can create new worlds that invite students to meaningfully engage complex disciplinary content and literacy practices. Students are motivated to learn because they experience the transformative potential that academic content can have on real-world problems. Games can establish worlds in which children are transformed into empowered scientists, doctors, reporters, and mathematicians who have to understand disciplinary content to accomplish desired ends. The *Quest Atlantis* project, described here, combines strategies used in mainstream video games with lessons from educational research on learning and motivation to develop a game-based curriculum.

Central to our work in the *Quest Atlantis* project has been designing a context for learning that sits at the intersection of education, entertainment, and social action. Designed to support social commitment and real-world action. *Quest Atlantis* is an immersive context with over 20,000 registered members worldwide. The project is intended to engage children ages 9–14 in a form of dramatic play comprising both online and off-line learning activities, with a storyline inspiring a disposition toward social action. The core elements of *Quest Atlantis* are (1) a three-dimensional multiuser virtual environment, (2) learning quests and unit plans, (3) a storyline, presented through an introductory video, novel, and comic book that involves a mythical council and a set of social commitments, and (4) a globally-distributed community of participants.

The activities of *Quest Atlantis* take place in registered centers, typically schools, under the direction of teachers who have undergone professional development and training. *Quest Atlantis* includes both curricular and optional projects that unfold both online and away from the computer, as children work alone or together to accomplish tasks within the international *Quest Atlantis* community. Questers form the heart and soul of the *Quest Atlantis* community. As questers, students have the opportunity to do meaningful academic work in a playful environment, socialize with students and teachers from around the world, participate in a variety of community structures such as blogs, polls, and bulletin

Figure 6.5 Map of Taiga National Park

boards and form relationships with the social commitments. While students in *Quest Atlantis* are always questers, for some of the activities they also get to play the roles of environmental scientists, reporters, and historians, among others. Students as questers become citizens in a community where learning, playing, and helping come together in exciting ways. The virtual Taiga National Park (see Figure 6.5), as one example of a *Quest Atlantis* unit, is focused on the following content areas: (a) erosion, eutrophication, water quality, and system dynamics; (b) graph (de)construction, hypothesis generation, water quality analysis, socioscientific reasoning, and scientific inquiry; (c) methods and concepts of statistical data analysis; and (d) environmental awareness. Students first receive a letter from

(Continued)

(Continued)

Ranger Mals Bartle, explaining a crisis in Taiga Park. The fish population, which is crucial to ensuring that the park is maintained and thriving, faces sharp decline—and no one is certain why. Students are commissioned by Ranger Bartle to investigate the decline and to determine how to stop it and how to balance the needs of everyone who uses the park area.

Students enter the Taiga three-dimensional world to begin the investigation and immediately meet Salik who acts as a guide as they progress through levels of the investigation. She explains that the first task is to talk with the different individuals in the Taiga Park to uncover their various perspectives on the fish problem, and she puts a map with their locations in the students' Q-Pack (a virtual backpack). As students navigate the three-dimensional space to encounter and talk with each of these individuals (see Figure 6.6), they find that most are affiliated with one of three groups of stakeholders each who have vested interests in the park: the indigenous Mulu (Ella and Norbe) live in the north end and use the land for farming and raising cattle; the K-Fly Fishing Company (Tom, Anna, and Markeda) operates a commercial fishing business; and the Build-Rite Lumber Company (Lisa, Hidalgo, and Lim) operates a logging site at the west end of the park. In addition, students interview Park Rangers and visitors to the park. These people all frequently provide more than just personal observations: they offer graphs, historical records, and diagrams, and they often respond with humor and wit as well.

Figure 6.6 Student's Avatar Approaching Character in Taiga Park

During this first quest, students are required to develop a hypothesis. They discover that each stakeholder has a different opinion of what is causing the fish decline and speculate who is to blame. They also discover that while each group of stakeholders may be contributing to a water quality problem, each also plays a valuable role in keeping the park running. Some of the people feel that the Mulu are to blame as their cattle and farming practices lead to fertilizers in the water, thus contributing to the green algae blooms observed floating. Others feel that the K-Fly Fishing Company is to blame, as their annual competition occurs during spawning season, reducing new generations of fish. Still others feel that the lumber company is responsible because the loggers have been clearing trees too close to the river's edge, resulting in erosion (see Figure 6.7). However, each group brings a legitimate benefit to the park as well, making it difficult to identify the problem. At the end of Quest 1, students are asked to make sense of all of the different perspectives and to develop a working hypothesis regarding the cause of the fish decline. Students then discuss with virtual scientists how they might go about investigating the state of the river and what kinds of data they would have to collect in order to better understand what is going on.

Figure 6.7 Logger Area

In Quest 2, students are introduced to the chemical indicators that they can measure in the water, which enable them to gather scientific data and inform and

(Continued)

(Continued)

test their hypotheses. A lab technician invites each of them into the lab to test and compare levels of pH, phosphates, nitrates, dissolved oxygen, turbidity, erosion, temperature, algae blooms, and eutrophication. These concepts are embedded and revealed naturally in the Taiga storyline. The technician sends each student back out into the park to gather water samples from three key sites along the river. Students then test these samples in the lab, compare the values, and interpret the occurrences at the different sites as causing the differences in values. In the conclusion of Quest 2, students use their data and interpretations to reevaluate and modify their previous hypotheses into explanations of the fish decline, which they now support with evidence. In these investigations, students are introduced to the statistical tools of calculating the mean, median, and mode of the data sets, and consider what each different measure of center tells them about the distributions.

Along the way, students can uncover three artifacts distributed around the park, left behind by scientists who previously studied the river. These diagrams and notes are somewhat cryptic, but after closer review they reveal a more complete picture of cycles that could be occurring at the different sites along the river—cycles related to water quality, chemical indicators, the food web, and the overall ecosystem. By deciphering these illustrations, students begin to understand the interrelationships between the chemical indicators and the environmental impact they reflect. Students can use these understandings to further inform their evolving hypotheses of what is causing the issues of water quality and fish decline. Students have now interviewed the stakeholders several times, at each occasion being given new information regarding social, economic, and scientific factors at work in the scenario. It is becoming clear that the solution to the fish decline is not merely a scientific issue but one that involves real people along with social and economic impact, and that a simply one-sided decision could actually lead to more problems later in time.

As part of Quest 3, students are asked to develop a final proposal for Ranger Bartle, outlining the cause of the fish decline with scientific and statistical evidence, a possible solution that takes into consideration the need to balance everyone's needs, as well as potential positive and negative consequences of such a plan. After submitting this proposal, the experience culminates when students are met by a man who in his secret cave helps them to reflect back on what they have learned while in the Taiga World and to apply that learning to new situations in order to solve novel but similar problems. Through this cave, students are able to teleport to the future, in order to observe the consequences of the recommendations that they made. In his conversation with the students, the man encourages them to focus on their ability to hypothesize, problem-solve, and generate solutions to issues that might be occurring locally in their own world.

In this future Taiga, students are given a chance to alter their recommendations, based on being given new data about the state of the river. In this investigation, students begin to consider the ways that variation in data measurements affect their understanding of the data, and in turn the recommendations that they make. At the end of this activity, the students make another recommendation, based on their analysis of data, about what kind of change the park might make in order to improve the quality of the water in the river. The ranger expresses gratitude and thanks the students for helping to better understand the socioscientific complexities.

How to Get Involved

Quest Atlantis supports teachers with a teacher manual, with professional development training, with novels and comics for their students, with continual monitoring of chat, with time-relevant blog entries, and with technology support and help in connecting students with other classrooms worldwide. In order to manage students, teachers also have access to a teacher toolkit so that they can register students in the program, assign classroom activities for their particular classroom, customize assignments for their students, access and review student work, and monitor student e-mail and chat entries. The toolkit also provides teachers with information about their student participation in voluntary activities; for example, completing system-defined missions, posting in blogs, signing up for jobs, and renting virtual lands.

With several years of development, implementation, and research behind us, the *Quest Atlantis* Project is excited to offer this experience to a broader audience. If you are interested signing up for *Quest Atlantis*, visit http://QuestAtlantis.org and click on the signup link to get a guest account or request a training for your school or district.

Additional Quest Atlantis Resources:

- *Quest Atlantis* for educators: http://atlantis.crlt.indiana.edu/site/view/Educators
- *Quest Atlantis* teacher resources (units in science, math, social studies and persuasive writing):
    - http://atlantis.crlt.indiana.edu/site/view/Educators#13
- *Quest Atlantis* video tour of the Taiga World:
    - http://atlantis.crlt.indiana.edu/#42
- *Quest Atlantis* worked examples of Taiga and two other units:
    - http://inkido.indiana.edu/barab_we

Visit YouTube and watch a short video on why Sasha Barab wanted to use virtual worlds as sites for learning (http://tiny.cc/teachtech_6_3).

Quest Atlantis is an amazing three-dimensional gaming environment in which students (and teachers!) can participate in real-world activities and watch the potential consequences and successes of their actions that are both socially and academically meaningful. This suggests that students experience words and concepts within an authentic context that has meaning outside of school. Sometimes school-based reading and writing activities lack a "real" context and only provide abstract situations and/or rote question and answer sessions. Since *Quest Atlantis* is an interactive learning paradigm, the literacy activities students engage in are meaningful and consequential. Thus, students are more apt to enjoy activities that are immersive and relevant to their everyday lives. As James Paul Gee (2003) argues, "We never just read or write, we always read or write something in some way" (p. 14). Thus, *Quest Atlantis* is an authentic learning environment and this is highly motivating to students.

Additionally, this interactive curriculum draws on youth's fascination with games and directs it toward academic outcomes. Its immersive environment positions learners as questers whose mission is to solve an ecological crisis in the virtual world of Taiga National Park. In the process of investigating this crisis, students experience opportunities to hypothesize, problem solve, and generate solutions.

Teachers who have adopted *Quest Atlantis* have shared their own observations of improved reading skills and sharpened higher thinking skills among students and how students are willing to collaboratively "co-quest" with their peers (even the students who usually dislike group work). Teachers have also discussed how their students help them when they get stuck on their own quests. *Quest Atlantis* and programs like it are beginning to be tested in schools across the country. These virtual environments necessarily complicate the role of the teacher as he learns to both facilitate and stand back, sometimes engaging as a peer and other times assuming a leadership or guidance role in the virtual as well as the actual world. Many teachers have moved some classroom activity into blended environments through the use of blogs, electronic bulletin boards, Web sites, and Internet research. Immersive environments will demand greater changes both in thinking and in performing the role of teacher.

PEDAGOGICAL IMPLICATIONS AND CLASSROOM PRACTICES

Virtual worlds and games may seem foreign to many educators who did not grow up using them as places to play or socialize. Popular television and news outlets have tended to focus on illicit and violent activity conducted in these environments and this has made many educators skeptical of their value. But there are educational uses for virtual environments that researchers, teachers, and students are beginning to uncover. In the fields of medicine and the military, virtual worlds have long been used not only as training tools to teach particular skills but also as simulated experiences through which participants develop their abilities to communicate effectively with others. In the field of education we are beginning to see programs designed to teach science, history, art, geography, and language arts in which a virtual world is designed to support problem-solving projects. Thus, the aspects of play and socialization that are important to youths are maintained in the virtual world while the overall content and learning is directly linked to academic outcomes.

One way to think about virtual worlds, and this has been helpful for both Jessica and Maryanne, is to see them as online spaces for organizing information and experience. In these virtual worlds, the purpose is to have users experience particular situations and meaningful information. As such, a virtual world that is designed with educational learning in mind can organize experiences so that students come to knowledge in a similar way that they come to knowledge in life.

Design

Design is an interesting term that Rachel Cody Pfister discussed in her Story From the Field. Ask your students what they think of when they hear the word design and their answers might be as varied as designer clothes and fashion, engineering design, graphic art design, designing Web pages, or "Top Design" or "Design on a Dime" television shows. Design is also an important concept for teachers. Designing a great lesson or project can provide an amazing experience for students and reinforce one's love of teaching, while a poorly designed lesson can force a teacher to revisit the mishaps and mistakes and make drastic changes the next time around.

For students, to take on an identity as a ***designer*** is to immerse one's self in a project-based environment. While game-based virtual environments such as *Quest Atlantis* clearly offer rich opportunities, not all virtual environments for learning will be game based. Some worlds are being designed as centers of history, art, culture, religion, and science where the interactions are unscripted but focused by intellectual curiosity and shared interests. Maryanne Berry's article below describes a project that involved designing this kind of alternative world building. University students collaborated with younger students in building models of three virtual libraries.

A TEACHER'S PERSPECTIVE

Virtual Models of Future Libraries

A Collaborative Project of Youth and University Students

By Maryanne Berry, English Teacher

I have always thought that to be successful as a teacher, I needed to meet students where they live. These days they live largely online, playing games, listening to music, chatting with friends, and shopping. To many teachers, the online activity of today's youth seems to have very little to do with academic or intellectual endeavors. But, as texts, films, photographs, and artifacts become available in digital form, teachers need to consider how digital media can provide opportunities for students to interact with media in ways that stimulate critical thinking as well as creativity. While some educators fear that engagement in virtual worlds will diminish students' interest in traditional forms of reading and writing, I believe that students are ready to participate in the design of virtual worlds that support learning.

As a teaching assistant in a university architecture class whose aim was virtual world building, I had the opportunity to test my beliefs by facilitating partnerships between university students and three Bay Area grade and high school classes. Like video games, virtual worlds are computer-generated simulations that can be accessed by people through avatars, virtual characters representing themselves. Though video games necessarily take place in virtual worlds, virtual worlds are being constructed for purposes other than games. Architects are building virtual conference centers, museums, historical sites, and laboratories, in short, places where people can gather to socialize, work and learn together.

University of California, Berkeley, Professor Yehuda Kalay's Virtual World Building course set out in teams to construct models of three libraries in cyberspace. As more and more of the holdings of libraries are being converted into digital files, virtual libraries are being developed as sites affording people the chance not only to access documents and artifacts as they could via a Web site but also to meet and discuss books, attend readings and lectures, view collections, and conduct research with colleagues. Many universities are currently testing the effectiveness of virtual libraries in *Second Life*, a world populated by several million adults.

The U.C. Berkeley architecture students set out to build customized libraries for their young "clients" in the community. They divided into three teams and selected a class of students in one of three Bay Area schools. One team worked with fifth-sixth graders who participated in an elective class called Structures and who were engaged in making books. The second team worked with an honors ninth-grade English class who were conducting group reading projects. The third worked with a twelfth-grade Advanced Placement Literature class focused on the social aspects of literacy and learning. At the beginning of the semester, while the college students were learning the software and principles that would allow them to design libraries, students in the grade and high school classes were asked to imagine not only how they might enjoy reading and discussing books in a virtual environment, but more specifically, how they would enjoy the particular books they were reading with their fellow classmates in a virtual library created especially for them.

All students watched a short film of the Virtual Smithsonian created by Yehuda Kalay's fall 2008 Advanced Studio lab in collaboration with the Smithsonian Museum. The film was used as a springboard to prompt the grade and high school students to think about virtual places devoted to learning. Teachers asked students to discuss, write, and sketch their ideas about a virtual library that they would want to visit. While some envisioned classic architectural spaces, others suggested highly inventive places. One student imagined a giant toaster from which books popped. Others emphasized that the use of space afford both opportunities for small group encounters as well as open space where events for large groups could take place. A number of students focused on the aesthetic qualities of the libraries, the light, and interior design. Others focused on the access to information and resources; they imagined viewing films with friends of the books they enjoyed or listening to the authors read from their works. The younger students demonstrated more interested in creating a game-like environment while many of the older students expressed concern over the social networking possibilities of the libraries.

The opportunity to participate in the design process generated important discussions not only about the nature of places designed for learning but about the experience of reading. The project encouraged the grade and high school students to imagine reading as not only a solitary pleasure but also one that could be highly social. They envisioned themselves in virtual environments discussing books, role-playing characters from books they read, entering into places that suggested the landscape of the books they read, meeting nonplaying characters or NPCs from the books, taking quizzes on books to earn points or prizes, displaying titles, and writing reviews of their favorite books, mixing elements of books they loved in order to find new books, clicking on objects or icons that provided them with background information, historical data, links to other sites related to the world at hand. The discussions were rich, the ideas creative, and the critiques insightful.

The models that the university students ultimately produced spoke to the needs and the imaginations of their young clients. The fifth-sixth grade library took the shape of a giant vending machine where students could concoct the world of a book in a bottle and explore that world by climbing into the bottle. At the entrance to the ninth-grade library, readers found a maze in which artifacts such as Harry Potter's flying golden snitch prompted interest and discussion of particular books. The twelfth-grade space, named Mybrary, was a cosmic place where planets formed when two readers' interests intersected.

(Continued)

(Continued)

While the development of virtual libraries that students can actually use is only in its earliest phases, the experience of collaboration between university and younger students demonstrated that it is an idea worth developing. Both grade and high school students imagined extending the traditional activities of reading, writing, and researching into virtual libraries that offered greater access to resources, an enhanced ability to share texts and artifacts, and the opportunity to develop communities supportive of learning. We shortchange students when we think that they are only interested in virtual worlds that allow them to escape the intellectual demands of the actual world. Students can become deeply engaged in social media that encourages them to think critically, act collaboratively, and express themselves creatively.

Online Resources for Teachers

While most schools currently lack the technology to build the digital libraries described in this piece, students can learn about projects and programs devoted to learning in digital worlds by investigating the following sources:

- American Library Association (www.ala.org): By visiting the site's Web page, ALA Island in *Second Life*, students can learn how this national organization is using a virtual environment to spread a love of libraries (http://tiny .cc/teachtech_6_4).
- Youtube's Virtual Smithsonian_Studio 101: By viewing this YouTube video, students can image how they might experience and access information on treasures from the national museums (http://tiny.cc/teachtech_6_5).
- The Smithsonian Latino Virtual Museum (LVM): Visit this Web page to see how the Smithsonian Latino Center, in partnership with the Virtual Immersive Technologies for Arts and Learning Lab at Ohio University and Linden Labs, created a virtual environment to access collections, research, and exhibits related to U.S. Latinos and Latin America. From this page http://tiny.cc/teachtech_6_6 is a link to create your own avatar in *Second Life* and entry into LVM.
- Global Kids has developed a *Second Life* curriculum for teachers at http://www.rezed.org to learn more. You will have to sign up to use their Web site.

Critical to the success of virtual environments for learning is the inclusion of all stakeholders in dialogues about design. As the process of building the libraries unfolded, designers customized the libraries for the varied age groups of their users. As Maryanne demonstrates in the article, the project created an opportunity for youth to imagine libraries that "offered greater access to resources, an enhanced ability to share texts and artifacts and the opportunity to develop communities supportive of learning."

Though the word *community* is frequently used to describe virtual environments, not every virtual environment becomes the site of a community. One might read a Web site or a blog and never interact with the community of other readers. Because visits to a site can be easily recorded, the sponsors of a site like to describe the number of people who visit that site as members of an online community. Likewise in an immersive environment one might don an avatar and stroll the streets in a game such as *Grand Theft Auto* or a world such as *Second Life* but never speak to another inhabitant. The act of visiting a virtual environment does not make one a member of a community, just as the act of shopping in Paris does not make one French. But visitors sometimes do become members and communities do exist in virtual worlds. Some virtual environments like *Second Life* are so extensive that a participant could never meet all of its members. In these worlds as in games, there are rules, protocols, and repertoires that are different from the way participants interact in actual worlds. The differences between actual and virtual communities are part of their appeal; through one's avatar, one might enact a persona very different from the ones she assumes in actual life. As educators it behooves us to look closely both at the features of virtual environments that are making learning more compelling through the development of virtual and actual communities. Additionally, we should continue to investigate virtual environments in order to have a voice in how learning is changing in the digital age.

For many of us, crossing the threshold to greater use of emergent technology will involve simple but often surprising steps. Roman Gonzalez and Leslie Finamore were looking for innovative ways of increasing students' motivation to learn when they wrote a grant that allowed them to purchase two Nintendo Wii video game consoles for their special education students. They believed that the games would help students to enhance both motor skills and attention spans. To their astonishment, enthusiasm for the game changed the dynamics between their students and mainstream students by creating a place and an activity that could create commonalities rather than reinforce differences. Below, Roman Gonzalez and Leslie Finamore discuss how the popular Nintendo Wii console was able to bring two populations of students together and foster a school culture based on fun, collaborative exercise.

Virtual environments are already affording participants the opportunity to create, shape, and maintain communities of people who share the same classroom, school, or planet. How we come to think of school communities will depend on how we leverage the affordances of virtual environments to

A TEACHER'S PERSPECTIVE

Wii Did It!

Bringing Special and General Education Students Together

By Roman Gonzalez and Leslie Finamore,
High School Special Education Teacher and Staff

When you think of education you think of students sitting in their seats with paper and pen, listening to the teacher talk as they take notes. I teach in a special education classroom with several students that have IQs below 40, so we teach life skills, social skills, and vocational skills. We try to create lesson plans that are not of the norm, bringing in new ideas and something that is going to catch our students' attention. Motivation is key in our class, the one thing that works today or even this minute may not work tomorrow or in 10 minutes. So creativity is essential. Our students are integrated in general education as much as their skills will allow them. Reverse mainstreaming, when students from the general education come into the classroom and help our students, is a better option. This is something that is hard. There are some students who will come in and help just out of the kindness of their hearts; however coming across kids like this is not easy.

This past year we applied for a grant through Break the Barriers, a nonprofit organization in Clovis, California, that works with kids in special education. Through this grant we were able to purchase two complete Nintendo Wii video game systems with a handful of games such as bowling, tennis, golf, and baseball. We thought that we could use the strength of this generation's video games to help improve students' fine and gross motor skills while gradually increasing their attention span. We installed the Wii in our classroom and told a group of students from the general education that they could come in and play games before school and at lunch. Next thing we knew the classroom was full of students from around the school who wanted to play! Now we have students from leadership and peer counselors coming in during class time to help with our students. It started with learning how to interact with one other and playing together and now everyone comes together just to visit and socialize. This is something that cannot be taught. Our students have to listen to us talk and give them directions all day, but to have someone there who is of their own age interacting as a peer is something we cannot give them.

When we first received the Wii we tried to help our students play the games. These are kids with attention spans of seconds. We have nine students, and out of the nine, we have three that can play the Wii with some assistance and two that can play it independently. This took a few weeks to achieve, but it worked. It started with hand-over-hand assistance, pressing the buttons on the wand, and showing them how to maneuver through the Wii. Now when the kids from general education come in to play, some of my students can help set up the game for them. Additionally, some of my students no longer need any assistance maneuvering through the games, and sometimes they beat everyone!

The Wii is something that no teaching activity can reproduce; the social integration is something that no lesson plan can achieve. We have students come into our classroom asking to play; without even being told they include our students in their Wii games. Regardless of how our students play, the general education students will help them in any game. If they are playing tennis and beating them 40–0 they tell them that they won. If they can't beat them, then they tell them how good they are playing. Witnessing such development in social interaction between the two populations of students is phenomenal. The Wii has also helped our students with their physical education. Their fine and gross motor skills are not as strong as others. So finding something that they can get involved in is more difficult then just kicking a ball and telling students to go play. Some are in wheel chairs while others have muscular problems, so being enrolled in regular P.E. class is rare. When my students are enrolled in general physical education it is great, but sometimes there are students who will stare at my students and not want to involve them due to their inability to physically keep up. Now that the Wii is up in our classroom, our students feel more comfortable. Their classroom is a safe zone for our students and other students to come to their world, so to speak.

Also, the Wii has had multiple uses such as regular education students using the Wii as positive reinforcement for having them finish their essays or projects. As soon as they finish they are able to come down and challenge the staff or other kids in other classes. Other teachers will use my classroom as an incentive to complete their work also. We now have school tournaments that involve students and their teachers. On those same guidelines we have a student with an emotional disability who will not work for anything on campus and the high school doesn't have any extracurricular activities to pull him into a more positive direction. The school psychologists are using the Wii as enticement for constructive growth. We started two months ago with him working independently as an incentive and now he's coming in once a week, working 15 minutes on his own and then *with* students for 15 minutes.

When we first set up the Wii, we were hoping for little more than playtime. We had no idea the growth that would happen, both socially and physically, for our students. Our students have made friends while gaining mental and physical strength as well as nurturing their self-esteem.

support and extend collaboration to potential partners in learning. As designers and educators and users we have important decisions to make, but we must begin with the realization that young people have already begun the work. Respecting their contributions, honoring their practices and understanding their needs will be key in the developing the trust necessary for building amazing and durable structures that support our highest ambitions for youth. Additionally, teachers must begin to collaborate with one another regarding virtual worlds. Check out this wiki created by Linden Labs (http://wiki.secondlife.com/wiki/Education).

Yet as educators we cannot forget to analyze social and cultural issues that can affect student learning. It is easy when discussing "video game success stories" to forget how much video game consoles, games, and their extra gadgets can cost. Sometimes video game consoles can start at $400 dollars and then the games are usually at least an additional $25 dollars. To help us think through the economic side of digital media, Megan Finn provides some bits and bytes from her research.

Bits and Bytes: An Additional Perspective

Bits and Bytes of Research is a sidebar designed to further our understanding of a topic. In this instance, Megan Finn discusses her insight into the purchasing of a personal computer.

Class Matters: Purchasing a Family Computer

By Megan Finn, U.C. Berkeley, Doctoral Candidate in the School of Information

Sometimes it is easy to take for granted access to and the decision to buy technology. Here are my findings from an interview study I conducted with freshmen at U.C. Berkeley from low-income backgrounds:

One marked difference between students in the lowest income group and students in higher income groups was in the purchase of a family computer. Typically for those with the lowest income groups, the computer was bought for educational purposes for the kids. This is quite unlike students from other income levels where parents might use a computer for work and therefore have one at home. Some of the lowest income students regularly used the Internet at school or at the library until their parents got it at home (sometimes not until late in high school). Similar to the purchase of a family computer, getting the Internet at home was typically driven, at least as a discussion topic, by the students needing the Internet for educational purposes. Although many students used the Internet for recreational purposes, it seemed that most felt that it was necessary for school purposes. The most important lesson I learned with regards to technology purpose in low income homes was that the decision to buy the family's computer was driven by the perceived needs of the kids. In many instances kids ended up knowing the most about the computer and how to troubleshoot.

Implications for Teachers

- Make sure the economic backgrounds of your students do not sway your opinion of their "assumed" ability to work with technology.
  - o In some cases students from working-class families frequently have to rely on teachers and peers in school for technological assistance since they may not

be gaining this experience at home. On the other hand some youth from higher-income families may seem more independent and focused when working with technology at school because they are more likely to gain resources and assistance from family and peers at home.

- Class backgrounds can also connect to other literacy issues such as students' access to books and reading at home. With higher-income families, a discussion at home around narrative and storytelling can take place long before children enroll in school.

- If students do not have access to the Internet at home, then not all students have an "equal opportunity" to engage in creative endeavors and interest-driven practices online.[6]

SHARE YOUR INSIGHTS, STORIES, AND OPINIONS!

We want to hear about your thoughts on and experiences with video games. Join our community of teachers by visiting our Web site at www.teachingtechsavvykids.com and posting your responses to this chapter. Here are some questions to address:

1. Roman and Leslie discussed how the Nintendo Wii brought different student populations together through video game participation and also provided a fun and entertaining way for students and teachers to exercise. Are there ways in which to bring consoles like the Nintendo Wii or video games like *Dance Dance Revolution* into schools for students and teachers to enjoy during lunch or after school? What have you done at your own school to generate school community?

2. Sites such as *Second Life* and Wikipedia are popular because of their reliance on user-generated content. How can classroom teachers harness the appeal of this feature? And how might user-generated content challenge and support a teacher's authority within a classroom?

3. If we think of students' participation in virtual worlds and games as places of self-expression and creativity, are there ways that

6. Currently after-school programs provide leadership and resources for kids to access the Internet and the means for digital production. These organizations are examples of public institutions' providing basic access to technology tools and skills training since technical, economic, and social resources are not always available. Visit http://digitalyouth.ischool.berkeley.edu/report to read more.

teachers can provide opportunities for academic assignments to be addressed with artifacts created in a virtual environment?

4. Despite the popularity of video games, the content of games and some virtual worlds is extremely limited. Throughout these fictional worlds, a remarkably narrow range of stories and perspectives is presented (Jenkins, 2006). The content of video games might be a great way to start discussions around issues in our lives such as the portrayal of women and other minorities, violence, or even sports. Are there ways teachers and students can use the content of some video games as a starting point to talk about society?

REFERENCES AND HELPFUL RESOURCES

Education Arcade: http://www.educationarcade.org

Educause. (2008). 7 things you should know about Second Life. *Educause Learning Initiative*. Retrieved September 28, 2009, from http://www.educause .edu/ELI/7ThingsYouShouldKnowAboutSecon/163004.

Foreman, N., Boyd-Davis, S., Moar, M., Korallo, L., & Chappell, E. (2007). Can virtual environments enhance the learning of historical chronology? *Instructional Science: An International Journal of the Learning Sciences, 36*(2), 155–173.

Freire, P. (1970). *Pedagogy of the oppressed.* New York: Continuum.

Gee, J. P. (2003). *What video games have to teach us about learning and literacy.* New York: Palgrave Macmillan.

Gee, J. P. (2005) Learning by design: Good video games as learning machines. *E-Learning, 2*(1), 5–15.

Gee, J. P. (2007). *Good video games and good learning: Collected essays on video games, learning, and literacy.* New York: Peter Lang Publishing.

Ito, M. (2007). Education Vs. entertainment: A cultural history of children's software. In K. Salen (Ed.), *The ecology of games: Connecting youth, games, and learning* (pp. 89–116). The John D. and Catherine T. MacArthur Foundation Series on Digital Media and Learning. Cambridge, MA: MIT Press.

Jenkins, H. (2006). The war between effects and meaning: Rethinking the video game violence debate. In D. Buckingham and R. Willett (Eds.), *Digital generations: Children, young people, and new media* (pp. 19–32). Mahwah, NJ: Lawrence Erlbaum.

Lave, J., & Wenger, E. (1991). *Situated learning: Legitimate peripheral participation.* Cambridge, England: University Press.

Moll, L., Amanti, C., Neff, D., & Gonzalez, N. (1992). Funds of knowledge for teaching: Using a qualitative approach to connect homes and classrooms. *Theory Into Practice, 31*(2), 132–141.

National Research Council and the Institute of Medicine. (2004). *Engaging schools: Fostering high school students' motivation to learn.* Committee on

Increasing High School Students' Engagement and Motivation to Learn. Board on Children, Youth, and Families, Division of Behavioral and Social Sciences and Education. Washington, DC: National Academic Press.

Nelson, B. C. (2007). Exploring the use of individualized, reflective guidance in an educational multiuser virtual environment. *Journal of Science Education and Technology, 16*(1), 83–97.

RezEd: The Hub for Learning and Virtual Worlds: http://www.rezed.org

Salen, K. (2007). Toward an ecology of gaming. In K. Salen (Ed.), *The ecology of games: Connecting youth, games, and learning.* The John D. and Catherine T. MacArthur Foundation Series on Digital Media and Learning. Cambridge, MA: MIT Press. pp. 1–20.

Shaffer, D. W. (2006). *How computer games help children learn.* New York: Palgrave Macmillan.

Squire, K. (2006). From content to context: Videogames as designed experience. *Educational Researcher, 35*(8), 19–29.

Warren, S. J., Dondlinger, M. J., & Barab, S. A. (2008). A MUVE toward PBL writing: Effects of a digital learning environment designed to improve elementary student writing. *Journal of Research on Technology in Education, 41*(1), 113–140.

Wenger, E. (1998) *Communities of practice: Learning meaning and identity.* Cambridge, England: University Press.

Remix Culture

Digital Music and Video Remix, Opportunities for Creative Production

Erin B. Reilly

INTRODUCTION

This chapter discusses the tools and strategies such as remix that our students are using today to make their voices heard. We will explore how to adapt these tools and strategies to classroom activities that encourage everyone in the classroom to participate in their own learning. Since education is not a single or solitary occupation but a collective, embracing, and transforming process of engagement, this chapter focuses on opportunities for creative production through remix.

THE IMPORTANCE OF STORYTELLING

Think back to the stories your parents told you as a child, stories sampled from reality and combined with make-believe. Each time our parents retold a story, they embellished it, adding dramatic twists and turns that created a new story from the original source. As children, my cousins and I would bunk up on the third floor where my mother sent us to sleep with stories from the Greek myths. I still remember her calling, "No man! No man has blinded me!" swaying to and fro, and adding a tremulous voice to emphasize the poor Cyclops' plight. Each retelling became more dramatic, ensuring that we would anticipate and laugh at Polyphemus' foolish attempt to out-trick the greatest trickster in literature. With Odysseus, we escaped the third floor room and sailed to the Land of Forgetfulness.

In the morning, our minds would teem with remembrances as we claimed a small part of the beach as our own island and transformed the bedtime stories into our own creations. Sometimes we would create new adventures where Menelaus and the Greeks lost the battle of Troy, and Paris and Helen remained lovers forever. Sometimes Odysseus would land on a new island and befriend our favorite movie character, E.T., who would point a shortcut home where Odysseus would romantically reunite with his lovely Penelope.

My mother's stories were elaborately retold from the literature she taught to her high school students—stories we knew when we reached the classroom but in a very different fashion from the texts we read in English class. Fortunately for me, the remixing of myth and reality I shared with my mom and cousins gave me a deeper understanding of the characters, plot, and the morals of the stories because they were a part of my lived childhood experience.

This recipe for adapting bedtime stories to elements of our own culture and adding a dash of personal creativity transformed the Greek myths into repositories for entertainment, self-identity, and the creation of a subculture within my family where I felt accepted and fulfilled. Stories are just as important to us today as they were when we were children. They have the same ability to transform our culture and to help us adapt to the world we live in. Just as when we were children, we use stories to be entertained, to explore our identities, and to create a subculture that gives us a sense of belonging.

Pew Internet and American Life Project noted in their Teens and Social Media report that nearly two-thirds of online teens are content creators (Lenhart & Madden, 2007). But they are not just creating content for themselves . . . Students lose track of time as they spend hours navigating the Web for material to create their stories and feel a sense of belonging through encouragement by their peers to post their stories on Facebook, illustrate them on Flickr, and share them with friends and the public at large through the multiple resources available on the Web. This participation in new media environments is a way to be creative and innovative, but it is also new opportunities for our students to acquire and synthesize information in a meaningful way.

One in four online teens remix content they find online—like songs, text, or images—and remix them into their own artistic creations (Lenhart & Madden, 2007). By remixing texts, teens re-create and redefine them to share with others. In the process they are acquiring new habits of expectation, meaning, and credibility; new ways of acting, interacting, and doing; and gaining the competencies to become part of this digital world. These gained experiences are the new equivalent of a hidden curriculum.

The learning ecology teens participate in today is similar to the hidden curriculum educational theorists in the 1960s who said that children whose parents took them to museums, had dinner conversations on politics and civic engagement, had encyclopedias in their home and listened to opera records would perform differently in school than those who didn't have those opportunities. Students who grow up in households with access to Wikipedia, Facebook, and YouTube have different experiences in the classroom than those who don't. Project New Media Literacies refers to this divide as the "participation gap" and that means educators in afterschool programs, library programs, and classroom programs have to help solve the gap by giving access to skills, such as remixing, and encouraging learning in a participatory culture.

Students today often **remix** original texts based on their own interests in order to create a new work that encapsulates their ideas and concerns about the issues that matter most to them. It is up to us as educators not to leave some students behind but to encourage them as media-driven explorers, sparked by social and cultural experiences, which play an important role in fostering creativity in the classroom.

WHAT IS REMIXING?

Remixing is building upon a work that already exists and using it to make new meanings and express new ideas. To develop a remix, the creator must first consider how the original source is related to a new context. When I transformed the fall of Troy into my own story of love and triumph, I remixed the *Aeneid* with romantic characters and images that were part of my life experience. The original source held the key for me to interpret and reinvent, through my own imagination and analysis of the original text, the story for my contemporary world.

History shows that the great authors are great remixers. William Shakespeare could not have written *Henry IV* without Holinshed's *Chronicles of England, Scotland, and Ireland*. William Blake could not have created *The Marriage of Heaven and Hell* without the *Old Testament*. It doesn't matter to the reader that Shakespeare's Richard the Third is based on misinformation from Hall's *History of England*. The character is so transformed for the contemporary audience that the original source is now intimately bound to the new creation and they are no longer separate but one. The Teachers' Strategy Guide is a set of curriculum modules for English and language arts classrooms created by Project New Media Literacies, a research project first established at MIT and now at the University of Southern California, states that teachers need to understand how their students work together to "think, critique, and create." Students do this by taking existing information and transforming it for their own needs through a multitude of strategies that encourage students to appropriate what exists, remix it into something new, and post it to their peers for immediate feedback.

A second consideration in building a remix is to determine how the meaning of the remix embodies and relates to the meaning of the new creation. A remix is not borrowing. In other words, the form and content of the original is acknowledged even as they are transformed into something that is distinct from, but reminiscent of, the original. It is not only literature that has a history of remix. During the late 1950s, early '60s, contemporary fine art artist, Robert Rauschenberg created a series called *combines*, which incorporated trash and found objects into his art. He chose to incorporate trash and found objects because he wanted something other than what he, himself, could create. His goal with combines was to transform the objects into something new. An example of these fine art remixes includes *Retroactive I* (1964), which incorporates publicly available printed images with mixed media to create a ***collage*** of related images. Rauschenberg discovered the synchronicity between the images and brought them into juxtaposition to create a new and contemporary statement on the condition of humankind at midcentury. This remix allows viewers to experience a sense of recognition that leads to reflection on our history and our ability to build upon our past.

Rauschenberg often remarked that the combines' series allowed him to work "in the gap between life and art." This work was a reflection of Rauschenberg's shift from creating art for his own individual expression to involving his community into his artwork by writing into meaning his views on the state of society—to represent what was happening in history.

We are in a paradigm shift in the classroom where educators need to work in the gap between life and school. Across multiple art forms, youth are immersed in the remix culture. This provides teachers an opportunity to offer learning objectives in their classrooms in a new way, while at the same time offering students opportunities to read and write their cultural practices that are central to their own everyday experience (Jenkins, 2006). Incorporating participatory practices into the classroom, such as remixing, allows for a blurring of boundaries between informal and formal learning and harnesses the power of digital technologies for students to reflect on the participatory culture that they live in.

Often hanging out and messing around encourage geeking out on something you're really passionate about (Ito et al., 2010). This happens by accessing an interest-driven network and learning happens from the culmination of all people you have met and all you have learned and discovered from them along the way. The George Lucas Educational Foundation released the Digital Generation Project 2009 that gives voice to children of the digital generation. Instead of adults talking for them, this project profiles a variety of children of all ages as they geek out on their passions. What this project provides to teachers is a glimpse into our students' lives and the strategies they engage in to communicate, socialize, and learn—not just from us but from their peers and larger community.

Jalen is a 12-year old artist, the epitome of a young creator of media and an active member of the Digital Youth Network located in Chicago, Illinois. Jalen says he was on the computer painting pictures by the time he was three, playing games on his Gameboy at five, exploring different drawing techniques by the age of seven, and creating his first comic book by the time he was 10. And in sixth grade, he received his first laptop, which opened up new doors of discovery and the tools to remix culture for his own purposes. Now his assignments at school, such as a book report transformed into a comic book, encourage the practice of remixing the knowledge required with the knowledge that has meaning to him, creating a more lasting impact on what he will remember in his learning experience (http://tiny.cc/teachtech_7_1).

We can clearly see that Jalen is geeking out on his passions and using them to influence his learning across the subject areas he studies during an average day in school. Jalen combines his talents and uses them to reflect on what matters to him, as he poignantly described in the poster he created on *Division 101*. The poster reflects a film about the racial divide he worked on.

Jalen is not alone in his quest to use new practices in learning.

Why Are Remixes Important?

So remixing is not new. Throughout human history, we have borrowed, reinvented, and remixed texts. However, remixing today is not an individual endeavor, especially among youths. Whether teens are sampling from a favorite song, television show, film, game, or a combination of media, they are having fun and learning from each other. They are forming communities based on the task of bringing together disparate elements and forming new creations. They are motivated to create—not to receive a prize—but to be part of a peer-based learning community.

Teens are drawn to the practice of remixing because it enables them to explore music, art, and video, reinterpret it, remix it, and produce their own versions to share immediately with their peers. Creating a remix requires youths to take the position of author, to be made aware of one's audience, and to contextualize one's intended meaning within a particular setting.

Take, for instance, the 15-year-old Atlanta hip-hop artist known as Soulja Boy, who rocketed to fame by not following the traditional standards for making a record (Driscoll, 2009). He took his music right to his peers by posting his songs and dance steps on YouTube and encouraged everyone to participate by offering a dance to go along with his song—similar to the Macarena or the Electric Slide that had been popular a few years before. Soulja Boy encouraged people to take up the dance and make it their own, and he created a phenomenon (http://www.youtube.com/).

People instant-messaged the latest dance video on YouTube, downloaded it to their iPods, and copied the routine. Teens quickly mastered the dance moves and added new steps, which created a new dance remixed from Soulja Boy's original moves. Between classes they videotaped others doing the new dance, loaded it back on YouTube, and tagged it to others who also participated in the Soulja Boy phenomenon.

Because Soulja Boy allowed anyone to remix their own dances, he connected them with others who had joined in on the craze. At the same time, he circulated to fame, rising to the top of the charts for seven weeks and getting a record label and Grammy nomination. Soulja Boy benefited from sharing his work with others and allowing them to adapt it for their own purposes. Those who participated in this community learned how to appropriate and transform the content of the original dance video. This process engaged young and old alike in what is known as **collective intelligence,** the ability to pool knowledge and compare notes with others for a common goal. This is achieved both **synchronously** with those in their own community and **asynchronously** with others in the YouTube audience.

By bringing remixing techniques into the classroom, students can collaborate and collectively create substantive learning challenges using the new media literacies available to them on the Web. As the community who participated in the Soulja Boy phenomenon shows, some students already think and work collectively. These students have already formed communities of learners. Teachers can channel this grassroots methodology to lessons presented in the classroom.

Additionally, incorporating remix into everyday classrooms offers teachers and students a chance to think creatively and encourage appropriation, a new media literacy skill. **Appropriation** is the ability to meaningfully sample and remix media content to make it one's own (Jenkins, 2006). The contemporary use of appropriation seen as a new literacy originates from music terminology and refers to transforming existing music into new versions by adding, subtracting, or modifying elements of the original. Appropriation is practiced across various disciplines and each discipline has a diverse array of methods. In traditional literature, for example, methods include parody, adaptation, or translation, and for the music culture, methods vary from sampling to mashup. Through practice, students will have a deeper understanding of how remixes exist within a large network of media and practice encourages students to acquire the habits of mind as well as the skills and competencies to become part of this digital world.

According to Jenkins (2006), the focus of literacy is changing from individual expression to community involvement where creative manifestation and active participation are the hallmark. The new media literacies (NML) are becoming increasingly important. When thinking about new media literacies, such as the skill, appropriation—one might interpret the language of the words *new media literacy* to refer to a new era where we build upon our interactions with media to analyze and critically consume media so that we're no longer consumers but producers of media. Remixing is synonymous with new media literacies appropriation. By practicing this art form we interpret and better understand the social and cultural world.

Access to new media encourages a wider population to remix. This new form of literacy helps teachers understand that our students are reading and writing in new ways. Reading and writing was once relegated to reading books and writing papers (lessons commonly found in English and language arts classrooms). However, a possible hypothesis is that the educational system has not caught up with the shifting landscape of participatory culture where there are new ways to read, write, and compute numbers.

Shifting Landscape	
Past	**Present**
Reading a book	Reading a transmedia story
Writing alone	Networked writing
Memorizing formulas	Gaming as problem solving

Students are seeking more active participation in learning. Our classroom practices must change if we are to encourage and expand on these new habits of thinking and value the new forms of participation and learning that have become a social construct for teens. In a participatory learning environment, knowledge happens by encouraging learning as emergent rather than prestructured; transmedia rather than unified; situational rather than universal; and collaborative rather than hierarchical.

Project New Media Literacies believes that the new media literacies should be integrated across the curriculum—not as an added subject but as a paradigm shift in how we teach and think about traditional school content. Each discipline needs to take ownership of those skills that are central to conducting research and practice in their area. The sciences may want to take up issues of ***visualization*** and ***simulation***; literature could take up the issue of ***appropriation***. To offer a model of how these skills can be integrated into the curriculum, Project New Media Literacies has developed a series of teachers' strategy guides that can inform and inspire teachers working in multiple disciplines, and spark further experimentation and innovation. For access to these resources, see http://newmedialiteracies.org/educators/.

POPULAR KINDS OF REMIX

There are a variety of subcultures of people who participate in remixing content because they are passionate about a specific style of production, whether it's mixing music or editing videos or performing backyard theater. These amateur productions are drawn from multiple sources and illustrate the practice of remixing media as a form of participation. Thus, youth have online spaces where participants share and build upon each other's ideas, where they pool their knowledge and are engaged and connected because of a similar interest.

Music Remix

Music helps define who we are. Music is one of the top modes of expression for bringing youth together and building a sense of community. We sing songs around the campfire and lull our babies to sleep. We learn our first form of literacy by singing the ABCs. We see the importance of music in how Soulja Boy used the power of social media to encourage a community beyond his peers to dance to his song and help build a visibility that made him a phenomenon of participatory culture.

The practice of remixing as we define it today gained popularity in the music industry as a result of the Jamaican dance hall culture of the 1960s where a **DJ** with microphone in hand would rally the crowd to get the party started. The DJ would often encourage a battle of the bands to determine which had the better sound. Using two turntables, the DJ would mix his favorite parts of multiple songs to force certain sounds and rhythms to stand out in relief. As DJ Spooky explains, "A DJ is a hunter and gatherer— collecting sounds, collecting images. We go off and hunt them down and gather them. It's not a passive relationship where you sit there and press play. The whole idea is to make things change; have them transform. You're changing a found sound, a found record, a found file." (View the What is a DJ? video at http://tiny.cc/teachtech_7_2.)

Geek Out on DJ Culture!

You can find out more about DJ Spooky and other artists by visiting Project New Media Literacies' Media Producer Profile Series: Learn about DJ Culture! at http://tiny.cc/teachtech_7_3

Combining two very different genres creates a surprise for the listener while introducing a new style of music. This type of sampling is called a *mashup*. I first realized I liked hip-hop when artist, Eminem, collaborated with pop artist, Dido, to sample the chorus of the song "Thank You" and incorporate it with the lyrics of "Stan" (http://tiny.cc/teachtech_7_4). Often, we like a certain genre of music or are attracted to one style over others. Eminem laid rhythmic hip hop with a slow bass line underneath the lyrics that attracted me more than the other range of hip-hop I had heard. This is an example of how an alternate music culture moved beyond the walls of the clubs into mainstream America, winning a 2002 Grammy for best remix.

Creating remixes provides a way to update the old and invoke enjoyment of the lyrics and sounds of yesterday. American Film Institute nominated "Somewhere Over the Rainbow" as the greatest song of all time. Not surprisingly, this song has been remixed and adapted for every genre from alternative to blues to dance (http://same-melody.com/category/over-the-rainbow). "Jawaiian" (Hawaiian reggae) artist, Israel Kamakawiwo'ole, known as Iz to his many fans, has one of the most popular remixes of "Somewhere Over the Rainbow," which he has remixed with a totally different rhythm and ukulele accompaniment (http://tiny.cc/teachtech_7_5).

STORIES FROM THE FIELD

Reason, FL Studio, and a Laptop

Digital Revolution in a Back Pack

By Ron Nobu Sakamoto, Instructional Media Technician and Specialist

A new golden age of music has emerged with the revolution in digital technology. Advancements in new media and digital technologies have transformed the music industry and the rules of the trade. The tools of the new music trade have never become more accessible for youth today. Anyone can become a music producer with the right audacity, talent, and entrepreneurial spirit. Equipped with only a laptop, a pair of headphones, and a microphone, youth, can create a portable recording studio that can all fit within a school backpack. Urban kids today are converting their bedrooms, closets, garages, and sheds into micro-recording studios and are now able to produce their own music beats and lyrical songs, upload them to their iPods, MP3 players, to the Internet and share them with their peers and to a worldwide audience. The creation of new digital audio recording software programs such as Logic, Pro Tools, Reason, and even free shareware software programs like FL Studio have helped to spawn a whole new generation of "cultural creatives" forcing the recording music industry to redefine itself.

As a classically trained pianist, I enjoy reading, playing classical music, and love all genres of music. I am always amazed at how adept students are with how quickly

(Continued)

(Continued)

they learn how to create rhythm, tempo, cadence, without even knowing how to read a single note of music! I especially love the improvisational nature of Jazz music and think some head musicians in hip-hop are at the forefront of one of the most improvisational music forms emerging today.

Students as Beat Makers

I want to share with you my experience with one student in particular. His name is DeAndre, and to outsiders, he appears to be just a normal high school kid: He walks down the school hallways, looking all fresh with his black hoodie, sporting an unmarked NFL cap as he listens to his iPod. He socializes and contributes to class discussions like any other normal teenager. Ask him to compose a five-paragraph essay and he would come up short for words and really struggle to organize his thoughts in grammatically correct sentences. But ask him to compose a song and he'll deliver you rhythmic verses that have deep philosophical truths about his struggles with class, race, and the injustices he sees in society.

DeAndre is a very industrious kid who is very mature for his age, not from choice but out of necessity. He had to raise himself basically in the shelter of his grandma's house without parents. He worked at a local bakery almost every day after school to support himself financially. It was in the beginning of his senior year when he finally achieved his goal of purchasing a new laptop to start producing his own beats in his granny's backyard shed. The storage shed contained a collection of old furniture, torn up rugs, and cobwebs that hung low from decades of dust. DeAndre ran a 50-foot AC cable that powered his laptop from the main house and accompanied a professional microphone and stand I gave him to record his vocals on. I think his only escape from the turmoil that constantly surrounded him was to immerse into his own creative self and produce music whenever he could.

After we returned from holiday break that winter, I found students huddled around DeAndre's iPod, as they listened to a song he had just produced with another student Nick. The song was about Nick scoring an almost perfect 2400 on the SATs. The song expressed Nick's commentary about the educational system and the meaninglessness of his test scores. Nick, who is white, is an exceptionally gifted academic student, and also quite socially awkward, lanky, and lives in an affluent neighborhood. That day, DeAndre and Nick illustrated to their fellow peers that music *can* bring the most unlikely students together and bridge the cultural class divide.

Producers of Music

DeAndre like almost every youth creating beats today are using Reason, FL Studio, and any audio software program and sound effect plug-ins they can find to experiment and create original works of art with. Reason is a professional audio software program for both Apple computers and PCs. Reason has become synonymous with hip-hop music as the main software program youths and professional musicians alike have adopted both for its affordability and its capability to be able to integrate with other software programs such as FL Studio and audio hardware from midi controllers to professional audio mixing boards. For a novice or untrained person looking at the interface of the program on a computer screen, it appears extremely complicated and full of dials, buttons, switches, and level meters (See Figure 7.1).

Ironically, to become a good producer of music you have to inherently develop a skill for listening, isolating instruments and sounds, instruments, beat tempos, all composited on multiple tracks in a single song, any Reason producer will tell you that. So while students may appear totally checked out walking through the hallways with their hoodies down below their eyes and earphones plugged in, I would argue perhaps all their creative synapses have kept them up all night long listening, learning a new beat, intuitively developing rhythmic algorithms. I have observed how music and beat making is all-pervasive in the hearts and mind of youth culture today. If public education can find innovative ways to bridge the cultural gap and explore new ways of teaching, both educators and students may come to a new understanding of learning and listening.

Figure 7.1   Reason Interface

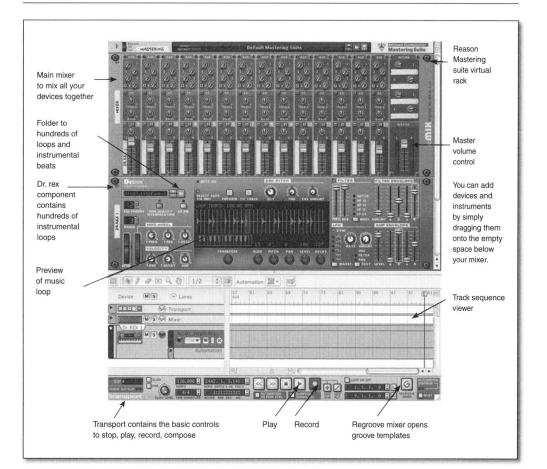

BECOMING A MUSIC REMIXER

A music remix is a reinterpretation of a pre-existing song, which dominates the sound in the remixed version. With the increased availability and use of the creative tools found on the Web, such as Mixx, Scratch Live, and Traktor and in software such as Reason, Pro Tools and GarageBand, we can mix and manipulate audio files and publish our own songs. So what inspires you? What song do you sing when you're in the shower or alone in the car? If you're looking for inspiration, begin at ccMixter (http://ccmixter.org/), a great community for entering into the world of music remixes.

Most music on ccMixter is made by people who aren't professional musicians. However, famous musicians like My Morning Jacket, David Byrne, and the Beastie Boys have posted their music on ccMixter to be remixed. Although you might not find most of your favorite songs on *ccMixter*, you will certainly find a new favorite!

Users post content to ccMixter in three different categories, each of which is noted by a tab at the top of the Web page. The first is Samples of instrumental elements, such as a drum beat or guitar solo. The second is A Capella, singing or rapping without background music. The final category is finished Remixes that pull both elements into one track. Everything on ccMixter is available for remixing, so users can collaborate on music without ever meeting each other, and can work together from around the world and across languages.

Music Remix Activity

Project New Media Literacies Learning Library challenge, *New Versions, New Visions* provides an interactive activity that encourages you and your students to explore the new media literacy, *appropriation*, by browsing through audio remixes on ccmixter.org, a community remix site. Find the challenge at http://www .newmedialiteracies.org/library/#/challenge/38.

The cc in ccMixter stands for **Creative Commons**, and the site is all about (re)mixing common material. At ccMixter, people make, share, and listen to music remixes—legally. The music on ccMixter is licensed under Creative Commons, which means that it can legally and ethically be used in various ways, as long as the creator of the new work follows any rules attached to the license of the work that he or she is remixing. Some rules say the creator can't make money from what is sampled, and often the work that is being remixed asks to be given credit as the original source.

Even though one in four teens are remixing content online, it is often relegated to their social setting outside of school. Remixing is usually not used in the classroom because of the ongoing debate about copyright and freedom of expression. Teachers are rightly concerned about ownership and authorship; but digital tools have increased the ability of users to sample and remix content to make it their own and it is not a subject that should be avoided or ignored. Instead of encouraging educators to better understand fair use of copyright and tools such as the Creative Commons, schools tend to reject remixing out of hand and dismiss it as a new form of learning.

It's understandable that a lack of clarity around copyright and fair use can cause frustration but don't dismiss these opportunities! Put your mind at ease and arm yourself with these resources that help set the record straight.

- "The Cost of Copyright Confusion" by Renee Hobbs, Peter Jaszi, and Pat Aufderheide (http://tiny.cc/teachtech_7_6)
- "Code of Best Practices for Fair Use in Media Literacy Education" (http://tiny.cc/teachtech_7_8)

Participating in creating remixes does raise legal questions. Remixed creations use material that has some type of copyright from the original author; however remixes recontextualize the original source and create new meaning and are highly eligible to be a fair use of copyrighted material. For example, it is legal, due to the transformative nature of the work. However, remixers must be aware that fair use is a case by case judgment call, which they can help make themselves based on the Code of Best Practices in Fair Use for Online Video (http://tiny.cc/teachtech_7_7). Knowing your rights as a remixer is key to protecting your free speech and thus, a key component of media literacy.

Schools can often misunderstand what copyright allows and does not allow. Identifying ownership and authorship is an important part of media literacy. One only has to look at the 2008 presidential campaign to see the influence of remixing media to help transform political campaigning. The professional photographer, Manny Garcia, makes his living by selling his best photographs to the press. **Copyright** allows Manny to have control over how his photographs are reproduced, adapted, and distributed in the United States.

At one of the press events during the 2008 elections, Manny Garcia took an infamous photo of Barack Obama. Artist Shepard Fairey was looking online for photos of Obama to use in a poster and created the famous Hope poster by remixing the photo taken by Garcia. The Associated Press (AP), Garcia's employer, owns this photo, and AP wanted to be credited for the image and paid for any poster sales. Shepard Fairey believes that the use of the photo comes under *fair use*. According to fair use, four key features need to change to legally use an original source: the nature, the purpose, the amount, and the effect of the original. By changing these key features, the artists transformed the original into a remix, which created an original in its own right.

Anyone who produces creative works such as images, videos, or music, might want people to remix them. Using a Creative Commons' license allows artists to communicate with others about the specific ways that they can or cannot use their work. The license gives people the freedom to make copies of a work and distribute it, with some restrictions, which combine the following elements:

- *Attribution,* which means people are allowed to use the work as long as they give the artist credit for creating it.
- *Noncommercial,* which means that people can use the work as long as they don't make money using it.
- *Nonderivative,* which means that people can use the work as long as they don't modify or change it.
- *Share alike,* which means that people can use the work as long as they offer their remix under the same license as the artist's.

VIDEO REMIX

In addition to music remixes, people are also remixing videos. A diverse subculture has developed on the Web centered on creating and sharing video remixes. Armed with free programs, such as http://jaycut.com/, or software programs such as iMovie or Windows Moviemaker, teens are learning from each other how to remix videos. Teachers can bring this creative production into the classroom. A variety of video remix styles, including movie trailer **recuts**, political remixes, and remixed music videos, allow students to build upon the originals and create new meaning, such as a parody, alternative messages, as well as new forms of music with subliminal messages.

Video Remix Activity

Project New Media Literacies Learning Library challenge, *Total Recut: Transformations* has you explore a video recut of *The Shining* that transforms the classic horror film starring Jack Nicholson into a romantic comedy. This challenge explores how appropriating content, specifically sound, can transform meaning. Find the challenge at http://www.newmedialiteracies.org/library/#/challenge/40

Fan vidders (vidder originates from song vid, vid short for video) create fan-made music videos derived from television shows or movies. If you've ever created slideshows set to music, then you are part of the precursor to fan vidding. Fan vidding has a rich history of vids, aesthetics, and technologies and is the earliest music video remix culture having been in existence since 1975 and is recognized having been established by Kandy Fong who created a remix with Star Trek slide images set to Leonard Nimoy's song, "Both Sides Now" (http://tiny.cc/teachtech_7_9). Most notably, this is a genre that is primarily practiced by women and something very important to understand since video making has been associated as a male-dominated movement. But this is a misconception that we need to squelch in order to ensure equality in participation and statistically there is no gender difference in teens remixing and creating online (Pew Internet and American Life, 2005).

Today vidders edit clips of their favorite television show or movie and transform them into a music video. Television shows such as "Heroes," "Supernatural," or "Buffy the Vampire Slayer" or movies such as *Star Trek* or *Twilight* inspire us to participate in telling more of the story or redefining it to share with others. Fan-vidding is our visual poetry, an interpretation of the television shows and movies that vidders love. The viewer will understand the vid better if they are familiar with or have seen the television show or movie that is being represented. With this knowledge, a viewer can move beyond the storyline to see the nuances of what a vid is trying to represent both in story, aesthetic, and technical remix.

Often vidders work collaboratively on a project. They usually become interested in the process after they find a vidder willing to teach the technique or by accessing a well-known vidding forum found on Live Journal (http://www.livejournal.com/). Live Journal is a discussion forum and social network site and hosts one of the biggest fan vidding communities. This peer-to-peer mentoring community is very welcoming and willing to share their expertise.

The best vids have a fully thought out concept with layers of meaning; but the song choice must fit the tone of the story and still be entertaining.

Point of view is vital to a successful video remix and vidders must consider the role of the characters and the message projected through them.

The novice vidder should watch many videos to learn vidding techniques and Live Journal's vidding archive has worked to gather vids from the Internet into one place (http://community.livejournal.com/vidding_archive/profile).

To get started, here are two vid classics that have had widespread interest and have been critiqued and analyzed by the vidding community as an excellent representation of what makes a good vid:

- "Vogue" by Luminosity (http://tiny.cc/teachtech_7_10) which spread to the mainstream in 2007, brought new attention to fan vidding by being voted Best Online Video in *New York Magazine* bringing the very underground world of fan vidding and media literacy to the forefront and turning sexism in the movie *300* on it's head. Luminosity objectified the male characters in *300* for the female characters to admire, and Madonna was portrayed as the pagan goddess.
- "Buffy versus Edward: Twilight Remixed" by Jonathan McIntosh is inspired by vidding history, but is considered a political remix because it doesn't rely on music to narrate the story. It constructs a political message using the format of a television show, instead of a music video. This remix is a clever mashup that brings one of the all-time powerful female characters, Buffy the Vampire Slayer, up against Edward Cullen from *Twilight*, the popular book and film series, to portray a feminist critique of Edward's patriachal attitude (http://tiny.cc/teachtech_7_11).

PEDAGOGICAL IMPLICATIONS AND CLASSROOM PRACTICES

In his book, *Understanding Media,* Marshall McLuhan (1994) says that a medium is "any extension of ourselves," (p. 7) suggesting that a hammer extends our arm. Tools we have today, such as the ability to sample music, capture video, and edit media encourages students to use that which they are comfortable with to socially construct meanings of the world. Remixing allows us to find ways for people to connect around common interests and encourages the expertise of both youth and adults in the learning process, where contributing to knowledge building is the reward for their inputs.

We as teachers have a new role to play in the classroom. Taking the apprenticeship model, we cannot continue to be on the sidelines of participation in the new media environment. We have to participate as well to produce and create alongside our students and to become facilitators of their learning. We also need to realize that as teachers, we do not need to hold all the knowledge. Social media provides teachers an avenue to bring new knowledge into the classroom by inviting experts and other perspectives to the discussion. Where this used to be a costly field trip or stipend to bring someone in, we can now harness new media to create a globally connected world of participants. Our relationship with students is to offer guidance, establish mutually agreed upon norms in the classroom, and provide learning goals to accomplish. It is not about providing all the answers or giving them specific directions but instead giving our students a map for them to achieve. The idea of remixing might be foreign to the classroom, but there are ways to wade into participation.

Over the past few years, Project New Media Literacies located at University of Southern California's Annenberg School for Communication has developed curricula for use both in school and out of school. One of New Media Literacies's resources created is the Learning Library, a Web-based platform for teachers and students to collaborate, share, and design new knowledge by remixing media to serve their specific context or learning purpose (http://www.newmedialiteracies.org/library/). What's unique about using this platform in learning is it encourages both teachers and students alike to see and use media in a different context than what its original purpose was for.

For example, the Web site—One Million Monkeys Typing (http://www.1000000monkeys.com/) allows you to create collaborative stories or choose your own adventure narratives while harnessing the power of collective intelligence. The original intent of this site was for fun, a way to read, write, and publish your story ideas and have the audience participate and add to your ideas. One Million Monkeys Typing wasn't intended for the classroom but as teachers, we can remix its purpose and envision this site as an engaging tool to bring into the classroom to learn about history, reflect on our world, or develop our skills in storytelling. As teachers, we build the context, the learning objective.

The Learning Library is made up of two primary features, media elements and challenges and offers a robust set of tools and media-focused activities, which are designed to get learners (teachers and students alike) exploring and experimenting with the new media literacies and in the process, producing and sharing media-related activities (challenges) with each other.

New Media Literacies has seeded the Learning Library with the Media Makers Challenge Collection that features exemplary new media makers and offers members rich opportunities to learn about and practice the new media literacy skills. The goal of the Learning Library is that, ultimately, users will produce and share their own content with other members of the Learning Library.

Teachers in a pilot program used the challenges in a range of different ways. Some sought to gain a better understanding of the new media literacy concepts and practices. Others took the challenges directly into their classrooms and applied them to texts they were studying with their students. Most adapted the challenges to different curricular contexts, using core Learning Library principles to develop their own challenges. In short, the teachers appropriated and remixed the challenges for their own ends.

EXPRESSING CHARACTERS

The Learning Library challenge, Expressing Characters (http://newmedialiteracies .org/library/#/challenge/37), encourages exploration by the learner to consider how a character can be expressed through different media. Each media focuses unique elements of the character. For graphic illustrations, the learner has to think about movement, color, the character in one time and space. In video, the learner reflects on the character in motion, as a live being in a real world. In theater, learners have to think of the character as interacting with other characters. All three express character in very different ways but the goal with transmedia storytelling is to make each expression and present the *same* character. Similarity in multiplicity is a great way to get students to think about how an author expresses character and remains consistent.

Once a teacher learns how to navigate the Learning Library, it becomes a valuable resource for stimulating classroom participation in forming and "teaching" the lesson. Starting the lesson with a character the students already know will let them buy in to the class project and increase their willingness to add to the learning environment and objectives.

Integrating expressing characters into a larger lesson would be a way to incorporate popular culture into the classroom and could be tied to a character in a literary text that the class is reading by practicing transmedia storytelling. This could be used as an introductory activity or extension by having the class collaborate on creating a *Twitter feed* for the different characters from *The Great Gatsby* over a few weeks. How would Jay Gatsby speak? What if Jay Gatsby hadn't taken the blame for Myrtle's death, how would the others act? What would each of them write in 140 characters over a couple of days of storytelling, especially if this story were of today's American Dream instead of the 1920s?

This twitter activity is only one example of how to remix *Great Gatsby* but with the knowledge of music and video remix—what other ways can teachers extend this classic? For example, one English class encouraged music remixes of the *Great Gatsby* (http://tiny.cc/teachtech_7_12).

Visit http://tiny.cc/teachtech_7_13 to find out about expressing characters and other media makers' challenges.

ANALOG REMIX

For many of today's youth culture, remixing is native to the digital tools afforded to them. However, you do not need to have technology in order to encourage remixing in the classroom. Remixing, like all the new media literacies, is on the development of skills and mental models rather than on the tools and techniques of new media. So one can look across disciplines and see how they apply.

Project New Media Literacies has developed the Teachers' Strategy Guide: Reading in a Participatory Culture to study authorship in relation to a range of literary works, pushing us to reflect more deeply on how authors build upon the materials of their culture and in turn inspire others who follow to see the world in new ways. Theater director, Ricardo Pitts-Wiley, engaged incarcerated youth in a deeper understanding of the classic literature in Melville's *Moby-Dick* and was the inspiration for the strategy guide. Ricardo's process had youth adapt and interpret *Moby-Dick* for their language. What emerged from the process was *Moby-Dick: Then and Now*, a play that combines two narratives: the original Melville story, i.e., Ahab seeking revenge on the "great white whale," and a present-day narrative about urban youth on a quest to hunt down an elusive character named WhiteThing, which loosely represents the social and cultural forces surrounding the cocaine trade. By remixing the original text to the gang culture they knew and understood, these youths had a better understanding of the original. The original and the appropriated story were performed in parallel on stage, juxtaposing the language of the 19th century with the 21st century. As you can see from this example, Pitts-Wiley did not put technology first but instead helped to encourage a new mindset of how to read deeply the classic literature of *Moby-Dick*.

Learning to remix is a basic skill for the production of culture. By applying analog remixing techniques students become aware of the degree to which all cultural expression builds upon what has come before. One method to try in the classroom is William Burroughs' the **cutup method**. A *cutup* is performed by taking a finished text (printed on paper) and cutting it into pieces with a few or single words on each piece. The resulting pieces are then rearranged into a new text (Lombana, 2007).

Ask your students to bring in their favorite song lyrics to cut up and remix with other lyrics or poems in order to create something new based on a theme you suggest. For example in my recent gender and media course, I had my students remix women poets and music lyrics to represent what it means to be a feminist in today's media culture. As you can see from Aonya's example, there were certain works of art that she sampled from, such as Maya Angelou and Riot Grrrl's song lyrics from "Bikini

Kill," and then there were influences, such as a patriarchal view of society and Aonya representing herself as a Christian woman, that helped to shape her cutup.

Aonya McCruiston discusses her process of remixing the varied texts to interpret what she thinks it means to be a feminist today:

In my poem (http://tiny.cc/teachtech_7_14), I wanted to sample life-defining texts and create something that reflected my thoughts and concerns about the future of the feminist movement and my involvement in it.

I wanted to take extremely tough sounding lyrics about revolution and reaffirm my identity as a woman. I think it's easy to take for granted that men are the revolutionaries since so much of history defines them as the owners of all its great revolutions, such as American, communist, and industrial.

I wanted to make a statement that women do change the world, which is why I added the truth quote about Eve. Women have been changing the world ever since, but I don't think it gets recognized enough. My generation might disagree, but I think that giving women a voice that is at least some say in all aspects of public and private life definitely revolutionized the American way of life. However, I think that there's still a lot more to be done which is why I added that the revolution's coming.

I believe that equality is obtainable.

Little girls have been raised with the idea that they can do anything they want. More women are graduating with more degrees than ever before. I think there will come a point when these educated, confident women will fight back against inequality.

I think we're all just waiting for some driving force, but I don't know what that is.

I ended my poem with the Audre Lorde quote "wondering which me will survive all these liberations" from "Who Said It Was Simple." In it she seems to be worried about losing her identity, but when I wrote it, I was actually wondering how I will change if a third/fourth wave does come? Do I have to change? Are there aspects of me that are unfeminist? I don't know the answers to those questions, but I think the answers will come as the feminist movement and I continue to grow and change.

ORIGINAL VERSUS REMIX

Becoming familiar with current remixes is a way to help you understand the aesthetic. Encourage your students to bring in remixes, mashups, collages, and recuts that interest them and share these links that provide a history of each music video remix genre and offer sample remixes to review. As you review examples with your students, have a discussion relating the original source to the remixed version.

Examples of fan-made music video remixes

- *Vidding* see examples, check out http://www.video24–7.org/video/vidding.html
- *Machinimists* are artists who use three-dimensional graphic engines from video games. To learn about fan machinima and see examples, check out http://www.video24–7.org/video/machinima.html
- *Political Remix Videos* (PRVs) use video clips from popular media such as new clips, speeches, TV shows, and movies to convey alternative messages not just on political structures but on social issues as well. To learn about PRVs, check out http://www.video24–7.org/video/political_remix.html
- *Anime Music Videos* are edited animated Japanese cartoons that add to a song or tell a story. To learn about AMVs, check out http://www.video24–7.org/video/anime_music_video.html

Using the following template, have students identify the original source and in review of the remix share the media influences and the media that was sampled from the original to create the remix.

Remix Template:

_____ is the remix; _____ are the influences of the remix.

The remix is inspired by and appropriates from the influences (media content) by sampling _____ (elements).

Example:

The film *Shrek* is the remix; *fairy tales* are the influences of the remix.

The remix is inspired by and appropriates from the influences (media content) by sampling characters (such as an evil lord) and situations (such as sleeping princess).

Template from NML's TSG: Reading in a Participatory Culture

CREATE A REMIX

Through peer-based learning and supportive adults in a model that is defined more as an apprenticeship community, teens are acquiring educational experiences they are a part of their larger learning ecology that expands beyond the classroom walls. This is the most important pedagogical practice I can suggest for all teachers—*get involved* and be part of the promises of this learning ecology.

You don't have to learn on your own or feel your way through this blindly by yourself. There is a community out there waiting for you to participate and not just as a lurker on the sidelines anymore. Use this as an opportunity to make time in your schedule to create change in your classroom.

Each genre of video music remixes has a community and offers opportunities to begin participating in remix.

- *Total Recut* (http://www.totalrecut.com/index.php) provides online resources and social networking opportunities for fans and creators of video recuts, remixes and mashups.
- *Political Remix Video* (http://www.politicalremixvideo.com/) hosts a blog to critique power structures, deconstruct social myths, and challenge dominant media messages, as well as share the most innovative and inspiring political remix videos.
- *Organization of Transformative Works* (OTW) (http://transformative-works.org/projects/vidding-history) supports all fan works and provides a history of vidding as well as many projects that document this culture.
- *Machinima* (http://www.machinima.com/) showcases thousands of trailers, videos, gameplay, montages. and original machinima using game engines such as *World of Warcraft* and *Sims2*.
- *Anime Music Videos* (http://www.animemusicvideos.org/home/home.php) welcomes all to share, learn, and create AMVs together, offering many technical guides on how to acquire the knowledge and techniques to create anime music videos.

SHARE YOUR INSIGHTS, STORIES, AND EXPERIENCES!

We want to hear from you. Join our community of teachers by visiting our Web site (http://projectnml.ning.com/) and posting your responses to this chapter. Here are some questions to address when reading a remix:

1. What constitutes the primary source material?

2. What is the media form of the remix?

3. What is the context of the remix?

4. What elements of the primary source material are being remixed?

5. Are the works of the same genre or different ones? How do you know?

6. What techniques are deployed in reworking the original material?

7. What is the intended purpose of the remix?

8. How does the remix build from, add to, or alter the cultural meaning of the original work?

REFERENCES AND HELPFUL RESOURCES

Clinton, K., McWilliams, J., Jenkins, H., & Kolos, H. (2010). Reading in a participatory culture: A model for expanding the ELA domain by bringing in new media mindsets and practices. Project New Media Literacies. Work in progress.

Coppa, F. (2008). Women, Star Trek and the early development of fannish vidding. *Transformative Works and Cultures* (Vol. 1). Retrieved on February 17, 2010, from http://journal.transformativeworks.org/index.php/twc/article/view/44/64

Driscoll, K. (2009). Stepping your game up: Technical innovation among young people of color in hip-hop (Master's thesis MIT). Comparative Media Studies.

Ito, M., Baumer, S., Bittani, M., boyd, d., Cody, R., Herr-Stephenson, B., Horst, H. A., Lange, P. A., Mahendran, D., Martinez, K., Pascoe, C. J., Perkel, D., Robinson, L., Sims, C., & Tripp, L. (2010). *Hanging out, messing around, and geeking out: Kids living and learning with new media.* Cambridge: MIT Press.

Jenkins, H. (2006). Learning by remixing. *Media Shift.* Retrieved July, 13, 2006, from http://www.pbs.org/mediashift/2006/07/learning-by-remixing194.html

Jenkins, H. (with Purushotma, R., Weigel, M., Clinton, K., & Robison, A. J.). (2006). *Confronting the challenges of participatory culture: Media education for the 21st century.* Cambridge: Macarthur/MIT Press. (http://newmedialiteracies.org/files/working/NMLWhitePaper.pdf)

Kelley, W. (2008). Reading Moby-Dick through the decades. Expert Voices, Reading in a Participatory Culture, Teacher's Strategy Guide, Project New Media Literacies. Work in Progress.

Lankshear, C., & Knobel, M. (2006). *New literacies: Changing knowledge in the classroom.* London: Open University Press.

Lenhart, A., & Madden, M. (2005). *Teen content creators and consumers.* Pew Internet & American Life Project. Available at http://www.pewinternet.org/Reports/2005/Teen-Content-Creators-and-Consumers.aspx

Lenhard, A., Madden, M., Smith, A., & Macgill, A. (2007). *Teens and social media.* Pew Internet & American Life Project. Available at http://www.pewinternet.org/Reports/2007/Teens-and-Social-Media.aspx

Lombana, A. (2007). *Appropriation, transformation and remix: Cut-ups.* Exemplar Library Lesson.

McLuhan, M. (1994). *Understanding media: The extensions of man.* New York: McGraw-Hill.

Pitts-Wiley, R. (2008). Reading Moby-Dick as a creative artist. *Expert Voices, Reading in a Participatory Culture, Teacher's Strategy Guide.* Project New Media Literacies.

Project New Media Literacies Resources: http://projectnml.ning.com

- Learning Library
- Teachers' Strategy Guide: Reading in a Participatory Culture
- Teachers' Strategy Guide: Reading in a Participatory Culture, Expert Voices
- Our Space: Being a Responsible Citizen of the Digital World (a collaboration with Harvard's GoodPlay Project)

Pryor, T. (2008). *Hip-hop.* Retrieved January 14, 2008, from http://worldmusic .nationalgeographic.com/worldmusic/view/page.basic/genre/content.genre/ hip_hop_730

Rauschenberg, R. (1964). *Retroactive I.* [Oil and silkscreen ink on canvas]. Wadsworth Athenuem, Hartford, Connecticut.

Thompson, C. (2009). *The new literacy.* Retrieved August 24, 2009, from http://www.wired.com/techbiz/people/magazine/17-09/st_thompson

Conclusion

Jessica K. Parker

Whether or not we choose to be, we are actors in the drama of technological progress.

—Andrea Oseas

New media, which incorporates the Internet as well as cell phones, video games, instant messaging, and virtual worlds, has come to stand for more than just access to information. New media has been defined in part by the active, economically feasible, and widely accessible participation of students (and others) to produce, remix, mashup, and recirculate multimodal texts. *Teaching Tech-Savvy Kids: Bringing Digital Media Into the Classroom, Grades 5–12* highlights the most current research on youth participation in new media environments and their peer-based learning practices. Insights from classroom teachers, counselors, and other voices throughout education complement these research-based vignettes to provide an account of learning and literacy in the 21st century. This collaborative work is a call to educators to see themselves as "actors" in the emerging field of new media and learning and to enter into discussions concerning technological change.

Unfortunately, some educators seem to be drunk on the hope of new technologies and its potential to reshape literacy and learning in an institution which appears to them to be anarchistic, while others point to a history of educational technology that tends to repeat itself as one unsuccessful medium after another is labeled the antidote to all educational ills.

Taking either side simply leaves classroom teachers alone to make tough choices as how to consolidate the latest research and negotiate whether or not it maps onto best teaching practices. It is essential that teachers take on leadership roles within the field of new media and learning in order to move from polemic views to more grounded discussions based on merging theory with practice. Teachers have a stake in understanding technological change because we, along with our students, will be directly affected by alterations to policy, funding, and current trends.

RETURNING TO THE THREE TOUGH QUESTIONS

In the Introduction of this book, I asked readers to consider three tough questions:

1. What does learning look like in the 21st century?

2. What does literacy look like in the 21st century?

3. What is knowledge in the 21st century? (Or what does it mean to *know* something in our mediated culture?)

These questions do not have simplistic answers. In fact, to grapple with these questions is to be a contemporary educator: to view learning as complex and socially constructed, to be open to new understandings of communication, and to appreciate a diversity of learning experiences. The excitement, sleekness, and allure of contemporary technology should not suggest that educators only have to incorporate laptops and webcams into their classrooms for students to magically acquire technical skills and understand academic concepts. For educators who are interested in creating engaging and motivating curricula in a digital era, technology is not at the core of pedagogy; at the core of pedagogy are the learning, knowledge, and critical thinking of a discipline (Beatham, 2008–2009). As Andrew Tucker (2008) argues, "Educational principles should drive change efforts, not technology" (p. 205). Therefore, it behooves educators to revisit and rethink key educational principles starting with notions of school-based learning and literacy and a definition of knowledge as static and unchanging. Through such analyses we can discuss how best to create new learning environments and refurbish traditional ones.

At the same time educators should address that norms regarding learning, literacy, and knowledge are inherently connected to teacher's roles, student agency, and traditional notions of authority and expertise. By allowing ourselves to take a reflective stance, we can confront how revisiting and broadening learning and literacy affects classroom practice. For instance, issues of ownership and personal creativity are connected to student media making. Integrating video production (covered in Chapter 3) into a classroom can flip traditional notions of authority and expertise on its head. Thus, this situation requires a shift in thinking: from a teacher teaching a lesson on video production to a teacher taking a journey with students through video production.

Ito et al. (2008) argue that educational institutions need to keep pace with the rapid changes introduced by digital media in order to stay relevant. In agreement, research from the National Research Council and the Institute of Medicine (2004) offers that a literate citizen must now have a higher level of critical and analytical skills than was true even a decade ago. With these pressures confronting us, educators must turn to frameworks for learning that place students' motivation and engagement at the forefront. New media environments offer a unique starting point to do just this. Participatory culture, networked publics, and peer-based learning are important tools for understanding the intense enjoyment and sustaining intrigue of new media environments.

I'VE READ THE BOOK. NOW WHERE DO I BEGIN?

You read the book. You are armed with the latest research. And you want to grapple with the issues the book raised but don't know where to begin. Below is a list of ideas that range from creating change at an institutional level to fostering change on an individual scale.

- Read the technology vision at your school (if you have one; if not, go forth and create) and see if it is in need of revision.
- Does your school have a literacy vision? If not, propose that a small number of teachers with you leading the way would like to think through such a project. If your school has one, are there areas that need revision? (And how can educators link a school's literacy vision with its technology vision?)
- Join the technology committee at your school (or start one yourself) and plan for both short- and long-term change.
- Reach out to a local media organization or an after-school program focused on youth culture and see if it possible to establish a mutually beneficial relationship.
- Start a reading group focused on new media technologies and education literature and blog about your discussions.
- Embrace your inner teacher-researcher and document your efforts at integrating an idea from this book.

(Continued)

(Continued)

- Dream about alternative learning spaces centered on broadened notions of learning and literacy and be brave enough to share your ideas online.
- Our profession is known to burn people out. Don't try and tackle these technological changes by yourself: Reach out and find like-minded educators with whom to collaborate and create partnerships.
- Think of education as a process of guiding kids' participation in public life more generally—a public life that includes social, recreational, and civic engagement (Ito et al., 2008). Share your ideas on your own educational wiki.
- Continue to be curious about new media environments and youth culture and discuss your insights with colleagues.
- Find a student who seems to be geeking out over an interest-based topic. Take this student out to lunch and ask them about their experiences: What is so great about their time spent online? What keeps them motivated to contribute?
- Go to a youth film festival even if you don't know any of the students participating.
- Start your own Facebook profile and friend at least five people.
- Upload a video response to YouTube.
- Be bold. Go to Wikipedia and create an entry regarding your school.
- Read the latest blog posts by danah boyd and Henry Jenkins and post your opinion.
- Find the self-proclaimed **Luddites** at your school and tell them that you are more than willing to walk them through some of this high-tech stuff.

Have other ideas for creating change in your school or for personally embracing technological change? Share your ideas on the online community forum at www.teachingtechsavvykids.com.

CHANGING SCHOOL CULTURE

When I first heard that researchers from the University of California, Berkeley, and University of Southern California were studying kids and their informal learning practices, practices that were primarily found in the home, in after-school programs, and other venues outside of school walls, I was frustrated that schools were not the sites where learning and participation with new media took place for students. These types of fun, experimental, peer-based practices were happening outside classrooms. My initial frustration quickly turned to curiosity and excitement when I listened to Mimi Ito discuss her experiences researching *learning* in out-of-school settings as compared to her experiences with *learning* in schools. In a video posted on YouTube titled, "Why Time Spent Online Is Important for Teen Development," Ito (2008) states,

I think the potential is really there for us to be raising a new generation of young people who have grown up with technologies that allow them to pursue self-directed learning on their own terms and on their own time schedules. This is very different from how kids learn in school, where they are handed a set body of knowledge they are asked to master and the expertise really resides in the teacher. When kids go online in these more informal contexts where they are pursuing their interests, they can really go, look around and connect with knowledge, people, online communities that really enable them to tailor and customize what they want to learn and when they want to learn it. And that is tremendously empowering for kids and motivating for them to learn.

Watch Ito's video interview at http://tiny.cc/teachtech_8_1 and also visit the MacArthur Foundation's Digital Media and Learning Initiative at http://digitallearning.macfound.org or its YouTube channel at http://www.youtube.com/user/macfound.

Ito's comparison of informal, online environments with traditional school environments struck me as insightful and thought provoking. I realize Ito is speaking in a general sense and that not all schools promote knowledge as a set body of information to be mastered or that not all teachers present themselves as the "expert" in class. But it is true, as she points out, that students want to pursue subjects that interest them and can become immersed in an online, networked environment in which to *connect* around interest-based subjects and friendship-driven practices. Teachers, parents, and administrators can attest to the massive amounts of time and energy students put into playing video games, texting, writing blogs, surfing the Internet, role playing, and making media. These activities are "tremendously empowering for kids and motivating for them" (Ito, 2008). And teachers usually agree that motivating kids is a fundamental aspect of the job.

Ito's words should also push teachers to think about student empowerment—that is the ability of students to choose an area of interest, pull from both online and offline resources other than a textbook and feel a sense of control over their education. Students are heavily invested in online communities because of this. Hence, these online spaces become about the students themselves—about how they came to define their creative abilities and their personal hopes and interests—with positive results for growth and learning.

Many secondary students look forward to increased autonomy; it is a sign that they are maturing intellectually and that their interests are acknowledged and respected. But increased autonomy should not imply that they seek only independence. In fact, new media environments are examples of the degree to which young adults also want to be part of a community of learners. For classroom teachers, these issues translate into offering students increased autonomy while supporting them with collaborative spaces, both face-to-face and online, designing assignments that are flexible in terms of topic and form, and providing access to richer learning resources (Kleiman, 2000). Additionally, inquiry, interdisciplinary, and project-based learning can provide avenues for deep, participatory learning.

Broadening the notion of education to include multiple facets of knowledge and expertise beyond the classroom opens up space for intergenerational relationships (Ito et al., 2008; Jenkins, 2006). Listening and learning from youth is our best response to a mediated culture. As adults, we have an important role to play in helping kids pursue their interests, discuss ethics of online behavior and model healthy and productive friendships. Since notions of expertise and authority can be tested and even reversed when it comes to digital media and youth, we have the ability to be part of reciprocal relationships based on learning and enjoyment and not limit ourselves to traditional power dynamics within school.

Education is not only about learning specific content. Arguably, education is more about developing and navigating relationships: personal relationships to learning, social relationships among peers and teachers, and relationships to the world. It is my hope that educators, classroom teachers, and students can create the relationships needed to promote characteristics of new media environments in a moment in which the potential exists for school-based notions of literacy and learning to serve many more functions and therefore to be more deeply implicated in thinking processes (Hull & Schultz, 2002). In fact, being *educated* and *literate* in a digital age depends on this.

REFERENCES AND HELPFUL RESOURCES

Beatham, M. (2008–2009). Tools of inquiry: Separating tool and task to promote true learning. *Journal of Educational Technology Systems, 37*(1), 61–70.

Hull, G., & Schultz, K. (Eds.). (2002). *School's out: Bridging out-of-school literacies with classroom practice.* New York: Teachers College Press.

Ito, M. (2008). *Why time spent online is important for teen development.* Retrieved on August 25, 2008 from http://www.youtube.com/watch?v=58X7YPebJVo

Ito, M., Horst, H. A., Bittanti, M., boyd, d., Herr-Stephenson, B., Lange, P. G., Pascoe, C., J., & Robinson, L. (with Baumer, S., Cody, R., Mahendran, D., Martínez, K., Perkel, D., Sims, C., & Tripp, L.). (2008). *Living and learning with new media: Summary findings from the Digital Youth Project.* The John D. and Catherine T. MacArthur Foundation Report on Digital Media and Learning. Download the report at http://digitalyouth.ischool.berkeley.edu/report

Jenkins, H. (with Clinton, K., Purushotma, R., Robison, A., & Weigel, M.). (2006). *Confronting the challenges of participatory culture: Education for the 21st century.* The John D. and Catherine T. MacArthur Foundation. Retrieved August 18, 2007, from http://digitallearning.macfound.org

Kleiman, G. (2000). Myths and realities about technology in K–12 schools. In D. Gordon (Ed.), *The digital classroom: How technology is changing the way we teach and learn.* (pp. 7–15). Cambridge, MA: Harvard Education Letter.

National Research Council and the Institute of Medicine. (2004). *Engaging schools: Fostering high school students' motivation to learn.* Committee on Increasing High School Students' Engagement and Motivation to Learn. Board on Children, Youth, and Families, Division of Behavioral and Social Sciences and Education. Washington, DC: National Academic Press.

Oseas, A. (2003). Introduction: An invitation to ask ,"What if . . .?" In D. Gordon (Ed.), *The digital classroom: How technology is changing the way we teach and learn* (pp. 3–6). Cambridge, MA: Harvard Education Letter.

Tucker, A. (2008). *Transforming schools with technology: How smart use of digital tools helps achieve six key education goals.* Cambridge, MA: Harvard Education Press.

Glossary

Anime (n): Japanese-style animation that emphasizes visual styles

Appropriation (n): the ability to meaningfully sample and remix media content

Asynchronous communication (n): online communication in which both parties do not have to be present at the same time. Information is saved and can be viewed at a later time. This includes sending e-mail, blogging, and responding to posts on bulletin boards or in online forums

Synchronous communication (n): the opposite of *asynchronous communication* in that two or more people communicate at the same time but not necessarily in the same place. Examples include Web conferencing, instant messaging, and online chat rooms

Avatar (n): a computerized representation of a person usually as a two-dimensional icon. View examples from Mr. Freccia's avatar in WikiFreccia in Chapter 4 and Rik Panganiban's in the What Are Virtual Worlds section in Chapter 6

Blog or **weblog** (n): a Web site usually maintained by an individual or an organization with regular entries related to the theme of the blog. These entries can include commentary, descriptions of events, or other materials such as photographs or videos

Blogging (v): used to describe the act of maintaining or adding content to a blog. Visit danah boyd's blog at http://www.apophenia.com/ or the MacArthur Foundation's blog titled Spotlight on Digital Media and Learning at http://spotlight.macfound.org. One of Jessica's personal favorites is Henry Jenkin's blog at http://www.henryjenkins.org

Collage (n): a combination of different things to create meaning

Collective intelligence (n): the ability to pool knowledge and compare notes with others toward a common goal

Copyright (n): a legal concept used by *most* national governments that gives the creator of an original work exclusive rights to it, usually for a limited period of time. It gives the copyright holder the right to be credited for the work, to determine who (if anyone) may adapt the work to other forms, to determine who may perform the work, to benefit financially from the work, and other related rights

Creative Commons (n): a nonprofit organization devoted to expanding the range of creative works available for others to build upon legally and to share. This organization has released several copyright licenses to provide more choice in ownership for creators to share their work

Cutup method (n): a remix method performed by taking a finished text (printed on paper) and cutting it into pieces with a few or single words on each piece. The resulting pieces are then rearranged into a new text

Designer (n): someone who designs how a webpage or video game looks and how it functions. Taking a position as a ***designer*** means that you are taking a step back from reading the content and trying to understand how a wiki, Web page, video game or any digital content is designed to look and function

DJ (disc jockey) (n): a person who selects and plays recorded music, no matter the source, for an audience

Fair use (n): a defense used in cases to decide whether or not someone has violated copyright laws. The idea of fair use of materials began as a way to allow for people to use copyrighted materials in very specific ways: "criticism, comment, news reporting, teaching (including making multiple copies for classroom use), scholarship, or research" (Copyright Act of 1976, 17 U.S.C. § 107). Whether or not using the copyrighted materials is fair use is determined by four principles, found in the Copyright Act of 1976:

- The purpose and character of the use, including whether such use is of a commercial (for profit) nature or is for nonprofit, educational purposes
- The nature of the copyrighted work
- The amount and substantiality of the portion used in relation to the copyrighted work as a whole
- The effect of the use upon the potential market for or value of the copyrighted work

Fandom (n): a community of people who share an interest. Fandoms can range from fans of a particular sports team to fans of a television show, movie or book series. Online fandoms are most often based around media

Flagging (n): the flag button on a particular YouTube video alerts the administrator's attention that a video may contain inappropriate material such as excessive violence. YouTube's Web page says that it does not automatically remove a video that is flagged, but it will investigate the issue

Friendship-driven practices (n): a phrase used by Ito et al. (2008) in their final report, Kids' Informal Learning with Digital Media. It refers to the networks that are youth's primary source for affiliation, friendship, and romantic partners (pp. 9–10). Visit http://digitalyouth.ischool .berkeley.edu/report to download the final report

Game world (n): a fictional setting in which characters interact to accomplish certain goals as defined by the parameters of the game

Instant message (IM) (n) or **instant messaging (IMing)** (v): a type of real-time communication based on typing someone a message through a network such as Yahoo! Messenger or AOL Messenger. It is a form of *synchronous communication*

Interest-driven practices (n): a phrase used by Ito et al. (2008) in their final report, Kids' Informal Learning with Digital Media. It refers to networks that support youth and their specialized activities and interests (p. 10). Visit http://digitalyouth.ischool.berkeley.edu/report to download the final report

Linkshells (n): player-created communities that happen in-game and require invitation, have dedicated chat channels, and often have their own organized activities. They are similar to guilds of other *MMORPGs*

Luddite (n): connotes a person or group who opposes technological progress. For a discussion of the social movement of British textile artisans known as Luddites, visit http://en.wikipedia.org/wiki/Luddite

Mashup (v): to borrow elements from a number of different sources to create a new message

Massively multiplayer online role playing game (**MMORPG**) (n): this genre of role-playing games has garnered global popularity due to the large number of players who can interact with one another in virtual worlds. *World of Warcraft* boasts over 11 million players worldwide; read about Andy Maul's experiences with the game in Chapter 5

Meme (n): a small, flexible bit of cultural information that is shared in informal (or viral) ways (See Chapter 5 for an example.)

Multiuser dungeon or **domain (MUD)** (n): in the very early days of the Internet (before it was the World Wide Web), MUDs provided players with a virtual space for social interaction based on textual commands and description

Networked public (n): a networked public is both the space constructed through networked technologies and the people who are connected by those technologies. Networked publics are spaces that share many of the same properties as unmediated publics like parks, cafes, malls, or parking lots

Offline resources (n): resources that are accessed somewhere other than the Internet or other online services. Some examples are books or journals in a library, encyclopedias, and hard copy papers

Online resources (n): resources accessed on the Internet, online services, or internal networks. Examples include Wikipedia, articles on the Web, and reference materials

Participatory cultures (n): a term used by Professor Henry Jenkins to describe groups that encourage contribution of cultural material (such as fan fiction or videos) to the group. People often find encouragement and support and feel that their contribution will be valued

Post or **posting** (v): the act of sending an electronic message, article, or video to a site. In most instances this allows other *users* to view the posting. Patricia G. Lange discusses how she posts her videos on her *video blogs* in Chapter 3

Recut (v): a parody trailer for a movie created by editing footage from that movie or from its original trailers and thus is a form of mashup

Relational perspective (n): the view that technological practices are bound to social life and not simply "neutral" skills

Remix (v): to take an existing work and make a new version by including new elements such as audio or narration

Remix (n): a new form of media inspired and adapted from an original source

Search engine (n): a Web search engine designed to search for information on the Internet. General examples include Google.com and Yahoo.com, but even YouTube can have its own search engine embedded into its Web site. For a brief history of search engines, visit http://en.wikipedia.org/wiki/Search_Engines

Simulation (n): the ability to interpret and construct dynamic models of real-world processes

Social network sites (SNSs) (n): Web-based sites that allow individuals to construct a public or semipublic profile within a bounded system, articulate a list of other users with whom they share a connection, and view and traverse their list of connections and those made by others within the system. Popular examples include MySpace and Facebook

Traffic (n): the amount of activity a Web site such as YouTube receives during a given period of time

Tweet (n): a short text-based post that is no more than 140 characters sent to a group of people. It is a form of micro-blogging and used through the social networking site Twitter

Twitter feed (n): a series of tweets similar to a threaded discussion by one or more authors

User (n): someone who uses a computer to access Web sites or logs into e-mail accounts. Users are different from *designers* in that they are interacting with the site for its content and resources and are not necessarily attentive to the organization or function of the site itself

Video blog or **vlog** (n): a version of a blog or weblog, a personal video site that uses video as the main way to communicate messages. Although it foregrounds videos, video blogs often contain other media such as photographs and text comments that people post to a video. Video blogging includes many different genres that range from the professionally-oriented narrative with actors, scripts, and editing to more diary or communicative forms in which people address a camera directly to share intimate thoughts. There are video blogs centered around certain themes, such as citizen journalism, how-to videos for tasks such as cooking, and video blogs targeted toward youth. Visit Patricia G. Lange's video blog at http://www.youtube.com/user/AnthroVlog

Virtual worlds (n): computer-generated, two- or three-dimensional, multi-user spaces, where people interact with each other and the environment through their *avatars*. Some examples of virtual worlds are *Second Life*, *Whyville*, *World of Warcraft*, and *Webkins*. These environments often mimic characteristics of the real world, including having land, water, space, gravity, buildings, and even weather. Read Rik Panganiban's vignette on virtual worlds in Chapter 6 and visit http://www.rezed.org to learn more about virtual worlds and education

Visualization (v): the ability to interpret and create data representations for the purposes of expressing ideas, finding patterns, and identifying trends

Wiki (n): a collaborative Web site that allows users to add and edit content

Index

Page references followed by (figure) indicate an illustrated figure.

Active reading activity, 104–105
Active writing, 105–106
Adventures with Role-Playing
    Games (Maul), 85–86
Aeneid (epic), 145
Amanti, C., 3, 122
American Film Institute, 151
American Library Association, 134
Analog remix, 161–162
Angelou, M., 161
Anime Music Videos, 163, 164
Anime series, 88
Annenberg School for
    Communication (USC), 159
AnthroVlog, 39–40 (figure), 42
AOL Instant Messenger, 100
Appropriation concept, 148, 149, 154
Are Kids Different Because of Digital Media?
    (YouTube), 6
Aristophanes, 103
Arya, D. J., 96, 98
Associated Press (AP), 156
Asynchronous conversations, 21
Asynchronously remixing, 148
Atticus Factor, 80 (figure)
Aufderheide, P., 155
Avatars
    creating a virtual world, 123
    Kalipea's Journey (Pfister), 116–122
    Quest Atlantis: A Game-Based Curriculum
        (Barab) use of, 124–130
    See also Virtual worlds
Ayers, P., 78
Ayers, R., 25, 27

Barab, S. A., 115, 124
Barman, C. R., 97

Barnes, M., 87
Baron, N., 5
Beach, R., 109
Beastie Boys, 154
Beatham, M., 49
Beathman, M., 168
Bebo
    student story on their experience
        with, 20
    youth space created by, 19
Becquerel, H., 97
Bedtime stories
    creativity of, 144
    remembering the magic of, 143–144
Behavior. *See* Student behavior
Berkeley Repertory Theater, 103
Berry, M., 10, 113, 131, 132
"Bikini Kill," 161–162
The Birds (Aristophanes), 103
Bits and Bytes of Research
    Class Matters: Purchasing a Family
        Computer (Finn), 138–139
    description of, 23
    Interactions with Media at Home (Horst),
        57–58
    Safe Spaces to Connect: GLBTQ Teens and
        New Media (Pascoe), 23–24
Blake, W., 145
Bledsoe, G., 100
Blogger (Web site), 109
Blogging activities, 106–109
*Blogs, Wikis, Podcasts, and Other
    Powerful Web Tools for Classrooms*
    (Richardson), 79, 109
"Both Sides Now" (Kandy Fong), 157
Bowker, G. C., 97
boyd, d., 15, 16, 19, 32, 36

Boyd-Davis, S., 115
Brave New World blog prompt, 107
Break the Barriers, 136
Breaking Through the Mystique of Science
    (Arya), 96–98
Brecht, B., 103
Buckingham, D., 13, 63
"Buffy versus Edward: Twilight Remixed"
    (McIntosh's video remix), 158
Burbules, N., 2
Burroughs, W., 161
Byrne, D., 154

Callister, T., 2
Carver, G. W., 97–98
ccMixter, 154–155
Center for Digital Storytelling, 52
Center for Social Media, 54
Chappell, E., 115
Checklist for Wikipedia Evaluation, 78–79
Chronicles of England, Scotland, and Ireland
    (Holinshed), 145
Civic engagement YouTube videos, 45–48,
    49–50
Clarissa (student), highlights of story of, 8
Class Matters: Purchasing a Family
    Computer (Finn), 138–139
Class Video Page project, 53
Classroom activities
    Class Video Page, 53
    Digital Storytelling, 52
    Personal Video Essay, 54, 55
    Print Advertisement project, 54
    Public Service Announcement
        (PSA), 53
    Report the News, 53
    text-based projects, 54
    Textbook Entry project, 54
    video projects, 52–55
    for Wikipedia use, 77–81
    See also Role-playing activities; Teacher
        activities
Classroom practices
    media technology observations
        applied to, 33–35
    pedagogical implications of
        remixing used for, 158–160
    pedagogical implications of role-playing
        used for, 95–109
    pedagogical implications of SSN used for,
        27–31
    pedagogical implications of virtual worlds
        used for, 130–139
    pedagogical implications of Wikipedia
        used for, 76–77

pedagogical implications of
    YouTube for, 48–52
then and *now* comparison
    discussion, 34
Code of Best Practices for Fair Use in Media
    Literacy Education, 155
Collaboration
    media productions as opportunities
        for, 56
    One Million Monkeys Typing project for
        creating stories, 159
    script writing activities, 100
    Virtual World Building course
        (UC Berkeley) use of, 132–134
    Wikipedia's nature of, 71–72
Collage of images, 146
Collective intelligence, 148
Combines series (Rauschenberg), 146
Comments
    functions of, 19
    as SSN feature, 16, 18–19
Communication
    examining how new media technologies
        impact, 2
    feedback, 55–56, 94–95
    social network sites (SNS), 16–19,
        29–31
Communities
    fan fiction, 88, 94–95
    MUDs (multiuser dungeons), 88
    role-playing, 88
    virtual, 135
Community of learners, xiii, 7–9, 49,
    54-55, 71, 115, 172
Conlay D., 80
Copyright issues, 55, 59, 155–156
"The Cost of Copyright Confusion" (Hobbs,
    Jaszi, and Aufderheide), 155
Counselor's perspective, Escalating
    Emotions: Social Networking Sites and
    Youth (Lauriks), 29–31
Countless Hours of Freedom (Navarro),
    43–44
Crawford, A., 102
Creative Commons, 154–156
Cuban, L., 63
Culture Clash, 103
Curie, M., 97
Curie, P., 97
Curriculum
    creating space for peer/adult feedback to
        students, 55–56
    Global Kids' *Second Life*, 134
    how to begin using new media/new
        digital, 169–170

integrating social network issues into, 28–29
interest-based topics used in YouTube, 49
Project New Media Literacies on including new media literacies to, 149
Quest Atlantis: A Game-Based Curriculum (Barab), 124–130
theory on hidden educational, 144–145
Cutup method, 161–162

Dance Dance Revolution (video game), 139
Day for Night (film), 42
Deep participatory learning, 98–99
Design/designers (virtual world), 131, 134–135, 137–138Dido, 151
Digital audio recording software, 151, 153 (figure)
Digital Generation Project 2009, 146
Digital media
  description of, 4–5
  how to begin teaching using, 169–170
  learning implications of, 5–6
  as social-cultural forms (Buckingham), 13
  See also New media technologies
Digital Storytelling project, 52
Digital Youth Network (Chicago), 147
DJ Spooky, 150
Dondlinger, M. J., 115
"Drabble" writing, 106
Driscoll, K., 147
Dungeons and Dragons, 84–85, 86–87

Educators
  becoming familiar with social networking sites, 25
  Blogging 101, 106–109
  getting started on your own profile, 26–27
  how to begin teaching using new media and digital media, 169–170
  media production in school, 49, 52
  online resources on virtual worlds for, 134
  opportunities to tap into peer-based learning, 8–9
  TeacherTube.com to share with other, 102
  tough questions about 21st century learning for, 2–4, 168–169
  Wikispaces for, 79–81
  YouTube is banned. What do I do now?, 60–62
  See also Schools; Teachers sharing stories
Educause, 114
Ellison, N. B., 16
Eminem, 151

Emotional escalation issue, 29–31
Enciso, P., 98
Engaging Schools: Fostering High School Students' Motivation to Learn, 122–123
Escalating Emotions: Social Networking Sites and Youth (Lauriks), 29–31
Expressing Characters (Learning Library challenge), 160

Facebook
  meme on, 100–101
  peer groups of, 7
  a teacher's perspective on, 25–26
  youth space created by, 19
  See also Social network sites (SNS)
Fair use concept, 156
Fairey, S., 156
Fan fiction
  a beginner's guide to, 92–93
  beta-edited requirements of, 94
  "drabble" writing of, 106
  Harry Potter, 91–94
  "shipper fic" of, 92
Fan fiction communities
  Live Journal, 88, 94
  social aspects of, 94–95
Fan vidders, 157
Fan-made music video remixes, 163
Fandom (*Harry Potter*), 91
FanFiction.net, 93
Faraway Lands (role-playing site), 89–91
Feedback
  characteristics of new media environments, 8–10
  creating space for providing students with, 55–56
  fan fiction communities role in giving, 94–95
  in the production of digital video, 44
FictionAlley.org, 93
Final Cut Pro (software), 44
Final Fantasy XI (virtual world), 116–122
Finamore, L., 135, 136
Finding Wikipedia "*Before* it was Cool" (Robinson), 69–71
Finn, M., 138
Flagging YouTube videos, 40
Fleischer, S., 87
Flickr, 105
Fong, K., 157
Foreman, N., 115
Freccia, B., 79–80 (figure)
Freire, P., vii, 123
Friend-ship driven practices, 7, 8, 23

Friends list
functions of, 18
as SSN feature, 16, 18

Game world
MMORPG (massively multiplayer online
role-playing game), 84, 86,
87–88, 109
role-playing game characters in a, 84
social experience provided by, 84–87
See also Role-playing activities
GarageBand (software), 154
Garcia, M., 155–156
Gay teens, 23–24
Gee, J. P., 130
George Lucas Educational Foundation, 146
GLBTQ teens, 23–24
Global Kids' *Second Life* curriculum, 134
Gonzalez, N., 3, 122
Gonzalez, R., 135, 136
Good Morning America (TV show), 47
Goodall, J., 98
Google Chat, 100
Google Groups, 34
Google search engine, 65
Grand Theft Auto (virtual world), 135
The Great Gatsby Twitter feed project, 160
Greek myths, 143–144
Green, A., 105
Griffiths, A. K., 97

Halpern, P., 50-52
Harry Potter series
fan fiction of, 91–94
role-playing communities of, 88
Henry IV (Shakespeare), 145
Herr-Stephenson, B., 57, 83, 109
Hidden curriculum educational theory,
144–145
History of England (Hall), 145
Hobbs, R., 155
Hoch, D., 103
Hodson, R., 47
Holinshed, R., 145
Homebody, Kabul (Kushner), 103
Horst, H. A., 57
How I Got 798 Friends (Ayers), 25–26
How Wikipedia Works (Ayers, Yates, and
Klein), 78
Hull, G., vii, 172

"I Will Derive" (MindofMatthew's YouTube
video), 59, 60
iMovie (software), 156
In the Shadow of Man (Goodall), 98
Instant messaging (IM), 100

Institute of Medicine, 169
Interactions With Media at Home (Horst),
57–58
Interest-driven practices, 7, 9, 42, 88, 93
Introduction to Communication Technology
(ICT) course, 50–52
Ionesco, E., 103
Ito, M., 7, 8, 9, 10, 42, 44, 146, 169,
170–171, 172

Jalen's remixed project, 147
Jaszi, P., 155
Jenkins, H., 4, 7, 10, 25, 42, 55, 84, 109,
140, 146, 148, 172
Joe Turner's Come and Gone (Wilson), 103
John D. and Catherine T. MacArthur
Foundation, 6

Kalay, Y., 132, 133
Kalipea's Journey From Novice to Veteran in
Final Fantasy XI (Pfister), 116–122
Kids' Informal Learning with Digital Media:
An Ethnographic Investigation of
Innovative Knowledge Cultures project,
6–7, 71, 91
Killing Ifrit (Web site), 117
Kleiman, G., 172
Korallo, L., 115
Kress, G., 81
Kushner, T., 103

Lange, P. G., 8, 37, 45
Latour, B., 97
Lauriks, A., 29, 35
Lave, J., 122
Learning
deep participatory, 98–99
friendship-driven and
interest-driven, 7
peer-based, 8–9
tough questions about 21st century, 2–4,
168–169
Learning about Civic Engagement (Lange),
45–48
Learning Library (Project New Media
Literacies), 154, 159–160
Lederman, N. G., 97
Lemke, J., 96
Lenhart, A., 144
Lesbian teens, 23–24
Lewis, C., 98, 99
Linden Labs, 138
Literacy
concepts related to remix, 148–149
remix culture impact on, 144–165
shifting landscape of, 81,148–149

tough questions about 21st century, 2–4, 168–169
See also Reading and writing activities
Live Journal
fan fiction communities on, 88, 94
as vidding forum, 157, 158
Lohan, L., 59
Lombana, A., 161
Luminsoity, 158

MacArthur Foundation, 6
MacArthur Foundation's Digital Media and Learning Initiative, 171
McCruiston, A., 162
McGovern, M., 101
Machinima, 163, 164
McIntosh, J., 158
McLuhan, M., 158
Madden, M., 144
The Marriage of Heaven and Hell (Blake), 145
Martinez, K., 57
Mashup sampling, 150–151
Maul, A., 85, 87
Mean Girls (film), 59
Media Makers Challenge Collection, 159
Media production
appropriate curriculum applications of, 49–50, 52
collaboration opportunities through, 56
creating space for feedback to students on, 55–56
a teacher's perspective on curriculum integration of, 50–52
text-based project suggestions, 54
video project suggestions, 52–54
See also YouTube
Meme activity, 100–101
MIT, 145
Mixx (software), 154
MMORPG (massively multiplayer online role-playing game)
description of, 84
Everquest as, 87
MUDs (multiuser dungeons) communities and, 88
World of Warcraft as, 84, 86, 87, 109
Moar, M., 115
Moby-Dick: Then and Now (play), 161
Moby-Dick (Melville), 161
Moje, E., 98
Moll, L., 3, 122
MUDs (multiuser dungeons) communities, 88
Music remixes
copyright issues of, 155–156
description and popularity of, 150

digital audio recording software for creating, 151–152, 153 (figure)
examples of, 151
mashup sampling, 150–151
participating in creation of, 154–156
Reason interface for, 153 (figure)
Soulja Boy phenomenon using, 147–148, 150
My Morning Jacket, 154
MySpace
peer groups of, 7
school policies related to, 25
as teenage online hangout, 89
youth space created by, 19
See also Social network sites (SNS)
Myths. *See* Technology myths

National Research Council, 169
National Research Council Committee on Increasing High School Students' Engagement and Motivation to Learn (2004), 122
Navarro, R., 43
Neff, D., 3, 122
Nelson, B. C., 115
Networked publics
Bits and Bytes of Research examined to understand, 23–25
description of, 21
four unique properties of, 21–23
a teacher's perspective on using, 25–26
See also Youth space
New media technologies
communication practices changed by, 2
community of learners supported by, 7
description of, 4
GLBTQ teens connecting through, 23–24
how to begin teaching using, 169–170
key characteristics of, 6–13
tech-savvy students as symbol of changing, 1–2
See also Digital media
New Versions, New Visions challenge, 154
New York Magazine, 158
The New York Times, 89
Niaz, M., 97
Nicholson, J., 157
Nimoy, L., 157
Ning, 34
Nintendo Wii video game, 135, 136–137, 139

Obama, B., 156
O'Donnell, H., 104

O'Donnell, R., 104
Odysseus, 143–144
Old Testament, 145
Omni Outliner, 100
One Million Monkeys Typing, 159
Online Conversations Support Student
    Engagement with Literature
    (Berry), 10–13
Organization of Transformative Works
    (OTW), 164
Oseas, A., 167
Our Town (play), 102

Panfandom role-playing sites, 88
Panganiban, R., 114 (figure)
Parents
    ability to purchase family computer,
        138–139
    cautions against alienating your
        teens, 25
    concerns leading to banning of YouTube
        by schools and, 58–62
    inclusion in school activities, 56, 79, 81
    interactions with media, 57–58
Parker, J. K., 15, 37, 65, 83, 113
Pascoe, C. J., 8, 23, 88, 89, 91, 95
Pedagogical implications
    of remixing for classroom practices,
        158–160
    of role-playing classroom activities,
        95–109
    of social networks in classroom
        practice, 27–31
    of virtual worlds for classroom
        practices, 130–139
    of Wikipedia for classroom practices,
        76–77
    of YouTube for classroom practices,
        48–52
Pedia, 66
Peer-based learning
    educator opportunities to tap into, 8–9
    new media environments facilitating,
        7–8, 42–43, 116–122, 147
Performance-based activities
    description of, 99–100
    reenactments of events for, 101–102
    role-playing tools used for, 100–101
    teacher experiences with, 102–104
Perkel, D., 57
Personal Video Essay project, 54, 55
Pew Internet and American Life Project,
    144, 157
Pfister, R. C., 116, 122, 131
Photo-sharing networks, 105
The Play's the Thing (Crawford),
    102–104

Podcasting, 101
Political Remix Videos (PRVs), 163, 164
Popper, K. R., 97
Posting YouTube videos, 38
Print Advertisement project, 54
Pro Tools (software), 154
Profiles
    classroom practice of creating historical
        figures,' 34–35
    getting started on your own,
        26–27
    as SSN feature, 16–17
    status updates on, 18
    See also Social network sites (SNS)
Project New Media Literacies
    on integrating new media literacies
        across curriculum, 149
    Learning Library of, 154, 159–160
    New Versions, New Visions
        challenge of, 154
    Teachers' Strategy Guide developed by,
        145, 161
    Total Recut: Transformations
        challenge of, 157
    Web site of, 149, 159, 164
Public Service Announcement (PSA)
    project, 53

Quest Atlantis: A Game-Based Curriculum
    (Barab), 124–130
Quest Atlantis (virtual world),
    123, 124–130

Radioactive Substances (Curie), 97
Rauschenberg, R., 146
Reading and writing activities
    active reading, 104–105
    active writing, 105–106
    description of, 104
    Flickr as tool for, 105
    See also Literacy; Remxing
Reason (software), 151,
    153 (figure), 154
Recuts, 156
Reenactments of events
    description of, 101
    digital videos of, 102
    podcasting, 101
Reilly, E. B., 143
Relational perspective of technology,
    4, 13
Remix culture
    introduction to online, 144–145
    remixing original texts as part of the,
        145–165
    shifting landscape of literacy through,
        148–149

Remix Template, 163
Remixes
 analog, 161–162
 creating a, 163–164
 music, 150–156
 original versus, 162–163
 video, 156–158
Remixing
 appropriation concept of, 148, 149, 154
 considerations when, 145–147
 copyright issues related to, 155–156
 creating, 163–164
 description of, 145
 expressing characters for, 160
 fair use concept and, 156
 literacy concepts related to, 148–149
 pedagogical implications and classroom
  practices of, 158–160
 sharing insights, stories and experiences
  using, 164–165
 Soulja Boy phenomenon using,
  147–148, 150
 template for identifying, 163
Replicability, 22
Report the News project, 53
Retroactive I (Rauschenberg), 146
Richardson, W., 79, 109
Riot Grrl, 161
Robinson, L., 66, 69, 71
Rodriguez, M. A., 97
Role-playing activities
 blogging, 106–109
 deep participatory learning through,
  98–99
 fan fiction, 91–94
 fan fiction communities, 94–95
 motivating factors of, 95
 online role-playing games, 84–87
 pedagogical implications and classroom
  practices of, 95–109
 performance-based, 99–104
 reading and writing, 104–106
 role-playing through writing, 87–91
 school relationship with, 99
 sharing insights, stories, and
  experiences with, 109
 writing and performable
  practices, 83–84
 See also Classroom activities; Game world
Role-playing games (RPGs)
 description of, 84
 Dungeons and Dragons as classic, 84–85,
  86–87
 MMORPG (massively multiplayer online
  role-playing game), 84, 86,
  87–88, 109
 online, 84–87

 teacher's retrospective on, 85–86
 World of Warcraft, 84, 86, 87, 109
Romeo and Juliet (Shakespeare), 87
Rowling, J. K., 93

Safe Spaces to Connect: GLBTQ Teens and
 New Media (Pascoe), 23–24
Sakamoto, R. N., 151
Scalability, 22
Schindler's List (film), 47–48
Schools
 changing the culture of your, 170–172
 how to begin using new media/new
  digital curriculum in, 169–170
 media production and curriculum used
  in, 49–56
 MySpace policies of, 25
 role-playing relationship with, 99
 YouTube banned policy by, 58–62
 See also Educators
Schultz, K., 172
Science in Action (Latour), 97
Scratch Live (software), 154
Script writing, 100
Search engines, 65
Searchability, 22
Second Life (virtual world)
 communities in, 135
 creating an avatar in, 123
 generative nature of, 116
 sharing teacher experiences with, 139
 user-generated content of, 139
 Virtual Smithsonian build in, 132–134
Shaffer, D. W., 123
Shakespeare, W., 87, 145
The Shining (film), 157
Silverstone, R., 55
Sims, C., 5, 8, 9, 19, 20
Simulation, 149
Smithsonian Latino Virtual Museum
 (LVM), 134
Smithsonian Museum, 133
Social network sites (SNS)
 description and social impact of, 15–16
 escalating emotions issue of, 29–31
 friends lists of, 16, 18
 importance for today's
  students, 19–21
 main features of, 17 (figure)
 as networked publics, 21–26
 pedagogical implications and classroom
  practices using, 27–31
 sharing your insights, stories and
  experiences with, 35–36
 student purchasing practices and role of,
  32–33, 36
 teacher activity using, 31–35

testimonials, comments, and the
wall on, 16, 18–19
understanding, 15
what happens on, 16–19
See also Facebook; MySpace; Profiles
"Somewhere Over the Rainbow" (song), 151
Soulja Boy, 147–148, 150
Squire, K., 123
Status update as SNS feature, 17–18
"Stan" (Eminem and Dido song), 151
Star Trek (TV show), 157
Star Wars role-playing communities, 88
Stories from the field
Finding Wikipeida "*Before* it was Cool"
(Robinson), 69–71
Kalipea's Journey From Novice to Veteran
in *Final Fantasy XI* (Pfister), 116–122
Learning about Civic Engagement
(Lange), 45–48
Reason, FL Studio, and a Laptop
(Sakamoto), 151–152, 153 (figure)
This Is Not a Second Life (Sims), 20–21
You Have Another World to Create
(Pascoe), 89–91
See also Teachers sharing stories
Storytelling
bedtime stories, 143–144
different genres, 102
fan fiction form of, 88, 92–95, 106
The Great Gatsby Twitter feed project on,
160
Kalipea's Journey (Pfister) in virtual
world, 116–122
One Million Monkeys Typing project for
collaborative, 159
Quest Atlantis, 123, 124–130
remix culture of, 144–165
Street, B., 3
Student behavior
myths and realities about, 6
online behavior mirrored by social life, 24–25
rules of YouTube conduct
established for, 61–62
social network sites (SNS) impact on, 15–16
Student engagement
online conversations supporting, 10–13
and motivation to learn, 122–123
pedagogical implications of SSN for, 27–31
virtual worlds and, 122–130
Student Purchasing Practices (boyd),
32, 36
Student YouTube student videos, Frank's
raising Internet access awareness,
46–47, 50
Student YouTube videos
Frank's raising Internet access
awareness, 46–47, 50

Max's global political debates
participation, 47–48, 50
rules of YouTube conduct for working
with, 61–62
Wendy's documenting neighborhood
problems, 45–46, 49–50
Students
Countless Hours of Freedom (Navarro)
retrospective, 43–44
everyday digital media use by, 5–6
friendship-driven and interest-driven
practices of, 7
impact of family computer purchase on,
138–139
parental fears driving alienation of, 25
SNS (social network sites) importance for,
19–21
as symbol of ongoing media technologies
changes, 1–2
Synchronously remixing, 148

Taking Over: Mother Courage (Hoch), 103
Talking Science (Lemke), 96
Teacher activities
evaluating Wikipedia entries, 78–79
media technology observations applied to
classroom, 33–35
Student Purchasing Practices vignette,
31–33, 36
See also Classroom activities
Teacher's perspectives
Adventures with Role-Playing Games
(Maul), 85–86
Breaking Through the Mystique of
Science (Arya), 96–98
How I Got 798 Friends (Ayers), 25–26
Online Conversations Support Student
Engagement with Literature
(Berry), 10–13
The Play's the Thing (Crawford),
102–104
Virtual Models of Future Libraries
(Berry), 132–134
Why I Teach YouTube (Warburton), 59–60
Why Integrate Media Production into the
Curriculum? (Halpern), 50–52
Wii Did It! Bringing Special and General
Education students Together
(Gonzalez and Finamore), 136–137
Teachers sharing stories
on using remixing, 164–165
on using remixing activities, 164–165
on using role-playing activities, 109
on using social networking sites, 35–36
TeacherTube.com use for, 102
on using virtual worlds, 139–140
on using Wikipedia, 81

on using YouTube, 62–63
See also Educators; Stories from the field
Teachers' Strategy Guide: (Project New
  Media Literacies), 145, 161
TeacherTube.com, 102
*Teaching the New Writing: Technology, Change,
  and Assessment in the 21st-Century
  Classroom* (Bledsoe), 100
*Teaching Writing Using Blogs, Wikis, and other
  Digital Tools* (Beach et al.), 109
Technology myths
  "look at me" generation behaviors, 6
  media technology is complicated and
    scary, 66
  print encyclopedia as errorfree
    sources, 77
  negative effects of virtual worlds on kids, 115
  role-playing activities for only for
    children, 84
Technology realities
  media technology is user-friendly, 66
  role-playing activities is a fundamental
    new literacy skill, 84
  textual constructions, 77
  understanding digital media and behavior
    of, 6
  virtual worlds are dynamic and positive
    social space, 115
Ten Things Wikipedia, 69 (figure)
Testimonials. *See* Comments
Text-based projects
  Print Advertisement, 54
  Textbook Entry, 54
Textbook Entry project, 54
"Third place," 88, 89–91
This Is Not a Second Life (Sims), 20–21
Tolkien, J. R. R., 85
Total Recut: Transformations challenge, 157
Total Recut, 164
Traktor (software), 154
Transgendered teens, 23–24
Trojan War epic, 144–145
Truffaut, F., 42
Tucker, A., 168
Tweets, 83
21st century learning
  shifting our understanding literacy and,
    3–4
  tough questions for educators about,
    2–3, 168–169
Twilight (film), 157
Twilight role-playing communities, 88
Twitter, 100
Twitter feed, 160

Understanding Media (McLuhan), 158
University of California, Berkley, 6, 170

University of Southern California, 6,
  145, 159, 170
User/Designer perspective, 75, 131, 134

Vidding, 163
Video projects
  Class Video Page, 53
  Digital Storytelling, 52
  Personal Video Essay, 54, 55
  Public Service Announcement (PSA), 53
  Report the News, 53
  See also YouTube videos
Video remixes
  description and tools used for, 156–157
  fan-made music, 163
  Total Recut: Transformations challenge on, 157
Virtual Models of Future Libraries (Berry),
  132–134
Virtual Smithsonian (short film), 133, 134
Virtual World Building course (UC Berkeley),
  132–134
Virtual worlds
  characteristics of, 116–122
  description of, 114–115 (figure)
  design and designers of, 131, 134–135,
    137–138
  Grand Theft Auto, 135
  Kalipea's Journey (Pfister), 116–122
  learning through, 113–115
  myths and realities about, 115
  online resources for teachers on, 134
  pedagogical implications and classroom
    practices using, 130–139
  Quest Atlantis as, 123, 124–130
  Second Life as, 114, 116, 123, 132, 135,
    139
  sharing insights, stories, and opinions
    on, 139–140
  student engagement and learning
    through, 122–130
  World of Warcraft as, 114, 116
  YouTube video on teaching use of, 129
  See also Avatars
Visualization, 149
"Vogue" (Luminosity's video remix), 158

Wales, J., 68
The wall (feature of sns), 18–19
Warburton, M., 59
Warren, S. J., 115
Web sites
  Adam Green's Flickr gallery, 105
  American Library Association, 134
  Anime Music Videos, 163, 164
  Aonya McCruiston's remixing
    process, 162
  Blogger, 109

"Both Sides Now" (Kandy Fong), 157
ccMixter, 154–155
Center for Digital Storytelling, 52
Center for Social Media, 54
Code of Best Practices for Fair Use in
    Media Literacy Education, 155
Digital Media project, 58
Digital Youth, 91
DJ Spooky, 150
examples of public institutions' providing
    access to technology, 139
fan fiction, 84
fan-made music video remixes, 163
FanFiction.net, 93
Faraway Lands (role-playing site),
    89–91
FictionAlley.org, 93
Final Fantasy (virtual world), 116
Final Fantasy XI related information, 117
Flickr, 105
free video remix programs, 156
Global Kids' *Second Life* curriculum for
    teachers, 134
Google Groups, 34
How to Edit Page (Wikipedia), 79
Ito's video interview, 171
Jalen's remixed project, 147
Kids' Informal Learning with Digital
    Media Project, 71
Killing Ifrit, 117
Linden Labs, 138
Live Journal vidding archive,
    157, 158
MacArthur Foundation's Digital Media
    and Learning Initiative, 171
Machinima, 163, 164
Mike McGovern's 9th grade world history
    reenactments, 101
music copyright information, 155
New Versions, New Visions
    challenge, 154
Ning, 34
One Million Monkeys Typing, 159
Organization of Transformative Works
    (OTW), 164
Panfandom role-playing, 88
Political Remix Videos (PRVs), 163, 164
Project New Media Literacies,
    149, 159, 164
Project New Media Literacies Learning
    Library, 154
Quest Atlantis, 129
role-playing, 84, 88–91
Second Life, 123
Smithsonian Latino Virtual Museum
    (LVM), 134

"Somewhere Over the Rainbow"
    (song), 151
Soulja Boy's YouTube video, 148
Ten Things Wikipedia, 69 (figure)
Total Recut: Transformations
    challenge, 157
Total Recut, 164
Vidding, 163
Virtual Smithsonian
    (short film), 134
"Vogue" (video remix), 158
Wikipedia, 68
Wikispace, 79, 81
WordPress (blogging site), 109
www.teachingteachsavvykids.com, 29,
    35, 62, 76, 109,139, 170
YouTube, 37
Webkins (virtual world), 114 (figure)
Wenger, E., 122
Why I Teach YouTube (Warburton),
    59–60
Why Integrate Media Production into the
    Curriculum? (Halpern), 50–52
"Why Time Spent Online is Important for
    Teen Development" (Ito), 170–171
Whyville (virtual world), 114 (figure)
Wii Did It! Bringing Special and General
    Education students Together (Gonzalez
    and Finamore), 136–137
Wiki, 66
Wikibooks, 66
Wikifreccia, 80 (figure)
Wikimedia Commons, 66
Wikimedia Foundation, 66
Wikinews, 66
Wikipedia
    activity process of using tabs in,
        67 (figure), 68
    checklist for evaluating entries
        on, 78–79
    classroom activities for using,
        77–81
    description of, 65–66
    expert level use of, 75–76
    fun facts about, 68–71
    pedagogical implications and classroom
        practices of, 76–77
    sharing insights, stories, and experiences
        with, 81
    strengths and weaknesses of, 71–74
    Ten Things Wikipedia page on, 69 (figure)
    user-generated content of, 139
    utopian ideals of participation in,
        67–68
    Wikipedia 101 on getting started with,
        74–75

Wikipedia classroom activities
   1: discussion, 77–79
   2: adopt a Wikipedia entry, 79
   3: Wikis for educators, 79–81
Wikiquote, 66
Wikispaces, 79–81
WikiVoices, 75
Wiktionary, 66
Wilson, A., 103
Windows Moviemaker (software), 156
WordPress (blogging site), 109
World of Warcraft
   as MMORPG, 84, 86, 87, 109
   as virtual world, 114, 116
Wright, S., 87

Yahoo! Group, 100
You Have Another World to Create
   (Pascoe), 89–91
Youth space
   created by social networking sites, 19
   for GLBTQ teens, 23–24
   recognizing teens' need for, 22–23
   a teacher's perspective on, 25–26
   See also Networked publics
YouTube
   AnthroVlog responses to,
     39–40 (figure), 42
   "Are Kids Different Because of Digital
     Media?" project on, 6
   common misconceptions of, 38
   concerns leading to banning of, 58–62
   flagging feature of, 40
   MacArthur Foundation's Digital Media
     and Learning Initiative channel
     on, 171

origins and use of, 37–38
pedagogical implications and classroom
   practices using, 48–52
positive and negative
   aspects of, 40–41
rules of YouTube conduct for working
   with, 61–62
sharing your insights, stories, and
   experiences with, 62–63
social space features of, 38–40
teacher examination to understand, 25
on using virtual worlds as sites for
   learning, 129
See also Media productions
YouTube videos
   Frank's raising Internet access
     awareness, 46–47, 50
   "I Will Derive," 59, 60
   Max's global political debates
     participation, 47–48, 50
   posting, 37–38
   process for making, 42–48
   "Somewhere Over the Rainbow"
     remix, 151
   Soulja Boy's, 147–148
   "Stan" (Eminem and Dido song), 151
   Virtual Smithsonian, 133, 134
   Wendy's documenting neighborhood
     problems, 45–46, 49–50
   "Why I Teach YouTube" (Warburton)
     on, 59–60
   "Why Time Spent Online is Important for
     Teen Development" (Ito), 170–171
   See also Video projects

Zorro in Hell: Rhinoceros (Ionesco), 103

CORWIN
A SAGE Company

The Corwin logo—a raven striding across an open book—represents the union of courage and learning. Corwin is committed to improving education for all learners by publishing books and other professional development resources for those serving the field of PreK–12 education. By providing practical, hands-on materials, Corwin continues to carry out the promise of its motto: **"Helping Educators Do Their Work Better."**